SHAHANSHAH

A Study of the Monarchy of Iran

SHAHANSHAH

A Study of the Monarchy of Iran

E. BURKE INLOW

MOTILAL BANARSIDASS
Delhi :: Varanasi :: Patna

First Edition, 1979

ISBN: 978-81-2082-292-4

Also available at:

MOTILAL BANARSIDASS
41 U.A. Bungalow Road, Jawahar Nagar, Delhi 110 007
8 Mahalaxmi Chamber, Warden Road, Mumbai 400 026
120 Royapettah High Road, Mylapore, Chennai 600 004
Sanas Plaza, Subhash Nagar, Pune 411 002
16 St. Mark's Road, Bangalore 560 001
8 Camac Street, Calcutta 700 017
Ashok Rajpath, Patna 800 004
Chowk, Varanasi 221 0011

PRINTED IN INDIA
BY JAINENDRA PRAKASH JAIN AT SHRI JAINENDRA PRESS,
A-45 NARAINA, PHASE I, NEW DELHI 110 028
AND PUBLISHED BY NARENDRA PRAKASH JAIN FOR
MOTILAL BANARSIDASS PUBLISHERS PRIVATE LIMITED,
BUNGALOW ROAD, DELHI 110 007

In Support

The Mighty Pillars

Louise

Rush, Gerd, Brand, Shane

CONTENTS

PREFACE

This book is a study in political and legal theory. Its concern is with the power of the Shahanshah — its essential nature, its tradition, the exercise of its function.

The theoretical framework for this book is one that is known in academic circles as *Stufen theorie* or concretization. It is not a particularly popular theory in North America but then it doesn't apply to North America which comprises essentially a bargaining society. Capital, labour, government, professional societies, the armed forces — these are powerful political bodies, constantly seeking the ascendancy and as constantly being met by forces of opposite and equal magnitude.

In Iran, it is different. That country has always had a recognized hierarchy of power in which the various levels of society are united by tradition, religion, obligation, service and protection. The Shahanshah is at the apex of this structure. All things exist, therefore, as derivative of that great office. The theory of concretization speaks to this. According to Kelsen, the foremost propounder of this theory and a distinguished thinker under whom I had the privilege of studying many years ago, the science of law is a hierarchy of normative relations. It is not a sequence of causes and effects.

The law is a pyramidal structure. It devolves in a gradual process from the highest norm to the lowest. At each level, the process of concretization takes place. Here the theory stabilizes, setting its own limits and at the same time applying law and creating law at its own level. General principles, therefore, move from the abstract to the concrete as they come to be applied. Within the descending succession of norms, law becomes more and more specific until it reaches the lowest level — the administrative.

At the top of this vast hierarchy of levels — of successions of norms — is the *Grundnorm*. This is the highest norm and therefore the most abstract — as the lowest norm would be the most concrete. Americans, who tend to think in constitutional terms, would say that their Constitution would be the

Grundnorm. Kelsen, himself, preferred the English Constitution as being more abstract.

Abstractions, however, are never entirely satisfying in the world of legal theory. Ultimately we must face the reality of the concrete substance. In Iran, we are dealing with an enormous time span. The Fundamental Laws of 1906 are quite recent when compared with 2500 years of monarchical tradition. For that matter, even the Muslim law, as it obtains in Iran, extends over but half the time span of the more ancient rule. That being the case, history would suggest that the *Grundnorm* in Iran is better identified with the great office of Shahanshah than with any other reality. This book builds on this assumption. The Royal Tradition and the exercise of its power is, therefore, the concern of this book. So are the succession of norms that relate to it.

This book consists of 7 chapters, all of them directly identified and identifiable with the office of the Shahanshah. The first is a synopsis of the Iranian National epic and is an essential component in the monarchical tradition. The second chapter deals historically with certain aspects of Achaemenid history that relate to the establishment of the Monarchy. The third chapter deals with the aristocracy and is concerned in large part with the establishment of this very ancient supporting structure. Much of the material is drawn from the early Parthian and Sassanian periods.

The fourth chapter deals with the historic relationship in Iran between politics and religion. The office of Shahanshah is by no means a secular one as this chapter will show.

The fifth chapter is straightforward enough. The Armed Forces, everywhere, are in attendance upon the ruling force.

The Government itself forms the subject of the sixth chapter. Here I have accepted Blackstone's well known legal theory that the functioning government is an exercise of the royal prerogative. In England, of course, the term prerogative has a meaning at law. In Iran, it is not a familiar expression and certainly has not been defined by the Courts or elsewhere.

The final chapter deals with law, justice, and rule. Systematic studies of these subjects in Iran are non-existent. This is also a part of the tradition of Iran. Few monarchs would want their powers defined. James I addressed himself to the subject. The Shah himself in his interviews with Mr. Bayne and in his book *Mission For My Country* has similarly done so. But in the latter's case there has not emerged a systematic statement of his power and rule. In the case of King James, of course, the definition came not with the King but with a succession of great common lawyers. There is no such tradition, nor has there been such a succession in Iran.

No chapter on the peasantry has been included although it could be argued that because this large and important segment of Iranian society has been peculiarly identified with the Shahanshah over the centuries it deserves this consideration. My reasons for not so including this group are essentially conceptual. The peasantry of Iran has not been a self-conscious support group. It has traditionally had no structure or command position that would enable it to so serve. It does not fit into a Theory of Concretization as that theory is conceived here. This does not mean the peasantry has been ignored in this study. Quite the contrary is true. Its presence is a very real one as so many of the chapters will attest.

In a book of this compass, given its intent, only selected epochs in Iranian history can be considered. Consequently, this book does not read systematically as a formal history. Rather the book reads as a series of parallels in which the chapter headings provide the requirements for the materials used. Undoubtedly there will be a difference of opinion among experts as to whether this selection results in a balanced assessment of the lessons of history. I offer no defense of them. My choices seem good to me both in political science and in legal theory. One must begin somewhere and study and reflection must finally come to paper.

Shahanshah, as the highest principle — the Grundnorm— does not, I must emphasize, exist in a personal sense, a party sense, or even — except in abstract form — a political sense. It does exist in a transcendental logical sense. Perhaps one could say it is fiction, a legal fiction, as that term is understood in law. For this reason, it is important that the principle be not identified with an individual incumbent, whether the present Shah or that great conqueror, Nadir Shah. The fall from power is a fact of life and not a negation of principle. This raises the question of whether a fundamental norm could be established in defiance of an earlier one. Perhaps that question is unanswerable. Did the Weimar Republic, in succession to the Hohenzollerns establish a new principle ?

Shahanshah is not a book for light reading. On the other hand I hope it is neither difficult nor tedious. It is not written for the Iranian specialist. I have, in fact, built to a considerable extent upon the authority of these specialists whose names appear in the notes.

The people for whom I have written this book can be found in many areas of professional activity — in oil, commerce, law, literature, religious studies, politics. These people may live in many different countries: in India which has a long association with Iran dating back to the Aryan invasions; Pakistan with its Moghul heritage; England, with its generations of impressive and varied Iranian scholarship; France and Germany with their archeological, cultural and scientific associations; the United States with the Mutual Security Pact; Canada with its shared energy interests — all of these have an interest in Iran and a real association.

Hopefully, there will be a reading interest within Iran itself. This book is not, to use the vulgar modern terminology either "pro-Shah" or "anti-Shah". The matter does not concern me. People may ask, "what of the future". I do not know the future. It lies in the mind of God. All I can do is to trace what has happened and to think conceptually about it. In a sense, like most theory, this book looks backward in time and not forward and for that I make no excuse.

I was last in Iran in June, 1978 passing through, actually, on my way from Kabul to Frankfurt. My wife and I walked through the Bazaar and about the neighbourhood, drove past the University and had lunch at Farid's with friends. It was a quiet time and we were at ease. Since then, and after the text of this book was in galley, a new struggle for power — not a new thing in Iran — surfaced and at this writing had reached major proportions.

In the anglicized spelling of proper names and words that appear in the text I have tried to be consistent although I make no claims to being a linguistics specialist.

Acknowledgements for a book of this type can only be general. Over the years, I have known many men and women — in

Iran, in England, and in North America — whose great knowledge of Iran has placed me greatly in their debt. Some are now dead; most of them I have not seen for years. Whether they would approve of this book I have no way of knowing. Certainly it would be presumptuous of me to tie them in any way to this end product. For that reason, I do not name them individually. I do wish to acknowledge the financial assistance of the Canada Council for a recent year in Iran and for the assistance otherwise of the British Institute of Persian Studies and the Royal Society for Asian Affairs.

TABLE OF RULE

Dates	*Major Rule*
559 – 330 B.C.	Achaemenid Dynasty (Cyrus to Darius III)
330 – 129 B.C.	Greek Rule (Alexander and Seleucids)
129 B.C. – 226 A.D.	Parthian Empire (Arsacids)
226 – 651 A.D.	Sassanian Empire (Ardashir I to Yazdigerd III)
642 ca 800	Arab Conquest and Rule
932 A.D. 1050	Local revolts in Iran, Buyid rule
1050 ca 1200 A.D.	Seljuq Rule (Turkish)
1200 – 1375 A.D.	Mongol invasion and Rule of Ilkans
1375 – 1499 A.D.	Timurid rule (Tamerlane)
1499 – 1736 A.D.	Safavid Dynasty
1736 – 1794 A.D.	Minor dynasties — Afshar, Zand
1796 – 1925 A.D.	Qajar Dynasty
1925 to present	Pahlavi Dynasty

INTRODUCTION

Iran is the great plateau between the plain of the Tigris in the West and the Valley of the Indus in the East; the Caspian Sea and the Turanian Desert in the North and the Persian Gulf and the Indian Ocean in the South. It is surrounded on all sides by great mountain ranges with a great salt desert in the centre. As a single major physical region, the Zagros Mountains can be said to dominate the entire western portion of Iran. It is an imposing structure with some of the highest peaks in the Middle East. I can recall flying over these mountains in a light de Haviland plane in 1959 with no oxygen and a flight ceiling of 10,000 feet. A skilful pilot managed to get me from Kermanshah to Isfahan by ducking in through the various valleys amidst what seemed to be towering peaks everywhere.

The Alborz Mountains, over which my sons and I once drove our car in the dead of winter, lie between Teheran and the Caspian and are likewise grim and awesome mountains, stretching some six hundred miles along the Russian frontier east. They are dominated by Mt. Damavand (18,955 ft.) which is forty miles northeast of Teheran. This is the highest peak in the Middle East or Europe.

The so-called Eastern highlands march with the borders of Afghanistan and Pakistan. To the South lies the Gulf.

Above this land flies the Iranian flag. It depicts an Asiatic lion holding aloft in his forepaw a scimitar. Behind the lion in low profile is the Sun. Lions have always been associated with royalty in Iran. At Persepolis, one can see bas-reliefs of kings fighting lions. The lion provided royal hunting as the stag did for the English kings.

Within the volatile and explosive area that we in the West describe as the Middle East, Iran holds its central position year after year. No other nation in the region provides the mystique and the continuity of this very ancient land. In the current and recurring crises that mark the Arab-Israeli struggle, Iran affords an interesting example of non-alignment. There is an Israeli mission in Teheran and Iran makes no attempt to lessen economic ties with Israel despite Arab anger. A sizeable share of Israel's imported oil comes from Iran. There is an important — and old — Jewish population in Iran. In Hamadan — ancient Ecbatana — there lies, within a heavy stone enclave guarded by the local Jewish community, the remains of Esther, the Jewish girl of Biblical fame. She belongs in Iran. She was wife to the Shahanshah. On the other hand, Iran maintains close ties with moderate Arab leaders and has identified with the Arab cause by supplying armament and medical supplies when it was needed. During the October war of 1973, the Iranian press emphasized the religious nature of the struggle — "Moslem" soldiers were fighting, not Arabs. Yet within Iran itself, the government has been careful to control anti-Israeli propaganda as well as pro-Arab.

To a world not always accustomed to consistent policy, Iran's position in the Middle East is only infrequently understood. It is a country really that few Westerners know well. Teheran seems to be the goal of most tourists who arrive by air — with an occasional by-trip down to Isfahan and Shiraz if the tourist has the time and is reasonably well heeled. But, as in the old days when it lay along the silk route linking Europe and Asia, Iran is a country that people pass through. Not that the Iranians are unfriendly or inhospitable. To the contrary, they are the most sophisticated hosts in the Middle East. But they are also an exclusive people. Despite their striking linguistic and ethnic differences, the Iranians are politically and socially very cohesive. A visitor to Iran simply cannot forget he is an outsider. There is the mystery there, the sign you must not touch. More than any other country in the Middle East, Iran affords an example of how to balance and yet control. True, Iran, over the years, has lost important areas of its Empire. It has been often in the position an American Vice-President once described as "between the hammer and the hard place." Russia has been a formidable neighbour and England's special position was, up until recently, equally threatening. Despite this, Iran has endured and in fact has greatly strengthened its position in recent years. Not a little of this has been due to the strenuous efforts of Mohammed Reza Shah. History will assess his role as the architect of modernization in Iran. The risks he has taken have been very great and he has chosen the more difficult course of direct administration. On the other hand, his long (by Iranian standards) reign of over 36 years has been a period of almost unimaginable change that would be impossible to describe here. Anyone who has been in and out of Iran over this period — and the writer is one of them — will attest to this fact. During this time, foreign press releases have tended to reflect the impact of these changes. In recent years, particularly since oil prices began to rise, the western press in particular has had a field day with the Shah. Adjectives describing him have often been unflattering, sometimes cruel, occasionally condescending (the October 14, 1974 issue of *Newsweek* announced that "the Shah is no longer an object of ridicule"). Despite this, the Shah by and large keeps his sense of humour and goes his own way. He is, after all, a man who has faced assassination on more than one occasion; who has led his nation from poverty and occupancy by foreign powers to the strongest position in the Middle East in a single generation; who is not easily intimidated by even the greatest world powers; who has, as few men do, a sense of rule.

The Shah is also concerned with Iran. His policy — and the policy of Iran — is a simple one. It is for Iran. Iran's position is an independent one. The nation has not been drawn into the vortex of the Arab-Israeli conflict. Western leaders are entertained with enthusiasm but the Shah is constantly in touch with Moslem Heads of State. Iran welcomes tourism and would like to see it developed. But indiscriminate travel is not encouraged in Iran. Iran has, over the years, taken the lead in raising world oil prices. Yet, the Shah has not been interested in the boycott. When asked if there is a difference between position of the oil companies and that of Iran, he says there is : "this is our wealth, our natural wealth. For them, it's only a question of manipulation."

Consistently the Shah emphasizes Iran's self interest. His policy is one of relationships without involvement. To those who remind him of past debts, he turns a dry eye.

It is important then, in the first instance, to understand the singularity of Iran's position. It is different. That is not only its charm. It is its strength. The second thing to remember is that the Shah and his country have, for centuries, been indistinguishable. The interaction between these two principal actors in the Middle East is as old as the history of the area —

and it has been extremely important. The king and his realm. It is an important theme, perhaps the most important theme in Iran.

It is the purpose of this book to develop this theme along the lines indicated in the PREFACE, and to try to explain it to the interested and outside reader. So little is known generally of Iran that there has grown up in the West an aura of romanticism about it — the Rubaiyat, the minaret, Persepolis, *et al.* These are traditional aspects. There are also modern ones. One looks at the person of the Shah who has been over the years so attractive and once was considered quite racy. Here is a man who, though now in middle age, is a licensed pilot, likes fast cars, speaks fluent English and French, is not averse to granting audienccs, gets a good press, conducts himself with great sophistication and has chosen to give maximum exposure to a succession of three very beautiful wives. It would be pretty hard to be more modern.

But viewed in his native habitat, the Shah is something else again. And it is this something else which gives Iran its singularity, its exclusiveness, its key position in the Middle East. When the Shah is back in the realm from which he derives, he and the realm merge just as does the coin of the realm — the Shah's picture on one side — the Lion and the Sun (emblematic) of Iran) on the other. It is impossible to understand Iran without a sense of history. It is equally impossible to understand the Monarchy.

The Monarchy of Iran is not the present Shah only : Westerners, particularly tend to mistake individuals for institutions and to personalize the latter. But the Iranian Monarchy is not a mere personality cult. It is something that the writer has described elsewhere as "deep and timeless and gaunt with age.'[1] When Iran commemorated its 25th centennial as an established monarchy in 1971, the nations of the world paid tribute gladly to an historical phenomenon that is without parallel in our time.

[1]Inlow, E. Burke, "The Divine Right of Persian Kings", *Journal of Indian History*, Vol. XLV, Pt. II (August 1967), p. 400. See Savory, Roger M., "Iran, A 2,500-year Historical and Cultural Tradition," *Iranian Civilization and Culture* (ed. by C. J. Adams) Montreal, McGill University, 1972, p. 78.

It is important then to begin with this knowledge of great age and tradition.

Iran, as will be explained later, means "land of the Aryans." The early invaders into Semitic and Jewish land areas were a people apart — not indigenous. They took pride in their heritage — and still do. The very fine *Traveller's Guidebook to Iran* which is published by permit of the Ministry of Culture and Arts says on page 15 :

> "Persia is the homeland of the Aryan people, the forbears of the Indo-European races. A mixture of Turkish and Mongol blood in the Northeast and Arab blood in the Southwest has been noticeable since invasion by these races, but it is gradually decreasing and the pure Persian is beginning to dominate."

It was not so long ago that the Iranian Majlis voted the present Shah the added title of Arya Mehr — "the light of the Aryans." In a western world which is trying desperately to forget the implications of "Aryanism," surely the Iranian action appears as anomalous and even perhaps provocative. And yet that is the way it is. The Iranian, in a world of Jews and Arabs, claims his own ethnic heritage which can, once again as in the case of his history, only place him apart.

Despite a few small minority religious bodies — excepting, of course, Israel — the Middle East is Moslem. As pointed out above, Iran identifies with the Moslems — "Islam is our base" — and takes great pride in its mosques, observes the holy days, and gives special place to learned *mujtahids* and *mullahs*. But, once again, with a difference. While the rest of the Moslem world is Sunni, Iran is Shi'a. The distinction is very important and will be developed later in this book. Suffice it to say at this point that when the Moslem faith was imposed upon Iran at the time of the Arab invasion, it was brought by a relatively primitive tribal leadership to a much older culture. Further, the conquered Iranians found that far from being granted the expected economic and social equality with Arabian Moslems, they were instead reduced to the position of clients: What made them more discontented was the consciousness that they represented a higher and more ancient culture, a fact acknowledged even by the Arabians themselves. Inevitably, a new phase of Islam developed which will be elaborated in the fourth chapter.

The Shah, like the Queen of England, is presently the Defender of the Faith (Moslem) by specific constitutional provision. He is more, as will be pointed out later. But there is an important separation here as between the Moslem (Sunni) Middle East and Iran.

In 1906, a constitution was adopted by Iranians for Iran. The details of this will be recounted below. There have been other constitutions in the Middle East, but they have been short lived. Iran's is still in force. The question of the Shah's power under the constitution is more than a constitutional question — as will be seen later. The Shah has described himself — on occasion—as a constitutional monarch. As such, he identifies with certain other constitutional heads in the Middle East. On the other hand, his position is more than constitutional and here he identifies with a different tradition. In true Iranian style, the Shah's powers cut two ways.

In Iranian newspapers, the Shah is invariably titled the "Monarch" or the "Sovereign" in the press. He is as closely identified with Iran as is the beautifully minted gold coin mentioned above. The relationship is indigenous and authentic. Shahs have seized power but they sit on an ancient throne. Western observers like to describe the Shah variously as a national cultural tradition, or as an Islamic institution. Others see him as a legitimate constitutional monarch. Some think of him as the apex of a social pyramid only. To his own people, the Shah is this and more and perhaps the Iranian way is more expressive — and even more conceptual. When the earthquake comes, the peasant cries *Magar Shah mordast* (Is the Shah dead?). When the high official addresses his Sovereign, (one does not address the Shah directly), he may well use the classic form "May I be your sacrifice, Asylum of the Universe." The Shah belongs to all. He is the orderer, the arranger, the provider, the sustainer. Over the centuries the arrangements between the Shah and his people have been worked out in a *modus operandi* that has been tested again and again. The simile of the pyramid has some validity. But it would appear as if a more accurate description would be that presented in the PREFACE. No one institution can guarantee the Monarchy. But certain groups and institutions in Iran — generally described by the chapter headings — find it in their own interests to offer this support. In exchange the Monarchy guarantees their favoured position. This is not unusual. Most monarchies have moved toward the same arrangement. But the very efficacy of this one certainly suggests differences.

Contrary to popular assumption, the tribes — early very important — are not now a major force in Iran even though a considerable presence of tribal groups around the peripheral areas of Iran (as contrasted with the central area) still recalls the early protective role of the tribes that will be described in the first chapter. Even the term "tribe" is not in use in correct circles today. The present term is "nomad". With a modern army and a rising industrialism, the tribal manpower as it was traditionally used is no longer needed. Farm labour, the ancient peasant, is not a political force in Iran. The Urban worker has not yet measured his position or been assessed.

The present Shah is a centre of contention. He is the driving force for modernization in Iran. He is at once, a very present ruler and at the same time the custodian of something very old and precious to Iran. His is an extremely complex position. For that reason, this book does not confine itself to the present office or the reigning office holder. It rather places the office and the man in the perspective of history. That is the reason for the title of this book, *Shahanshah.* It is a title but it is much more than a title. It is an embodiment. It speaks to all men, in all times but to a particular place.

Chapter 1

THRONE OF JAMSHID

In 1971 Iran proclaimed the 2500th anniversary of the founding of the Persian Empire by Cyrus the Great. In every major country national committees were named to assist in celebrating this joyous occasion. An impressive number of conferences were held including an invitational Iranology Congress in Shiraz consisting of leading scholars and Iranologists from all over the world. In the Soviet Union there was a special exhibition at the Hermitage Museum, which houses probably the best collection of Iranian artifacts and coins in existence and the prestigious Institute of Orientology of the Academy of Sciences held a continuing series of special seminars. In the United States, New York State University inaugurated an eight-week program of lectures, films, and discussions on Iranian history. In Canada, "Iran Week" celebrations were conducted at the Iranian Pavilion at *Man and His World* in Montreal, a week of cultural activities initiated by the Empress herself when she visited Canada in June, 1971. A large number of books were published in that year and in the years immediately following dealing with Iran's culture and history that were commissioned or inspired as the result of this celebration.

But the big party came in October of that year when Iran hosted nearly fifty Heads of State including an Emperor, nineteen kings and queens, more than fifteen presidents, and almost unnumbered prime ministers, emissaries, sultans, sheikhs, princes and princesses at Persepolis in Iran. It was probably the largest gathering of its kind seen in modern times. Admidst what must have been unbelievable security problems, guests were flown in special planes from Teheran to Shiraz on October 13-14 and then motored to Persepolis where they were housed in a luxurious tent city. The caterer, naturally enough, was Maxims of Paris.

The whole thing was reminiscent of the great No Ruz (New Year's) celebrations held by the Achaemenid Kings on the same site, over two thousand years earlier. Roman Ghirshman describes these occasions[1] which are still depicted in part on the ruins of this mighty palace at Persepolis. For those who have only seen the Acropolis in Athens it is still an awe-inspiring sight to come to Iran and see the monumental gate-house built by Xerxes guarded by winged bulls and other genii; the fore-court of the Apadana; the two great stairways that gave access to the Apadana (or audience hall) with its bas-reliefs depicting processions of notables from the many nations of the Empire; the Tripylon with its famous stone doors showing Darius standing beneath a Sunshade, Darius and Xerxes seated, Ahura Mazda the great God; the Hall of one hundred columns with its Royal Heroes depicted fighting lions and other animals; and finally the Throne Room itself where the king is represented enthroned, seated in front of two fine altars surrounded by fly-whisk bearers, heralds, body guards and the masters of ceremonies. Gifts presented to the King in this room were at once removed to the royal treasury, also a part of the Palace. In addition — because it is difficult to really do justice to the sheer size and magnificence of this tremendous ruin — there were banquet halls, military areas, and broad terraces, all adding to the sheer size and scope of the site chosen for the pageant program, reception and banquet provided for the 20th century guests of the present Shahanshah and his Empress.

Actually for five years before the 1971 party, an annual Festival of Arts had been held at Persepolis so the lighting effects and general pageantry that could be provided among the ruins, particularly at evening performances was on a scale that could easily provide audible and happy entertainment to foreign guests — and this, of course, was done. For example, three hundred Baluchi, Kurdish, Azarbaijani and Turkoman tribal dancers staged a royal performance of music and dances that was not of the type often seen in the western world. There was a grand military parade on camel, foot and horseback of units of the Imperial Army dressed in period uniforms from Achaemenian times to the present day. There was a fireworks display. In these, and other ways, guests were shown cultural and intellectual aspects of a civilization that is not well known throughout most of the western world. Iran is half the world away from North America. What is known to those who have had some association in school or through personal contact with

Iranians, but who have not been there, it is a country of Persian rugs, Persian gardens, and highly individual art and poetry forms much of it not very understandable.

To people who live in newer and somewhat simpler cultures, even the names are difficult to comprehend — Achaemenid, His Imperial Majesty—Mohammad Reza Pahlavi Aryamehr, Persepolis, Shah. It is really all quite exotic. But to return to Persepolis which is but a short drive from the lovely city of Shiraz. This is the heart land of the ancient land of Parsa (*Fars* in Arabic) from whence the name Persia is derived. It is an ancient land to which only the knowledgeable western traveller goes. It is far from Teheran, the capital city, although over two thousand years ago Persepolis was the capital of the Persian Empire. There is a good highway from Teheran to Shiraz and Persepolis and the driving is easy. There is also regular air service. But it is out of the way and, hence, too many people limit their stay in Iran to Teheran itself.

The Iranians themselves do not call it Persepolis. They called it Takht-i-Jamshid — the throne of Jamshid. Yet nowhere is this personage mentioned in the official anniversary program issued for the celebration of the 2500th anniversary of the founding of the Persian Empire by Cyrus the Great. But, almost a thousand years ago, so famed was this great ruin that in far away Nishapur, Omar Khayyam, the mathematician and astronomer, penned his famed and poignant quatrain to a lost once great era that was presented to the English speaking world in Fitzgerald's well-known translation of the '*Rubaiyat*' in 1859.[2]

> They say the Lion and the Lizard keep
> The Courts where Jamshid gloried and drank deep
> And Bahram, that great hunter — the Wild Ass
> Stamps o'er his head but cannot break his sleep.

The explanation for this dual description of Persepolis and Takht-i-Jamshid is an interesting one. Modern historians tell us that the palace was built by Darius I and destroyed by Alexander. But, in the legendary history of Iran, its existence takes on an added dimension. The reason for this is that the history of Iran is a parallel history. On the one hand there is the actual world, recreated by recent distinguished generations of archaeologists, numismatists, geographers, philologists and historians. This is what we read in the various modern histories of Iran, specialized monographs and other works by scholars and researchers. It is the history that most moderns understand and with which they identify.

The other history of Iran is less well known in the West but it is no less real to the Iranians. It is a history of life and tradition in a highly romanticized setting but one which has its own reality. It is at once fabled and childlike and yet it is of titanic dimensions. All of man's feelings and desires are here, his triumphs, his failures. This history is what Iranians see of and in themselves and it is centered on the Kings and dynasties who ruled them. There is no concept of social history here, no concern with villages and peasants, and bazaar groups. It is truly heroic, serving an unbroken line of heroes. Takht-i-Jamshid itself is an example.

The sheer size and splendour of what remains of Persepolis can certainly explain why hundreds of generations of ignorant and superstitious herdsmen, shepherds, and even travellers of higher rank, who passed by in early times, would see in those gigantic pillar staircases, court yards, bas-reliefs of Kings and giant men fighting animals and genii, the work of superhuman forces. Whoever had built Persepolis, so they said, must surely have been the work, not of men, but of demons. And only Jamshid was known to have command over demons.

The term Iranian National Epic[3] is now generally used to describe this history of heroes and is identified today almost exclusively with the famed *Shahnameh*, or Book of Kings by Firdawsi, the Iranian poet. The Epic was put in completed form over a thirty to forty year period ending in 1010 A.D. It was an immense poem, consisting of some 60,000 couplets, longer than the *Iliad* and *Odyssey* combined. Upon completion it was dedicated by Firdawsi to Sultan Mahmud, the Ghaznavid, who represented a new royal house of Turkish blood. Although the son of a slave, Mahmud had gained a reputation as a patron of the sciences and was known to be of some learning. He was, however, a zealous Sunni Moslem and was probably completely unprepared for Firdawsi's strong defense in his Epic of the early Persian Zoroastrian faith. (The Zoroastrians had been badly persecuted by the Arab Moslems at the time of the Conquest and many had fled to India.) At any rate Firdawsi was rewarded so meagerly for what he regarded as his life work that he turned in anger against the Sultan, withdrew his gift, and coined a savage satire of his would-be patron that of course required his fleeing for his life. The first few lines ran as follows :

Long years this Shahnameh I toiled to complete,
That the King might award me some recompense meet,
But naught save a heart wrung with grief and despair
Did I get from these promises empty as air !
Had the sire of the King been some prince of renown,
My forehead had surely been graced by a crown !
Were his mother a lady of high pedigree,
In silver and gold had I stood to the knee !
But, being by birth not a prince but a boor,
The praise of the noble he could not endure !

This was considerably different than Firdawsi's original dedication to "the Prince whose like was never seen, not since the Creator created the world."

The *Shahnameh* was built, as do most massive literary achievements, upon other earlier works. There had been earlier attempts at compiling something similar to the *Shahnameh.* Firdawsi himself refers often to the "Book of Kings" or the "Book of Ancient Times." Other earlier antecedents were the "Book of Zarer", the "Book of Lords" and the "Khodhainameh." By far the most important, however, was a poetical version of the "Book of Kings," attempted by *Daqiqi*, a distinguished poet at the Court of one of the Samanids around 976—997 A.D. He was a zealous Zoroastrian himself and his story of the introduction of the new religion by Gushtasp and his knights is repeated in Firdawsi's version. Unfortunately, Daqiqi was killed by his slave male lover while he was still a relatively young man, so that there were only one thousand verses completed at the time of his death. Firdawsi says that he used them but he did make some minor changes (i.e., in the earlier work, Rustam was killed by Bahman avenging his father. The more romantic version which will be recounted below is Firdawsi's.).

Another younger contemporary whom Firdawsi mentions is one Mansur, a poet and scholar, who apparently had worked on a book entitled, "The Sparks of Records About the Kings of Persians and Their Lives." It is possible, although Firdawsi did not like Arabs — he called them "those snake devouring devilfaces who have no knowledge, nor shame, who are devoid of wealth, of fame, of luck and of nobility" — that he did use some Arab sources, most probably the historian Tabari. However, the Arabs, in general, had almost no familiarity with Persian Tradition. Rustam's great episodes, for example, are not found in Arab sources and no mention is ever made of his knightly son, Sohrab.

Of Firdawsi himself, quite a bit is known. He was born in Tus about the year 940 A.D. He was a well to do but not wealthy landowner. He seems to have been a man who enjoyed life. Like many of his countrymen, he enjoyed wine even though its use was enjoined by the Koran. He had one daughter for whom he was concerned to build an adequate dowry. Apparently as a young man he dabbled in epic poetry but did nothing substantial. He had been given a prose copy of an early "Book of Kings" when he was seventeen to translate into verse, but it was apparently not until 980 when he was forty and after the death of Daqiqi that he picked up the massive project to which he devoted the next thirty years. Obviously Firdawsi had the necessary qualities of patriotism, ability, and sheer physical strength that when he finally decided to make this great effort, he did it with pride. He finished the *Shahnameh* in his seventy-sixth year.

Firdawsi's old age was an unsettled one to say the least. His sharp satire on Mahmud may have been satisfying to him personally, but, of course, it kept him on the move. He was finally accepted at the provincial court of Tabaristan. There he continued to write, reproducing, among other things, a verse rendering of the legend of Potiphar's wife who is known in Persian literature as Zulaykha. (It is interesting that the Persians were much more sympathetic toward this lady than are the Old Testament authors. In Persian literature she emerges as a woman not only of great beauty but one of pathetic dignity. It is she, not the colder Joseph, who becomes a veritable symbol of self-sacrifice. Unlawful passion her's may have been, but

Joseph's cold virtue does not come off well by comparison with it — at least as Firdawsi draws it.)[4]

The aged writer of the *Shahnameh* finally returned to his native Tus to die. There is a story that as his corpse was being carried from the city a rich load of indigo from a repentant Mahmud entered the gates. It was a fine dramatic ending for such a romantic figure.

The Iranians see Firdawsi as having accomplished, through the *Shahnameh*, essentially three things. The first is that almost single handedly he "rescued from oblivion and preserved for all time our national history." The second is that, through his actual writing, he composed in classic form the beauty and majesty of the Persian language. Even today, the *Shahnameh* can be read by a modern Iranian with much more ease than is Chaucer read by English speaking people. In his verses, Firdawsi is able to not only produce a strong and solid piece: "it contains no weak or flaccid lines; from beginning to end, the style of the *Shahnameh* is uniform and consistent," but he is a master of dramatic delineation. Throughout, one sees in the Epic the tensions of humanity emerging again and again. The *Shahnameh* does not merely report confrontations. Firdawsi's overall conception is one of the tension of great drama. True kingship will, Firdawsi shows us, endure, but not necessarily individual kings. The prices must be paid and the sacrifices made.

Finally, Firdawsi himself, as a man and as a poet, is seen by Iranians as "a perfect embodiment of all that is meant by a Persian; he comprises all the characteristics of our Persian race."[5] Today Firdawsi's name and statue grace one of the great broad thoroughfares in Teheran, a national tribute to a very great man who gave back to his countrymen their history and their pride.

To turn now to the *Shahnameh* itself. This great Epic comprises a loosely connected history of Iran from prehistoric times up to the Arab conquest. It deals with four dynasties and some fifty reigns, all of very unequal duration. Space devoted to the separate reigns in the Epic, therefore, in no way corresponds to the length of the periods described.

The four dynasties named are the *Pishdadi*, the *Kayani*, the *Ashkani*, and the *Sasani*. The first two are entirely unhistorical although they comprise by far the greatest bulk of the writing. The material contained goes back to the mythology of the early Aryan *Avesta*,[6] a body of literature both oral and written (Gathas) that records very early Indo-Iranian legends that were probably brought to the land of Persia and were not native to it. There are also Zoroastrianisms contained in this section that were native. The next chapter will give a larger account of the Aryan movement but suffice it to say here that many of these older traditions are jointly shared by India and Iran even though the names may change.

The *Ashkani* dynasty corresponds to the Parthian period of history or the period between the death of Alexander (who is treated, but only briefly in the Epic) and the rise of Ardashir and the founding of the Sassanian dynasty. This is a brief and erratic part of the Epic. What few names are mentioned are without order or method. The Arcacids, who will be dealt with historically in the third chapter are considered as a single reign although as a dynasty of the Parthian period, they ruled for over three hundred years.

The fourth dynasty treated in the *Shahnameh*, the *Sasani* or the *Sassanian*, as it is more familiarly known, is generally historical in that the kings in this section are historical personages arranged in correct order. Naturally, there are a large number of deeds and adventures related which are of a legendary nature, however.

One of the favourite games of earlier scholars was to take personages from the first three dynasties listed in the *Shahnameh* and seek to establish parallels with actual historical figures. On an individual basis, this is very difficult to do and is really not very fruitful. What might be useful, however, in order to demonstrate the nature of Iran's early parallel history, would be simply to put down side by side the kings of Persia as described in the Epic and those that history gives us. Although it may not correlate, it provides the base upon which this and the next chapter builds.

The Mythical kings of Persia

Pishdadian[7]

Kayumarth

Hushang (Ushhang)
Tahmurath, known as Divband
Jamshid (or Jam)
Bayvarasb, known as Dahhak

Kayanian

Faridun (or Afridun)
Minuchihr (Navdar)
Ziv bin Tahmasb (Garshasb)
Kay Qubad
Kay Ka'us
Kay Khusraw
Luhrasb
Gushtasb
Bahman
Humay (widow of Bahman, mother of Dara)
Dara (= Darius III)
(Dara ibn Dara)

The Archaemenid kings and their reigns (B.C.)

Cyrus, 559 – 529
Cambyses, 529 – 521
(Pseudo-) Smerdis, usurper, 521
Darius, 521 – 485
Xerxes, 485 – 465
Artabanus, usurper, 465 –464
Artaxerxes I, 464 – 425, known as Longimanus
Xerxes II, 425
Sogdianus, 425 – 424
Darius II (or Ochus), 424 – 405, known as Nothus
Artaxerxes II, 404 – 358, known as Mnemon
Artaxerxes III (or Ochus), 358 – 338
Narses (or Arses), 338 – 336
Darius III, 336 – 330, known as Codomannus

This chapter will generally deal with the contents of the *Shahnameh* and, more particularly, with the meaning in Persian history of the Throne of Jamshid. The second chapter will deal with the coming of the Aryans and the rise of the Achaemenid dynasty as modern historians have reconstructed it. This parallelism is deliberate and in line with the earlier observation made that Iran's history is a parallel history.

Kayumarth, the first mythical Shah, is pure prototype. He has been described as the first man of the Avesta, Gayo Mareta, the Zoroastrian Adam. According to this version he dwells in the mountains, dresses himself and his people in leopard skins, brings the beasts of the field into subjection, wages war on the demons, rules as first king of the legendary Pishdadi dynasty and dies.[8] In view of the fact that Kayumarth is a Syric word which means a living being endowed with speech, there is also the suggestion that this first king introduced a written language (we know that the early Aryans had none).

Kayumarth was much loved of men and they prospered and grew strong in his reign. Only the Deevs or demons opposed his rule. They dwelt in the province that is now known as Mazanderan, to the north of Kayumarth's kingdom. Their kings were sworn enemies of the Shahs and in the Epic there are many stories of Shahs and heroes successively doing battle with these enemies of mankind. They are described as being a mixture of man, animal and evil spirit. They walked like men but they were possessed of horns and tails and long ears. Some were small and black but some were giants of tremendous strength. The Deevs were masters of sorcery and enchantment who could call up whirlwinds and fire in the midst of battle. Indeed, Kayumarth's own son was slain by them and his army dispersed. But the great Shah had a grandson, Hushang, who was wise as well as brave. Enlisting the aid of all the wild beasts of the land, as well as the faithful subjects of the Shah, Hushang did battle with the Deevs. His victory was great. He himself killed the King of the Deevs and the important members of his family.

Hushang succeeded his grandfather, Kayumarth as Shah and ruled for forty years, producing fire by flint and steel and other marvellous contributions to civilization. He was succeeded by his son who reigned for thirty years and who, in turn, was succeeded by Jamshid, grandson of the mighty Hushang. It is related that Jamshid reigned for seven hundred years. It was the great period of Persian history, the golden era from whom all subsequent reigns took their light. It was a period of great prosperity and glory. No one died or was ill. All remained in the prime of youth and strength. Old age and pain and sorrow were no more.

It was a period of great building, for Jamshid was a builder rather than a warrior. His dominion was entire, including the Deevs whom he used to construct marvellous palaces and fountains and to make silks and jewellery. Most famous was the throne they constructed for him to be transported through the air from one city to another in the twinkling of an eye. So gorgeously beautiful was this throne that it became the wonder of the world.

The Epic tells us that Jamshid discovered many things and gave them to his people — new weapons of war, textiles, perfume, medicine, ships. He separated men into classes and divided the year into periods. He established the great national festival of No Ruz which is still celebrated as the Persian New Year — at the vernal equinox when sun enters the Sign of Aries.

Learning and wisdom were at his court. There was wine and good living. Men flocked to his standard from all the corners of the earth. It was indeed a beneficent and glorious reign. But the time came when Jamshid's head was turned by the power he held. And the Epic tells us that pride took possession of his heart and he forgot the God Ormuzd, the source of all his blessings. It was even said that so great became his arrogance that he beheld only himself in the world and he named himself God, and he sent forth his image to be worshipped. The day came when Jamshid commanded all of his people to present themselves in the great square before the palace. It was an awesome sight, the palace that we call Persepolis. The Deevs had made it into nothing like the world had ever seen. It was not only the largest creation of its kind but it was covered with the beautiful tiles that are still to be seen in Iran. The windows and balconies were made of fretted stone work encrusted with cut and polished glass. Its towers reached to the Heavens, sparkling in the azure sunlight.

And in front of this palace there glittered something even more brilliant — the throne of Jamshid — Takht-i-Jamshid. The Epic tells us that this throne was studded, not with glass, but with every precious stone that the world had ever seen. It was so resplendent in the sunlight that it dazzled and danced in shimmering waves. Around it, standing guard were giant Deevs, proof of the power of Jamshid even to subdue these awesome creatures.

Awaiting the Shelter of the Universe, as the Shah was called, the people stood in eager expectation. What new wonder was to be given to them; what mighty acts were they to witness? It was truly a day to remember.

The trumpets sounded and slowly Jamshid mounted the throne. All fell on their faces in solemn obeisance, then rose to their feet and cried in admiration Bah ! Bah ! — an expression still heard today.

Jamshid raised his sceptre. There was silence, then the single question from the throne, "Long long, O my people, have you basked in the sunshine of a golden age. Now tell me, to whom do you owe this marvellous prosperity?" With one voice, the people shouted : "To Ormuzd the Blessed. Hail to the God of the Persians." This was not the answer he expected and the Shah thundered forth calling them foolish and blind and as worms. "There is but one God of the Persians Jamshid the Glorious," he said, "bow the knee to him, not to Ormuzd."

Never had the people seen such arrogance. A shudder ran through the crowd and they were afraid. Then to the north they looked, to Damavand, the sacred mountain that still guards the city of Teheran. "Damavand, look at Damavand." The snow covered crest was aglow with dusky red. And while they watched, a huge cloud flowed from the crater and moved swiftly south to hover like a giant bird over the palace and the people. There was no thunder and no lightning. But all at once it happened. The world's mightiest palace fell into a heap of ruins. The throne of Jamshid, glory of the world, turned to dust. Jamshid's royal robes became fluttering rags. And out of the ruins came snakes and lizards and from the clouds there rained scorpions and centipedes. Jamshid fled on a milk white steed and wandered for one hundred years before being brought before Dahhak, the Arab usurper, to be sawed in two on planks, making two figures of Jamshid out of one so that all the world could see the duality of this great king.

There is, of course, in the tale of Jamshid, much allegory as well as mythology. Dahhak, the usurper, under whom Persia groaned, is in the first instance, a throwback to the great dragon of Aryan mythology, found in the Avesta. Two snakes grew from his shoulders which required a daily meal of human brains. On the other hand, Firdawsi, to whom the memory of the Arab conquest was still very real and in whom racial hatred ran very high, converts the usurper into an Arab. Dahhak became the apotheosis of all the evil visited on Persia by the conquering Arabs. He was parricide, tyrant, an instrument of the devil. His demand for fresh victims to feed his snakes, ultimately after a period of one thousand years, drove his subjects to revolt under the leadership of the blacksmith Kavah. Knowing the people's needs for a standard around which to rally, Kavah took off his leathern apron and raised it aloft. "Behold, O my countrymen, the banner which shall lead us on to victory, delivering us from out of the hands of the evil Serpent King."

So Kavah led the people forth and the "Flag of Kavah" became a sacred symbol honoured by the early Persian Kings as the true sign of royalty. This flag grew over the centuries to a huge 22″ × 15″ banner adorned with gold and precious stones. It was taken by the Arab forces at the battle of Qadisiyah, cut up, and sold in pieces at Medina.

Kavah, however, was not royal and as happened so often in the stories of the Epic — and in actual history — it was required that the line of kingship remain royal. Instead of Kavah, the liberator therefore mounting the throne emerged as the grandson of Jamshid, Faridun, who was brought forth from a hiding place and hailed as King to bring final defeat to Dahhak.

This, Faridun the Glorious did. He seized Dahhak in battle and chained him, Prometheus-like, in a cave at the summit of Mount Damavand. And thereafter he ruled with great justice and splendour for five hundred years.

Faridun is the first king of the second dynasty listed in the *Shahnameh* — the *Kayani*. He had three sons who were the Iranian counterparts of Ham, Shem and Japhet of Biblical fame. To them, on their marriage, he divided and gave his vast domain. The youngest, Iraj, was given the land of Iran and because this was considered to be the choicest portion of the heritage, he was killed by his two older brothers, Tur and

Selim. This fratricidal conflict as recounted in the Epic was, as will be explained later, a real historical conflict between the Turks (the sons of Tur) and the Iranians.

For the murder of his favourite Iraj, the aging Faridun swore vengeance upon his two older sons. But it remained for his grandson, the son of Iraj, his youngest, and the Princess of Yemen to accomplish this deed. This young man, whose name was Minuchihr, and who was destined to become one of the great legendary figures in Iranian history, was early brought into the house of Faridun himself, so outstanding was his promise. But as Faridun was an old man, Minuchihr's education and training was committed to the celebrated house of Saum Swar, or Sam, which guarded the marches of Seistan. As the Epic says, there was no house greater than this and none which had such great influence in shaping the destinies of Iran. There was here bred a race of heroes that not only saved Persia again and again from the hands of her foes but "whose marvellous deeds have filled the world with wonder."

Minuchihr's education is described in the Epic as comprehending every act necessary to form the character and accomplishments of a warrior. His horsemanship excelled all others, his spear could pierce all shields, his arrow shot farther and straighter than anyone's at court. In wrestling, no one could put him down. Even so, it was his personal charm that endeared him to the army as did no other man. When Minuchihr came to his maturity, Faridun abdicated in his favour. The young Shah thereupon set in motion his plan to avenge his wicked uncles, Tur and Selim. Eventually the great battle was joined. The Deevs came in support of Tur and Selim but so strong was the might of Minuchihr that nothing could stand in his way. He returned, "conqueror of the world", beloved by his people. The Epic says that he ruled for one hundred and twenty years in wisdom and in strength. Minuchihr holds an honoured place, not only in the National Epic, but in other early sources as well. One has to assume his is still a position in the legendary. But he is closer to reality than is, say, Jamshid. Mirkhond, for example, a Persian historian of the 15th century, attached to the Court of Herat, credits him with an oration that is given in full text, so important did Mirkhond consider it to be.[9] While this is not repeated in the *Shahnameh*, it is worth at least brief consideration.

The oration begins, of course, in praise of Almighty God. After premising thanksgivings and prayers, Minuchihr gets down to business. "That Monarch," he says, "is the most fortunate ... who renders his flock most happy." It is the Monarch's responsibility to care for his subjects, to curb and punish oppression and to redress the injured. He is to avoid "capricious innovations which are invariably attended with small gains and great losses." He is also to avoid demanding more of his subjects than they anticipate.

There follows two sections, one devoted to the relationship between the Monarch and the Army and one to his relationship with the husbandman. Of the former, it is said that "the army is to the king what wings are to the bird." The king has a right to obedience but in turn he is to "supply their maintenance without delay or evasion."

The husbandmen may not withhold their persons or their properties from the Sovereign and they are to labour unceasingly in the cultivation of the soil and the improvement of the country. In return the king is to dispense "impartial justice" and not to place tyrannical governors over them. In years of drought he is to grant them exemption from taxation — and for the year following.

Minuchihr then sets forth the three qualities of a good king: (1) whatever he says should be spoken in truth; (2) he should avoid penuriousness "which renders everyone despicable,"; (3) he should not give way to anger.

A good king should rarely have recourse to punishment and he should not concern himself with the personal aspects of people's lives (i.e., what they eat and how they dress, etc.). Any accusations — even against governors — must be carefully investigated and a just punishment rendered.

Death is the end of all, Minuchihr says toward the end. "The people of this world are like travellers, laden with their respective burdens, who set out on a journey. All they have is borrowed, they must at last leave it behind them. Nor can any part of it accompany them except gratitude, recognition of the Divine Will and good works."

The king must conform to that Divine Will. He is only

a good ruler when he walks in the paths of righteousness, when his equity is administered, when his enemies are defeated and the frontiers guarded against every foe. "It only remains for you to obey," he concludes his admonition to his people.

It is in Minuchihr's reign that the famous Seistan legend begins to take form. In many ways the most attractive of the many recountings of the *Shahnameh*, this legend really sits at the heart of the National Epic. It is still the heroic period of the mythical *Kayani* dynasty and the name Pahlavi, after which the present ruling house of Iran takes its dynastic name, is associated with this era.

Seistan itself is a geographical area (now a province), that marches with present day Afghanistan. Early, it was the guardian area of the frontiers that push down from Central Asia. These were the routes followed by many of the great campaigners who invaded Iran over the centuries. Consequently, the area was one of constant strife because it was an area in which penetration had been the historic pattern. The penetration actually took two forms. When the Shah — who has always been responsible for defending the frontiers of Iran — was weak, the penetration became invasion, pure and simple. When he was strong, it became a controlled penetration. The control took this form. Iran was comparatively fertile by comparison with its neighbours. Thus, very early, it became essentially agrarian rather than pastoral. For the cultivator to work, however, he needed protection. Further, as Iran was an area with a limited water supply, the water had to be parcelled out on a time basis and this had to be ensured.

The pastoral people thus came to have a real utility. They could protect the tiller of the soil against destructive marauders and protect his work animals as well. They could also be used to impose a certain discipline on the use of water. And, finally, in times of real crisis, the pastoralists could be pressed into service as warriors in exchange for certain guarantees regarding themselves and their flocks. A wise Shah, therefore, could provide his country with a certain amount of security at very little cost. The traditional presence of tribal groups around the peripheral areas of Iran rather than in the central regions recalls this early protective role.

The Seistan legend is, therefore, in one sense, legend, but in another a part of this historic process. As mentioned above, Faridun divided his vast empire between his three sons, Iraj, the youngest receiving Iran. After his murder by his brothers and the avenging by Minuchihr, one would have thought the matter was ended. But, the fraternal strife went on between the descendants of Tur and Selim and those of Iraj. The former — the Turanians — were the Turks or Tatars of Central Asia, seeking access to Iran. The descendants of Iraj were the resisting Iranians. This resistance was led by the great house of Sam (which many associated with the great house of Karen the great Arcacid noble who will be described later) which was introduced above. Rustam, of course, was the greatest of the warriors of the House of Sam or Zal as it was later called, and is the most famous hero in the National Epic. He must have been a formidable man. He is described as "elephant bodied" with the strength of one hundred and twenty elephants. His horse, Raksh, would have put Babe the Blue Ox, of Pacific Northwest lumbering fame, to shame. When the conquering Arabs came to Seistan, ruins a mile apart were pointed out to them as having been the "manger" and "heel-ropes" of Raksh. Rustam's mother was said to be related to the devil king Dahhak who killed Jamshid, and which therefore gave Rustam an edge in subduing demons (Deevs). Rustam began life requiring the milk of ten nurses, so great was his hunger. When he was weaned, it was said he ate as much as five men. At three he rode on horseback and at eight he was as tall and powerful as a man. When he was ten the Epic tells us that the King's white elephant broke loose and went on a rampage. Rustam seized his grandfather's iron mace and went after him. When the elephant saw him coming, he rushed to him, trunk up, tusks out, trumpeting wildly, but Rustam struck him such a blow that the mace was bent in two. But the elephant fell at his feet with a crash. For this, as a reward, his father sent him to capture an enchanted fortress. Disguised as a salt merchant with his train, Rustam was admitted to the fortress from whence he stormed the treasure palace. So great was the booty when he finally gained access that two thousand camels could not carry it away. So Rustam burned what remained of the palace and returned to his father. Thus ended his childhood.

In the Epic, one of the characteristics of Iranian society that emerges so clearly is the family relationship — in this case illustrated by the house of Sam — and the relationship of the family to the Shah. Before recounting further great deeds of Rustam, therefore, it is important to understand something of these relationships.

Sam was the son of the great legendary chief Neriman who, on account of his intrepid bravery, had been made commander-in-chief of the Persian armies. Shortly before Minuchihr came to the throne, Sam — known as the great Pahlavan — had a son born to him with white hair and black eyes. This was considered a bad omen by the Persians and it took a week before the nurse had the courage to announce the birth to Sam. She did this with great cleverness, declaring that the stars had decreed for him a great destiny.

Sam, his heart overflowing with bitterness, decided to abandon the child — named Zal by his mother — in the Alborz Mountains. The baby was taken from his mother (who no doubt was in great disfavour by now as all assumed it was she who was of the demon race to which the child belonged) and left to die. But Zal was not forgotten by God, the Epic tells us, so a giant bird, Simurgh, found the babe and adopted him. The moons and the years rolled happily for the boy as he was growing up in his mountain home, while his father, Sam, and his mother, suffered the loss of their child. When the time was right and the suffering of the parents had come to repentance, the great bird brought back the boy and delivered him to his father. The latter, seeing his son's powerful body and beautiful countenance, asked his son's forgiveness, clothed him richly, put him on an Arab steed, and conducted him into the Army.

By this time, Minuchihr had taken the throne and upon hearing of these wonderful events, had his son Nuder go to Seistan at the head of a troop of horses to escort Sam, the great Pahlavan, and his son back to the royal palace. Minuchihr first received Sam, seated him at his left hand, and bade him tell the whole story which Sam did, "hiding not his own evil deed." The Shah then received the son, had his horoscope cast, and found that the stars said nothing but good would come to Zal and that he would outlive every warrior of the age and be the defense of Iran for hundreds of years.

These prophecies so delighted Minuchihr that he gave both

father and son rich presents and a charter investing the House of Sam with the sovereignty of Kabul, Zabul, and Ind which today would roughly cover the land from Afghanistan to the Indus Basin. The new grant caused a considerable flurry after Zal had distinguished himself in a few campaigns because he fell in love with the daughter of the King of Kabul (The House of Sam was not royal so could not assume a royal title). Her name was Rudabeh and the Epic describes her as having skin fairer than ivory, cheeks like pomegranates, arching brows like a raven's wings, and a body like a Sabin tree. Nevertheless, Sam was angry because she was not a Persian and this was mild by comparison with Shah Minuchihr's anger. The Shah recalled Zal to him and put him through a series of contests and combats in which Zal outstripped every competitor. Minuchihr therefore asked for another reading of the stars and once again an affirmative report came back :

> "O, Shelter of the Universe. Lo, in the Book of Fate it is written that the love of Zal and Rudabeh shall shine as the stars, for from their union shall spring a son, beside whom all the heroes of the world shall pale. Long life, courage, strength and honour shall be his, and in the hour of peril, the great Shahs of Iran will never call upon him in vain."

So the Shah relented, Zal returned for the great wedding, and from the union came Rustam.

Rustam was barely out of his childhood, as related above, when Minuchihr came to his death bed. The great Shah, known for his wisdom, called his son Nuder to him and gave him counsel before he closed his eyes, but Nuder was of a different temperament and soon the land groaned under his injustice and tyranny. The great nobles of the land finally came to Sam and asked him to take the crown from Nuder and place it on his own head. But, the old man, true to the tradition of Iran, refused to take such action, reminding the nobles of the oath of allegiance that they had all taken to the Shah. But it was a costly decision in a sense because as the news of Minuchihr's death and the new Shah's weakness spread into Turan, those of the race of Tur decided the time was right to resume the fratricidal feud. Afrasiàb, the Prince of the Turanians was a warrior of great reputation and he raised an army "which covered the ground like ants and locusts" to move against Iran. In turn, the Iranians raised an army to defend. Shah Nuder made the mistake of assuming command of his own army. Afrasiab killed him and seized his crown. What Iranian nobles were left alive from the great battle came to Zal for advice as they would not accept Afrasiab's claim to the throne of Iran. Zal was of a like opinion but realized the hazards of disavowing the Turanian's claim without a royal replacement. He called Rustam to him and asked him if he were prepared to take the field, inexperienced though he was. Rustam who by now had found his famous horse Raksh, was eager to prove himself as a warrior among warriors. He readily offered his service whereupon Zal began the raising of a new army. To test Rustam further, however, Zal asked him to go to Mount Alborz and find a hidden palace in which resided a young prince of royal blood, Kaikobad, a descendant of Faridun. It was Rustam's mission to offer the throne to the prince and return him safely to the army.

Rustam found the palace and the prince, gained Kaikobad's acceptance, and amidst many dangers, returned him safely to the army that Zal had meanwhile raised. For seven days, the nobles feasted and counselled together with the prince and on the eighth day placed the Crown of Iran on the head of Kaikobad, the "Hope of Iran."

So once again the battle was joined and though Afrasiab made one terrible onslaught in which so great was the clamour and confusion that it seemed as if heaven and earth had closed in deadly conflict, it was Rustam, who here established himself as the greatest warrior of them all. At one crucial point he closed in single combat with Afrasiab against his father's advice. He caught the Turanian by the girdle and dragged him from his saddle, but the leather of the girdle broke and Afrasiab fell to the ground to be immediately surrounded by his warriors. But not before Rustam had snatched the crown from his head.

So, among them all, none could compare with Rustam and the Turanians sued for peace and a boundary was set and Kaikobad sat on his throne as of old. He reigned beneficently over Iran for one hundred years, keeping the peace.

Kai Ka'us succeeded his father on the throne and at first, the Epic tells us, exercised many of the princely virtues of his illustrious predecessors. But, as his riches increased and his armies grew stronger, he became filled with self admiration and pride until he, like the great Jamshid, could no longer behold anyone but himself in the world. Indeed, he claimed to surpass the glorious Jamshid and all his predecessors. His announcement that he meant to move his armies into Mazanderan, and conquer the Deevs — something that even Jamshid had not done — brought fear to the hearts of his countrymen. They sent messengers to Zal telling him of the proposed expedition "O Gracious Pahlavi, once again Iran is in danger and in need of thee."

Zal was sorely distressed but spoke words of comfort to the messengers, telling them that though the Shah was like a child with a sword who expects the whole world to tremble, that the House of Sam (now known as the House of Zal) would not abandon him in his folly and that no matter what came, Rustam would safeguard the Army for the sake of Iran. He did, however, agree to accompany them back to court to seek to persuade the Shah against the action.

His words were in vain. In fact the Shah told Zal that his house would not be needed, that he and Rustam could stay home and guard the kingdom. Zal's answer was a model of Persian diplomacy: "May the great Shah never have cause to recollect the warning voice of his servant with repentance or sorrow. May his glory shine on undimmed for ever."

The campaign was short and disastrous. The Shah was taken prisoner and his army destroyed. He did manage to get a message to Zal, however, who called forth Rustam to deliver the king from the enemy.

What followed was a series of encounters that tested Rustam to the limit. Described as Rustam's seven labours, he emerged from them with the title "Champion of the World".

The journey to Mazanderan, the land of the Deevs was a succession of challenges from lions, dragons and beautiful enchantresses, ending in final victory over the Great White Deev himself and the freeing of the Shah. Mighty though he was in these single-handed efforts which stretched him to the utmost, Rustam constantly invoked the name of the great God,

Ormuzd, admitting his need for divine intervention. This is the same God, of course, whom Jamshid sought to displace and we are constantly reminded in the Epic that those who gain the victory are in service to the great God. Those who fail — and many of the Shahs did — were those who became so puffed up in their own vanity that they forgot him.

Howbeit, to return to the Great Pahlavan, as he was now known, Rustam received much acclaim and many gifts for his great exploits including a letter from the Shah written upon pages of silk, in ink made of wine and olives and amber and the black of lamps, naming him Champion of the World.

"Behold it is chronicled in the Book of Shahs, that Kai Ka'us and his folly parted not company."

Kai Ka'us, having been rescued from one disaster now invited another. Busy with triumphal marches through Iran demanding the homage of his subjects (can the lamb wage battle with the lion?) he was not properly attentive to his duties and the Syrians seized the opportunity to revolt. Kai Ka'us raised an army and moved against them and was victorious in his first encounter. But, in the feasting and victory celebrations that followed, the vain Shah failed to perceive that he was being lulled into inaction and he was finally seized and imprisoned by the King of Hamaveran who had been instrumental in raising the revolt. So once more, the Epic tells us, the King's folly left Iran with an empty throne. Afrasiab, the Turanian, ever wakeful and dangerous, learning that the Shah was imprisoned in a Syrian dungeon, raised a vast army, burst over the borders, took Syria first and then Iran. The Persians appealed for counsel and aid from the great House at Seistan and, although Rustam was angered at the Shah's foolishness, he recalled the oath that his grandfather Sam had sworn to Faridun that he and his House would support and uphold the glory of the Shahs forever. He took the army of Seistan, marched into Syria, liberated the Shah, and then wrote Afrasiab telling him to quit the land of Iran. Afrasiab responded with a caustic and witty reply recalling to Rustam that he was so busy extricating his glorious sovereign from his follies that he really had no time left to expel invaders and that he, Afrasiab, was not inclined to leave.

The newly released Shah responded with an instant call to

war and once again Rustam set forth to free Iran from its enemies. Afrasiab fought with his usual skill and bravery but Rustam watered the earth with the blood of his Turanians and Afrasiab was forced once again to retire behind the border.

Kai Ka'us was not finished. No doubt recalling the flying throne of Jamshid, he had constructed a chariot to which were bound four strong eagles. Extending in front of each corner was a javelin surmounted on the point with the flesh of a goat to urge the eagles on. With great pomp, carrying a goblet of wine in his hand while all the people shouted "Bah ! Bah !" in admiration, Kai Ka'us mounted the flying chariot and the eagles were released. Up, up, they flew, far into the clouds, hungry for the meat just beyond their grasp. Far beyond the borders of Iran they flew until their strength was spent and the chariot tumbled to earth in the midst of a desert in far off Cathay. Here, finally, the Shah suffered hunger and thirst, loneliness and despair with no one to minister to his needs. In his anguish he prayed to the great God, Ormuzd, confessing himself to be unworthy of his throne and of his people and he watered the desert with his tears of penitence. So Ormuzd finally returned him to his land to face the wrath of Rustam who spared his sovereign neither words nor reproaches. When the Shah heard the scathing tongue of the great Pahlavan, he listened with chastened spirit and his vanity evaporated leaving him humble and ashamed. After forty days lying in the dust before Ormuzd, he once more ascended the throne and finally ruled in wisdom.

With a chastened Shah on the throne and peace declared, Rustam was restless for the hunting which he loved. Mounting Raksh, he rode out toward the tiny kingdom of Samengan which was feudatory to Afrasiab, not knowing that a beautiful princess resided there in the King's palace who had all her life worshipped Rustam from afar. Tahmineh was her name and never in the Garden of Kings did there ever bloom a fairer flower.

When word came into the palace from a traveller who had passed by the Champion of the World during the hunt and recognized the Mighty One, Princess Tahmineh began to weave the pattern of her desire. Calling to her six of the wiliest horsemen of the little kingdom, she bade them go to the hunting grounds while Rustam slept, steal Raksh, his great horse, and bring it to the royal stables.

Never had man or demon overcome that glorious steed. But for the sake of the beautiful Princess, the stars decreed it and Rustam awoke the next morning to find the signs of the struggle and the tracks leading outward. He followed them to the castle where the king — not knowing of the night's events — greeted the great Rustam not as an enemy, but as a guest.

Rustam's anger was finally assuaged at the King's promise to help find Raksh and the thief and gave himself up to a day's feasting and drinking with his host.

When night fell and as he lay on his couch perfumed with musk and roses, there stepped into his chamber a slave bearing a lamp perfumed with amber and following after, a woman, the fairest that Rustam had ever seen. The Princess identified herself and confessed the theft in a long dialogue that brought Rustam up to the point. But she, knowing that no man—least of all a warrior—cares for what he wins too easily—held his fiery purpose off and left him finally alone. The next morning he asked the King for her hand in marriage and they were wedded that very day in a bower of roses and white lilies.

It was a lovely affair and the days passed for both like a happy dream. But, gradually, Rustam became restless and the Princess knew the time was not far off when he would leave her. The day came and amidst much bitter weeping Rustam left, taking from his arm at the end an onyx bracelet upon which was engraved the image of a Simurgh—to be worn, said Rustam, by a daughter on her curls and a son, if he should come, on his arm. It was the badge of Rustam and Zal to protect against the power of evil. Time passed and Tahmineh heard nothing. One day a present came from the Mighty One—three great rubies of priceless value and three wedges of the finest gold. But no letter and no word and Tahmineh knew she would never see her Lord again. But to her came a son and she called the babe, Sohrab, meaning Sunshine, and she was comforted though woman-like she let word return to Iran that a daughter had been borne to the Mighty Rustam.

Sohrab grew up a warrior under the tutelage of the famous Tatar General, Piran-wisa. When he came of age he was commissioned in the army of Afrasiab and fought many battles with great wisdom and valour. His horse, given to him by his mother, was a foal sprung from Rustam's glorious Raksh. His sword and shield—which he swore to keep untarnished—was given to him by the King of Samengan. On his arm he wore the amulet of the House of Zal. He represents, therefore, in the Epic, the conglomerate, the most vulnerable of men. For in his drive for fame, the dangers multiply for this man to the point of destruction. He belongs everywhere, but in a sense nowhere, to every one, but no one.

Afrasiab was growing old. He knew, through his spies, that Sohrab was in truth the son of Rustam. With Sohrab in his command, Afrasiab, therefore, set the machinery in motion to match Sohrab against his father. "The young lion will kill the old lion," he told his commanders, and with Iran devoid of Rustam, that rich country would finally fall prey to the Turanian armies.

It should not be necessary here to recount the titanic struggle between father and son. Matthew Arnold's masterly poem, *Sohrab and Rustum* has become, for the English speaking world, a part of its own literature, just as is Fitzgerald's translation of the *Rubaiyat.* Even Firdawsi speaks of the tragedy as full of "water for the eye." The battle raged between the two combatants for two days. At the end of the first day's encounter, Rustam feared for the victory. He sought audience with the Shah telling him that he had fought the Tatar Champion with sword, and spear, and arrow and mace, not once but again and again and in the warrior's art "he seems to be my superior." He conversed with Zuara, his younger brother and commanded him that should he fall on the next day, he, Zuara, should return his army in safety to Seistan and say to Zal that he had no cause to complain of fate for he, Rustam, had fought long and gloriously for Iran.

The next day the contest was resumed and Rustam with the wisdom and cunning of the years, finally as night fell, cut Sohrab down.

As Sohrab lay dying, Rustam saw the amulet of the House of Zal on the arm of his opponent and then it was that the two men knew each other. And lo, there broke from the heart of the Hero, a terrible cry of anguish, and the earth became dark before his eyes and Raksh the intelligent, gave forth a fearful cry — a cry so unearthly, so full of woe, that a shiver ran through all the Persian lines.

The Epic recounts, then, the dialogue between father and son as they discovered their love for each other. Finally, however, Sohrab's beautiful spirit departed this life and soared into the sunny gardens of the Blessed. All night, Rustam kept vigil by his dead son and none, not even the Shah, dared come near him. In the morning the procession was formed to take the body back to the home Sohrab had never known, in Seistan, the House of Zal. All the nobles of Iran marched before the bier, their heads covered with ashes, their garments rent and tattered. The mighty wailing of the army drowned even the cries of Rustam. And the drums of the war elephants were shattered and the cymbals broken and the tails of the horses torn to the roots. For thus did the Persians mourn their mighty dead.

Afrasiab's scheme had worked. But when Rustam had recovered, in vengeance he moved against his old enemy with all the strength he had ever known. He demolished the Turanian's capital and paused not in his work of destruction until the whole land was laid waste and Afrasiab became a wretched wanderer on the face of the earth.

New Shahs came to the throne. And Rustam, knowing only the warrior's life, continued to serve them in counsel with his aged father, the white-haired Zal, and on the battle-field. His last great combat was against Isfendiyar, still a distinguished family name in Iran. But time was running out for the Mighty One. Zal, in his old age, had a son of great beauty born to him. But the horoscope cast spoke of terrible things — that he would be the ruin of the house of his fathers and bring destruction on the land of Iran. Zal prayed to Ormuzd that he would avert this fate from the head of his son. But the stars do not lie and the day came when his young brother plotted Rustam's death. Working with the King of Kabul, a hunting trip was planned for the great Rustam over an area where pits had been dug with upright spears and lances and covered over, a device that jungle fighters of World War II recall, the only difference being the use of sharpened bamboo in place of lances and spears.

When the day came for the hunt, and as they drew near to the place of peril, Raksh drew back, refusing to advance. Rustam thinking him afraid, commanded him to go forward. When Raksh refused again, Rustam applied the whip for the one and only time in their long campaigns together — and it cost him his life. Maddened by the stroke, Raksh sprang forward only to fall into one of the pits. Sinking onto the cruel bed of pointed weapons, Raksh with a mighty leap escaped, only to fall into another. Seven times he went down and seven times he struggled on bruised and maimed until he could go no more. Finally as horse and rider lay exhausted, Shug'had, the younger brother came smiling in triumph. In one last mighty effort, Rustam drew his bow and sent an arrow into the black heart of his brother.

So fell Rustam the Mighty and never again did Iran achieve such telling victories, for with Rustam her glory departed.

The death of Rustam marks the end of the *Kayani*, or purely mythical period of the Epic.

Iran's parallel history continues on through the period of Alexander and his successors and into the Sassanian dynasty and it is at this point in time that Firdawsi begins to be historical even though his history is interlaced with all kinds of myths and legends. The coming of Ardashir or Artaxerxes is typical.

Ardashir was an historical figure of the first magnitude and he was even known to the Arab historians. The dynasty which he founded, the Sassanian, equalled in splendour the Achaemenid from which it claimed descent and its long wars with the Roman Empire kept the dynasty in constant touch with the West and with the Roman historians. Consequently we do know a great deal about the period.

It is the accounting of the *Shahnameh*, however, which concerns us here and which provides continuity to the National Epic.

As mentioned above, the death of Rustam brought an end to the heroic age of Persia. But it will be recalled that Rustam's last great battle was against Isfendiyar, whom he slew. Isfendiyar had a son, Bahman, who is identified as Artaxerxes Longimanus, a late Achaemenid monarch who was the first historical Shahanshah that Persian historians record. It was from Bahman that the Sassanian dynasty claimed descent and its right to rule in direct line from the Achaemenid kings.

As Firdawsi describes it in the *Shahnameh*, Bahman married his sister Khumani or Humay who bore him a son, Dara. Bahman's brother, Sasan, now being deprived of the succession by the birth of an heir retired to the mountains and became a shepherd. This son, Dara, interestingly, is the same one whom the Epic tells us married the daughter of Philip of Macedon from which union sprang Alexander.

So Sasan's house remained far from the strife of the Parthian period, which followed Alexander's death and so Sasan's house continued for four generations, the *Shahnameh* tells us "from sire to son the name Sasan descended," herdsmen and tenders of cattle but preserving nevertheless the true tradition and blood of the Achaemenid kings.

The Epic tells us that the last in the generation of Sasans finally came to the great Papak, no doubt having fallen on evil days, and asked for a job as head-herdsman.

Papak who was Governor of Fars and Warden of the Marches under Ardawan, the great overlord of Fars and neighbouring lands, hired the man and shortly thereafter dreamed one night about his new herdsman, Sasan, and that from his head emanated a sun that illuminated the whole world. The next night he dreamed that he saw his shepherd riding on a white elephant receiving homage from all the people. The third night he saw the Sacred Fire alight in Sasan's house.

Papak's advisers interpreted these dreams as indicating that Sasan or his son would become Shahanshah, King of Kings. Papak, no man to miss an opportunity, sent for his shepherd and heard from his lips the account of his illustrious descent. Upon receiving this information, he immediately clothed Sasan in a royal robe and gave his daughter to him in marriage. From this union came Ardashir.[10]

When Ardashir reached his early maturity,[11] Papak, sent him to the court of his great Parthian overlord, Ardawan, for his education. Ardashir's many accomplishments soon overshadowed those of Ardawan's own son. Ardawan, as a consequence, moves to put Ardashir down — the latter becomes the head groom. Ardashir complains to his grandfather about his treatment, but the old man reminds him that he is not even a relative of Ardawan and thus has no real claim to special position unless the great lord chooses to give it to him.

After all, his grandfather points out, Ardashir is still young and has a lot to learn.

In Persian literature, just as king's sons seem always to emerge in some special capacity to recognition, where formerly they were not known, — on the polo field or the hunting ground — so they are also the beneficiary, at the right time, of some godsend. In Ardashir's case, it was a woman.

Gulnar was Ardawan's mistress. She was also a highly intelligent, practical woman whom Ardawan saw daily and apparently greatly depended upon. Her one weakness seems to have been her great passion for Ardashir. Once their liaison is established, the Epic tells us, she continues to manage Ardawan's affairs with her usual skill but at the same time keeps Ardashir informed. Eventually she hears from the king's astrologers that Ardawan (although he is not mentioned by name) will be facing a revolt from a subordinate who will eventually surpass him in greatness. She sees that this must be Ardashir and she knows he is in danger. So the young couple agree to flee back to Fars.

There is nothing so apt to arouse a king's anger as stealing his mistress and Ardawan proves to be no exception. He sets forth with 40,000 horsemen in hot pursuit. Inquiring at a certain village on his way to Fars, if anyone had seen the couple, Ardawan is told that yes, they have seen a couple riding like the wind, one on a white horse and one on a black. Behind them ran a large ram, the villagers say. Ardawan asks his adviser what this mountain sheep was. "That royal splendour," replies the adviser, "which by his lucky star leads him to lordship." The adviser further admonishes Ardawan that he must not let the sheep overtake the fleeing couple. Ardawan and his men press on hard. The next day, they come to a hamlet and again inquire of the couple. The head man answers :

> "Hard by our hamlet two riders hastened,
> Dry were their lips with thirst, their raiment dust-stained,
> And behind one on the saddle, a sheep sat:
> In palace hunting scenes, ne'er was its like met."

Ardawan turns to his adviser but knew the answer before it

came. "King Ardashir's luck rides behind him." In true Persian tradition, Ardawan accepts his fate. He dismounts and gives thanks to God. He then sleeps until morning, then arises and rides.

> "And with cheeks sallow like a scorched reed-bed,
> Did he to Rey return in the dark twilight."

The theme of the Royal Splendour (Far) is most important in Persian literature. It occurred in the case of Sasan. It occurred in the case of Ardashir. It will occur later and re-occur in examples that will follow. Its significance is that to the Persians it is a manifestation of the Divine Right of their kings. The theme is repeated in coronation ceremonies. There is nothing quite like it in western experience. It is not, as seen above, simply something that passes from king to king. It can come to a shepherd or a groom. In fact the sub-theme of a royal scion being reared in very simple surroundings is an important part of Persian tradition. In fact it is almost essential from a political point of view — this marriage of royalty with the commonalty. The point is though, that the Royal Splendour marks the designation as in the two cases cited above. One does not have to worry about a royal presence when it is needed. It will manifest itself or be manifest. This, at least, is an article of faith among Persians.

In 226 A.D., Ardashir killed his overlord, Ardawan just as his great Achaemenid predecessor, Cyrus, killed his on his way to Empire. There followed a series of campaigns that eventually brought the House of Sasan to ultimate victory. Interestingly enough, however, the *Shahnameh* tells more of the other side of the coin.

Once Ardawan was killed, Ardashir according to the Epic, turned his thoughts to Ardawan's daughter. He marries her, hoping no doubt to consolidate his wins and get his hands on what he believes to be Ardawan's considerable fortune. She, in turn, at her brother's bidding tries to poison Ardashir. Quite understandably, Ardashir orders her death. But she is by child with him and the first minister, knowing the need for an heir if the dynasty is to continue, shelters her and eventually she delivers a son. The lad is kept from Ardashir for a few years as his mother's concealment continues, but ultimately Ardashir picks him out of a group of boys playing polo and recognizes him as a king's son. So Shapur I, as the boy was to be known in manhood, came to his high position as Crown Prince.

According to the Epic, Shapur eventually married the daughter of a rival tribal king and they have a child, so the dynasty is firmly established.

Firdawsi concludes his great Epic at the death-bed of Ardashir. Addressing his son Shapur, he says — and this is repeated many times in Persian history — "Consider the altar and the throne as inseparable. They must always sustain one another." He then gives his blessing and asks God's blessing upon his son's memory and that of his own.

NOTES

1. Ghirshman, R., *Persia*, London, 1964, pp. 154 ff.

2. Omar Khayyam (1038-1125). He was born and is buried in Nishapur. Bahram was a Sassanian king who ruled from 420-438. Because of his prowess as a hunter of that elusive animal, he was known as Gur (wild ass).

3. Noldeke's "The Iranian National Epic" or *Shahnameh*, Bombay (K. R. Cama Oriental Institute Publication No. 7), 1930, pp. 24 ff. The material immediately following is drawn from Noldeke.

4. Wickens, G. M., "The Imperial Epic of Iran : A Literary Approach" in *Iranian Civilization and Culture* (ed. by Adams, C. J.), McGill University Press, 1972, p. 141.

5. All quotes from Arberry, A. J., *Classical Persian Literature*, London, 1958, pp. 45-46.

6. For a detailed explanation, see the section on the *Avesta* in Browne, E. G., *A Literary History of Persia*, Cambridge University Press, 4 vols., 1969, I, pp. 95-102.

7. Ghazali's Book of *Counsel for Kings* (trans. by Bagley, F.R.C.), Oxford University Press, 1964, p. 48.

8. Browne; *op. cit.*, I, p. 112. See I, pp. 110-125. There are many narrative accounts of the *Shahnameh.* I have used Renniger, E. D., *The Story of Rustam* and other Persian Hero Tales from Firdawsi, New York, 1917.

9. *The History of the Early Kings of Persia*, translated from the original Persian of Mirkhond, London, 1832, pp. 177ff.

10. Sykes, Sir Percy, *A History of Persia*, 2 vols., London, 1958, I, pp. 392ff.

11. Wickens, *op. cit.*, pp. 133ff.

12. Browne, *op. cit.*, I, pp. 137-38.

13. Parallel passages are given in *Ibid.*, pp. 139-45

14. De Lorey, Eustache and Fladen, Douglas, *The Moon of the Fourteenth Night*, London, 1910, p. 59.

Chapter 2

THRONE OF CYRUS

The Persian Empire was created within the space of a single generation by a series of conquests that followed one another with a rapidity scarcely equalled except by Alexander and by the Arabs in the first generation after the death of Mohammed.[1] Between 550 – 549 B.C. when the Persians and Medes were joined and 525 B.C. when the conquest of Egypt was complete, the Persians conquered an area — and held it — which was far greater in extent than the more ancient empires of Babylonia, Assyria, or Egypt had ever known and was, in fact, the greatest Empire west of China that the world had ever seen. As will be pointed out later, it was, moreover, a true world empire by comparison with China's, which would more properly be described as a Chinese Empire.

Further, the Persian Empire was maintained by the same family that created it, undivided and unbroken, for two hundred years. By comparison, Alexander's Empire ended with his death and the unity of Arab rule lasted only a little more than a century.

Such remarkable achievement is comprehended in this Chapter under the title, "The Throne of Cyrus." It is essentially an account of the rise of the Achaemenids to power, although the Chapter following will continue to deal with certain aspects of this dynastic reign.

The land of Parsua, to the south and southwest of Lake Urmiyeh, now known as Lake Rezaiyeh — which lies in the large central basin of the northwestern Zagros and measures roughly ninety miles by thirty — is mentioned for the first time in the annals of the Assyrian King Shalmaneser III in 834 B.C. This appears to have been the region where the Persian tribes halted for a time before continuing their migrations southeastwards, following the valleys of the Zagros mountain range.

Clearly the Persians were an outside people. The Assyrians noted their presence but were content to leave it go at that. Their concern was always Babylon. Assyria and Babylon had grown up on the banks of the Tigris-Euphrates — to the west of where the Persians were infiltrating — in such close proximity that it is as difficult to separate them historically as it is geographically. Their history is so intertwined up until the rise of the Persian Empire that one can only say in brief focus that the power of one became the measure of the weakness of the other. In this overriding concern, even obsession, one with the other, the Persians found their early route to world power.

The Persians were a part of a far greater tribal movement, or rather waves of tribal movements, that have come to be described as the Aryan invasions. For unlike the more native peoples of the Middle East, the Aryans were a people apart who saw themselves as a people apart.

When the first Iranians began to appear within the outer limits of the Assyrian Empire, they came as a primitive, pastoral folk, owning horses, cattle, sheep, goats, and the watch dog. They had no written language but they were an extremely strong and hardy people, adaptable, and clearly exceptional. In some cases, their men seemed to have served as mercenaries in other armies, although this is not certain. What is certain is that they early appeared to demonstrate a competence as fighting men as well as pastoral people.

The Aryan family of which the Iranians were a part, was an extended family as we say today. It was based on patriarchal authority and polygamy. There was an awareness of class and position despite the fact that the families travelled much the same way in rude wagons with axles and wheels roughly hewn from a single stem. The fighting men used the horse and developed the chariot. They were a resourceful and courageous men and once on the move gained the respect of their enemies as illustrated by the fact that they were not only mentioned in other early annals of the Assyrian kings, but, as well, in Semetic sources.

The original home of the Aryans seems to have lain in the great steppe which stretches north of the Black Sea and the Caspian through southern Russia to Turkistan (ancient Turan) and the Oxus and the Iaxartes. They were all of one people bearing the name Arya. This included Indians as well as Iranians — of which the Persians were a sub-branch.

The causes of the Aryan migrations are not clear, but they seem to have been connected with events taking place on the northern coast of the Black Sea — possibly a massive drought of extended duration. At any rate, the conditions in their homeland were such that the Aryans fanned out across Asia in successive waves over a period of time. It was not a single invasion.

One branch of the Aryans skirted the Himalaya and eventually subdued the Punjab. We know that this was accomplished around 1200 B.C. in the Vedic era. They brought with them to India the tight knit caste system that has endured to our own day. The Brahmin caste, or the upper priestly caste, kept itself protected and apart with the result that they endured for centuries as a lighter skinned (like the late great Nehru who was of the Brahmin caste), proverbially "Aryan" type having their counterparts in Persia.

The other branch of the Aryans — which became subdivided and splintered — pressed south more directly into the area we now know as the Middle East. There was no single route taken. Some came through the interstices of the Zagros Mountains in Iran, some through the broad plains of what is now Iraq, and some more to the east, down through Afghanistan and into Iran through the area now known as Seistan province in Iran.

In short, the Aryan conquest of the Middle East in the initial stages was a fragmented series — not coordinated — of many Aryan tribal groups on the move. Later, as consolidation took place under a series of able Aryan leaders, the actual battles were joined out of which finally came the Persian Empire, the first great world empire.

The Middle East was ripe for the Aryan conquest. While there had been in the history of that area great rulers such as Sargon and Hammurabi who did some preliminary consolidation of Empire, they were extremely loose forms. The land to which the Aryans came was really an assemblage of small city states and petty kingdoms — Elam, Sumer, and Akkad, to mention the three best known — that made no pretense of being a broadly based imperial structure. Essentially the native peoples whom the Aryans confronted, consisted of two ethnic groups — the Sumerians, who were Assyrians, and the

Semites, who were Babylonians. The Semites eventually dominated although then, as now, they were continually quarreling amongst themselves.

Between 1800 B.C. and 1500 B.C., the Assyrians broke free from Babylonian rule and started their own road to conquest. For the most part the Assyrians were a free, agricultural people; masters of the horse and capable of fierce, sustained effort. They put together the most formidable army the Middle East had seen up to that time. Their commanders were great fighting kings whose names have come down in history — Tiglath-pileser I, Assur-natsirpal, Tiglath-pileser IV, Sargon II, Sennacherib, Assurbanipal. The last named king conquered Babylon — the dominant city of ancient times — in 648 B.C. He took the title of King of Sumer, Akkad and Elam and died in 626 B.C.

The Assyrians were as cruel as Byron describes them in his poem "The Destruction of Sennacherib" and as the old Testament recounts again and again (remembering that Babylon had been Semetic and the Old Testament writers were Semites). Assurbanipal, for example, who in the Middle Eastern manner tended to make his recordings on rock inscriptions, was a man of great cruelty who writes (he was an educated man for his time who could read and write cuneiform and even old Sumerian texts) of carving up a governor with his own hands, grilling prisoners on the fire, cutting off hands, fingers, ears and noses, ripping "thousands" of eyes of prisoners from their sockets and tongues from their throats, making huge mounds of the bodies of his enemies, etc. When he conquered Susa, he transformed into a vast desert all of a region over a march of a month and twenty-five days. "I sowed salt and thorns."[2] Plunder, destruction, terror and mass executions — hardly a basis for a lasting kingdom. So it was that the Assyrian Empire was already falling into decay as the invading Aryans moved into the region and began pressing for power.

The Medes were the first of the Aryan tribal groups to gain position. The fact that their Empire came into being earlier than that of the kindred Persians was due essentially to two things — location and early leadership.

The Medes had migrated down through the Zagros range and established themselves around modern day Hamadan (known anciently as Ecbatana). This was a very strategic location as can be clearly seen even today by the visitor. It commands the pass through the mountains from Mesopotamia to the Iranian plateau. It is a natural route and a good highway today follows it. Furthermore it is a location that was in close proximity to the power of Assyria — much closer than that of the Persians who had settled to the east of them. Hence, as the Median power expanded and the Assyrian lessened, the Medes were in position to take over when the time came.

Eventually the Median empire extended to the Caspian Sea in the north, and what is now the area around Teheran in the northeast, moving out from the centrally located Ecbatana. (A writer would be remiss in his duties if he were not to mention the famous Nisaean horses which bore the Medes to their many victories and became famous as probably the best horses in Asia. They were of dun, grey or white and were unrivalled for speed, endurance and beauty. The Greeks — Herodotus, Arrian, and Ammianus Marcellinus — all write about this famous breed. The white horse, incidentally, was the one used by the Achaemenid kings in the great horse sacrifice which was of ancient Aryan origin.)

Cyaxares (died 584 B.C.) was the second reason for the rise of Media to imperial rank. He appears to have been a military genius — of which the Aryans produced a good number — who not only consolidated the first Aryan Empire but beat off a vicious attack from the Scythians invading in from Asia. It was he who eventually broke the power of Assyria. A leading historian remarks that "at the beginning of his reign, the paramount power of the east was Semetic but when he died, it was Iranian."[3]

Unfortunately his son Astyages was not strong enough to hold the Empire together. He was also unpopular, possibly because he had no heir. Consequently when Cyrus the Great attacked him, supported by many of the Medes themselves, there was really no doubt as to the outcome. In 550 B.C., the Empire passed into the hands of the Persians. It is now necessary to turn back to the Aryan branch that finally created the greatest of early Empires on the shoulders of their Aryan brethren, the Medes. The reference is to the Persians themselves.

The Persians, as they are commonly called in the West,

call their land Iran and themselves Irani, a word which is the Airiya or Arya of the Avesta, meaning land of the Aryans. The term Persia simply refers to the ancient province of Parsa, now Fars, which was the cradle land of the early Achaemenid kings. This is the area around present day Shiraz.

The Greeks knew this land as Persia. The Parsis or Parsees of India, who migrated from Iran because of persecution by the Arabs at the Conquest, derives from the same root word. Farsi is the word used by Iranians to describe their own language, or in the case of a person, to an inhabitant of the region of Fars. The older term Parsi has the same meaning but as there is no letter "p" in the Arabic language, after the Arab Conquest when many Arabic words were introduced into the older language, changes of this type were not uncommon.

The Persian kings, first known as the Achaemenids, belonged to the southern branch of the Iranian stock which had settled in the province of Fars at the time of the Aryan invasions. They spread out over the plains of Elam which is a very ancient land north of the Persian Gulf and east of the Tigris. There appears to have been an understood border between this Aryan group and the Medes who occupied, as pointed out above, the lands to the west and north of that held by the Persians. At least there was no fighting between them and in fact there seems to have been considerable intercourse although the Medes, because their responsibilities of Empire came earlier, tended to look upon the Persians as their country cousins. This relationship is borne out, too, by the fact that after they came to power, the Persians adopted many of the Median customs.

Unlike the heroic period described in the first chapter, the period of the Achaemenian Dynasty is well documented. There are a number of cuneiform inscriptions composed in old Persian carved into rocks scattered around the country, into the side of a rocky mountain which can still be seen today on the road from Hamadan to Kermanshah. The Greeks and the Jews also provide a great deal of information about this period as both peoples tended to be sympathetic toward the Persians and, in the case of the Greeks, fascinated by them.

The fact that so much information is available may seem at odds with the fact that the heroic period is so factually non-historic. But the explanation is a relatively simple one — the early cuneiform writing of the type that is at Behistun became lost and incomprehensible for hundreds of years. In fact, it was not until the 17th century that travellers began to return to Europe with samples of a strange West Asian script that even the leading scholars of the day did not recognize as being of great significance. Before them in fact, in these few samples, lay the most widespread and historically significant writing system in the ancient Middle East.

The disappearance of the wedge shaped script that we describe as cuneiform had taken place with such swiftness that even the Greeks seemed hardly aware of its existence. Yet its active history covered the last three millenia before Christ and involved a long string of successive cultures and languages.

It was a hundred years before the mystery began to unravel.[4] In 1761, a Dane, Carsten Niebuhr, managed to reach Persepolis after a hazardous journey which claimed the lives of most of his companions. He copied the inscriptions he found there and found to his surprise that there were, in reality, three different scripts. Upon his return to Europe, and his release of the information to the scholarly community, the deciphering proceeded apace. A German Sanskrit scholar, Georg Friedrich Grotefend was the man who really cracked the code however, if we can use that expression. He guessed that the introductory lines would contain the name, titles, and genealogy of the king as early literature was largely confined to what the king did, or said (social history was still centuries away). He found a sequence that appeared over and over again which he translated as "King of Kings." From this he finally worked out the puzzle and names began to drop into place. It was clear then that the Old Persian was related to Sanskrit (the other two Persepolis scripts were eventually identified as new Elamite and Akkadian).

Years later, Henry Rawlinson, a British officer and a fine scholar in the tradition of so many of that elite corps, translated and published the inscription at Behistun and established beyond any doubt the relationship between old Persian and Sanskrit.

The demise of cuneiform in the face of the Mediterranean alphabets and the Phoenician script, left Aramaic as Iran's national language. Aramaic reached the peak of its popularity after the 4th century B.C., and was in use, actually, until the Arab Conquest, although during the Parthian and Sassanian periods, the Pahlavi language became the official language of Persia. The scorched earth policy of the Arabs who tended to be both ignorant and illiterate, saw the imposition of their alphabet, however, on the Iranians with the result that calligraphy came to be the standard, and present day Persian script is derived from that. Thus, to sum up, we can say that the language and source material of the Persian Empire moved from cuneiform to calligraphy.

Greek and Jewish sources of early Persian history are too well known to require much elaboration. In the Old Testament, Ezra, Nehemiah, and Esther offer important insights into early Persia while among the Greeks, Herodotus, Ctesias, Zenophon and Arrian, are the best known chroniclers of Persian history.

Plato tells us that "the Persians were originally a nation of shepherds and herdsmen, occupying a wide country such as naturally fosters a hardy race of people of supporting both cold and watching, and, when needful, of enduring the toils of war."[5]

Shepherds and herdsmen they may have been, but the Persians, like other Aryans, were a stratified people with a considerable difference existing between the life style of those at the top and those at the bottom. Essentially they were divided into ten tribes. Three only were noble; the Pasargadae, the noblest of them all, the Maraphii, and the Maspii. While the noble aspects of Persian life will be dealt with at length in a later chapter, suffice it to say here that within the Pasargadae tribal group, the noblest family was the Achaemenidae, from which the Shahs of Persia were always taken.

Both the tribe and family were as closely identified with the name Pasargadae as with the name Achaemenid and they reflect something of the relationship between the two. Pasargadae, which is only thirty miles north of Persepolis, was the Achaemenian capital in the province of Fars that was built by Cyrus the Great. It is also where he won his great victory over the Medes and it is also where he is buried. His tomb was built on the southern edge of the built-up area which covers a mile and a half from end to end which formerly housed the great palace built by Cyrus after he became the ruler of the Medo-Persian

Empire (550 B.C.) and which was undoubtedly the model for the later Persepolis. The tomb has been pretty well modernized by now since the celebrations of 1971 when the area around it was paved, staked out with flags and access roads. But for centuries, it stood in lonely splendour on the vast plain, visited by generations of pilgrims, one of whom was Alexander who failed to destroy it, probably because he saw himself as a true successor to Cyrus. The tomb sits on a rectangular court surrounded by a wall of unbaked bricks, the funerary chamber stands on a stereobate of six stepped slabs of unequal height. On its north side is a low aperture some four and a half feet high closed by an inner and outer door. The masonry of the tomb consists of carefully dressed blocks of fine white limestone that have really stood up remarkably well over the centuries. It has a gable roof made of five enormous slabs of stone. The overall height is about thirty-six feet, although it does not look that high when first approached.[6]

Over the years, Pasargadae, even though too far from the center of a vast Empire to be an active political center, remained the religious center of the Empire where the coronations of the early Iranian kings were celebrated for generations.

The name Achaemendiae, the noblest family within the Pasargadae tribe, took its name, of course, from Achaemenes, the first king of the small Persian kingdom that became the central core of the later Empire. His son and successor, Teispes (675 – 640 B.C.) expanded his title to "King of the City of Anshan" and added to his kingdom the entire province of Parṣa (Fars). He had two sons and when he died, he divided his kingdom between them. Ariaramnes became king of Parsa and Cyrus I (not the Great), king of Parsumash. Quite clearly two small Persian kingdoms could not stand against the rising strength of the Medes and the King of Media became the overlord for the area. Cambyses I (600 – 559), son of Cyrus I reunited the kingdom and thus the way was paved for Cyrus the Great. But the Persians were still sub-kings, noble though they were the power still lay with the King of Media.

Cyrus the Great, who ruled from 559 – 529 B.C., was thus the first imperial ruler to rise to power from the Achaemenid line. He so describes himself in an inscription at Parsagadae : "I (am) Cyrus, the King, the Achaemenian."

Although Cyrus has been reasonably well documented by historians, there was, particularly among the Greeks, a good deal of embellishment. For example, the story of his birth is no doubt apocryphal but it is of interest simply because the theme was repeated in the case of exceptional rulers down to and including the Roman period. Briefly it runs thus. King Ishtumegu, or Astyages as he is better known, the ruler of the Medes, had a daughter Mandane, out from whose womb — he dreamed — a great vine grew that covered all of Asia. His astrologers interpreted this as referring to a mighty son and conqueror that would be born to her. Astyages, fearing for his own throne, therefore, instead of marrying his daughter to a nobleman of the Medes gave her to a Persian, not in line to the throne, whom he considered of good family but distinctly inferior in rank. Astyages' dreams continued, however, so that when his daughter was expecting, the Median king summoned her to Ecbatana, his capital, took the baby boy from her at birth and gave it to a trusted servant to dispose of. The latter took it to the mountains for exposure, but a shepherd's wife, who had had a stillborn son, persuaded him to make an exchange which he did. Astyges, therefore, was presented with a dead boy whom he assumed was the son of his daughter and Cyrus was saved for posterity.

Two things appear in this story that are significant. One is that of a great man-child being suckled by a wolf — the shepherd's wife's name in Cyrus' case was Spako, the Median word for dog. This is the earliest version of the Romulus-Remus story of Roman fame.

The second is more important. In Persian history, in the case of Cyrus, and again in the case of Ardashir, the founder of the Sassanian dynasty, we have the motif of a man of Royal Splendour, as the term is described in Iran, who is raised by poor people who do not know of the true nature of the boy for whom they are responsible. But the circumstances of the boy's early childhood actually represents the union as mentioned above between the common people and the mighty that has always been so important politically —just as so many American presidents project the image of the humble surroundings — Lincoln is the best example — that hide the exceptional qualities required of a future leader.

Cyrus, of course, returned in due time to the Court, having raised an army, and eventually captured or killed his grandfather, Astyages (the chronicles are not clear). So began his long march into history.

The Behistun inscription of Darius the Great referred to above, has a sentence that long puzzled the early historians. It quoted Darius : "there are 8 of my race who have been kings before me, I am the 9th. In a double line we have been kings."

What Darius was talking about was this : as pointed out above, Achaemenes, had a son Teispes, who eventually occupied the district of Anshan assuming the title "Great King, King of Anshan". Upon his death, one of his sons succeeded to Anshan and the other to Fars, the traditional home and district of the Persians. So two lines began that look like this :[7]

(1) Achaemenes
(2) Teispes

Anshan line	Persian line
(3) Cyrus I	(5) Ariaramnes
(4) Cambyses I	(6) Arsames
(7) Cyrus the Great	(Hystaspes)
(8) Cambyses	(9) Darius the Great

The famous cylinder of Nabonidus, which along with the cylinder of Cyrus,[8] lies in the British Museum, gives accounts of the rise of Cyrus to fame. The former states that "Cyrus, King of Anshan," marched at the head of his troops against Astyges. In turn, Astyges' troops revolted against him and in 550 B. C., Ecbatana was captured. Astyges was delivered up to Cyrus and the silver, gold, goods and substance of the Median Empire was taken to the land of Anshan.

In 548 B.C., Cyrus is referred to in the cylinder of Nabonidus as King of Anshan. In 546 B.C., he is referred to as "King of Persia." Presumably — and after all the throne was in his own family — once the conquest of Media was complete the other throne was offered to him as well.

Herodotus credits Cyrus with more guile than the simple accounts of the cylinders afford. He claims that Cyrus, before the conquest of Media assembled the Persian tribes and exhibited to them a fictitious written order, as if from the Median king, appointing him overall Commander-in-Chief. The story then goes that Cyrus ordered them to reassemble on the following day in a field over-grown by thistles, each equipped with a reaping hook. He set them to work and they laboured the whole day clearing the field. The next day he invited them to feast for which purpose "he slew all the goats, sheep and oxen, which were the property of his father," and added to this rich wines and an abundance of delicacies. When they were satisfied, he asked them which day they had enjoyed the most. When they had no trouble expressing their preference, he put his purpose before them.

> "Men of Persia, you are the arbiters of your own fortune; if you obey me, you will enjoy these and greater advantages without any servile toil : if you are hostile to my projects you must prepare to encounter worse hardships than those of yesterday. My voice is the voice of freedom; Providence has reserved me to be the instrument of your prosperity; you are doubtless equal to the Medes in everything and most assuredly you are brave !"[9]

Cyrus' reference to "Providence reserving me" is re-stated in another way in his own famous Cylinder that will be described below where he tells the Babylonians that their God Marduk chose him. There is even another story that he thought he might be a God but was neither surprised or annoyed when Croesur suggested he was only human.[10]

What emerges from these brief accountings is that Cyrus recognized himself very early as being exceptional among men. When this belief is coupled with the many great qualities possessed by Cyrus along with his driving sense of purpose, it is hard to imagine the man not accomplishing what he did. He was truly one of the world's Greats.

The Conquests of Cyrus are : (1) those of Media and Lydia; (2) the East; (3) Babylon.

Whether the Greek story of Cyrus' birth is apocryphal or not, there seems no doubt but what he was either the son of Mandane, daughter of Astyages, the last Media king, or married to Amytis, another daughter of Astyages. He was definitely tied in by family. But neither this nor the fact that he was a vassal king kept him from overthrowing the Median ruler.

The Babylonian Chronicle, a contemporary source[11] says that as early as 553 B.C., Cyrus had moved against Astyages without success. Astyages, consequently, raised an army and took the initiative in a final campaign against his rebellious vassal in 550 – 49 B.C. It was a disaster. The Chronicle says that "he assembled his troops and marched against Cyrus, king of Anshan, to conquer him; and Astyages' troops mutinied, and he was captured, and they gave him over to Cyrus." It is probable, on the basis of what the Greek physician Ctesias tells us, that this last battle occurred at Pasargadae.

Cyrus then proceeded to Ecbatana where he met no opposition and transferred its treasure back to Anshan. No damage was done to the city and the Achaemenid kings maintained it as a summer residence. Today it is still a delightful city, the center of a great pottery industry and the recipient of electricity and irrigation from the huge Shahnaz Dam. Its present name is Hamadan. It is very possibly the oldest city in the world, although that honour is also claimed for Damascus in Syria.

The victory of Cyrus had little effect on the Medes and Persians as Cyrus was careful to combine them into a greater Empire which he titled, "Persia and Media and other lands." It did, of course, vastly enlarge his power base. At the time of his conflict with Astyages, he could really count on only three Persian tribes, although they were all noble. In addition to his own, the Parsagadae, Cyrus had the support of the Maraphii (Maraphians) and the Maspii (Maspians). With the conquest of Media, he could now count on the remaining seven Persian tribes who were largely agricultural and nomadic.

The rapid rise of Cyrus clearly threatened Asia Minor. Since 585 B.C., a treaty had been in effect setting the boundary between Lydia and the Medes at the Halys and there had been intermarriages between the royal houses of both kingdoms. But Croesus appears to have been nervous about the defense of his kingdom of Lydia so in 547 B.C., he secured alliances with Egypt, Babylonia and Sparta. Bolstered by this presumed addition of strength, he, not Cyrus, first crossed the Halys and invaded the kingdom of Cyrus. He should have had better intelligence. Cyrus countered in an indecisive action and as it was late in the year and as the winters of Anatolia are known for their discomfort, Croesus assumed that Cyrus would wait until spring to resume the counter-attack and he dismissed his mercenaries. Cyrus did not wait. He swiftly moved on Sardes, the Lydian capital. All Croesus had left was his cavalry drawn up on the plain facing the enemy — the plain known to generations of school boys as Cyrus' Field. By the simple expedient of driving his baggage camels into the cavalry — camels can be nasty as well as smelly in close quarters — Cyrus broke the lines of the cavalry, took Sardes, captured Croesus and his treasure ("rich as Croesus") before the alliance could even swing into operation.

The Kingdom of Lydia was overthrown in 546 B.C., and the whole of the interior of Asia Minor now passed to Cyrus. He left the work of subduing the Ionian cities on the Asiatic side to his representatives and generals and turned back — but not to Babylon which was expecting the attack. Instead Cyrus reversed himself completely and instead of moving against great Babylon, which was the strongest fortified city in Asia, he led his army back through the mountain passes into Ecbatana which by now was the commercial center of the new Achaemenid Empire and then proceeded on across his native lands to the East.

Little is known of Cyrus' Eastern campaign. Cyrus himself is almost lost sight of by the Greeks and others during those six years of fighting savage tribesmen. It was an unknown area to the historians of the day. But it appears now that Cyrus successively conquered Parthia, Chorasmia, and Bactria, most of what is now modern Afghanistan. The evidence would appear as if Cyrus made his way even to the Hindu Kush and to the Indus — a campaign repeated by Alexander many years later.

In 546 B.C., Cyrus reappeared in the west, ready now for the conquest of Babylon. On the Cylinder of Cyrus there is an account rendered by Cyrus himself of the occupation of Babylon, the great enemy, that is described by the present day Iranians as the first Declaration of Human Rights.[12] It is all of that and really much more. It is really a superb political piece showing all the facets of Cyrus' nature.

Cyrus begins by describing the ruler of Babylon as a weakling who removed the correct images of the local Gods from their thrones, imposed inappropriate rituals, "did blabber" incorrect prayers, changed the worship of Marduk, the king of the Gods, into abomination, and placed the yoke "without relief" upon the necks of the inhabitants. "He ruined them all."

So Marduk, as the Cylinder recounts, "scanned and looked through all the countries searching for a righteous ruler to lead them." Not surprisingly he finally pronounced the name Cyrus, King of Anshan, to become the ruler of all the world. Then Marduk saw to it that many peoples would submit to Cyrus and in turn Cyrus endeavoured to treat with justice those whom Marduk had delivered to him

Without any battle, Cyrus took Babylon and the weak king Nabonidus was delivered to him. And all the inhabitants of Babylon as well as the entire country of Sumer and Akkad bowed to Cyrus and kissed his feet "jubilant that he had received the kingship and with shining faces."

Having thus established himself (Cyrus, who was probably a non-believer, believing only in himself, had a real gift of getting all the Gods to work for him including the Judeo-Christian God Yahweh or Jehovah), Cyrus stretches himself a bit at this point in the Cylinder and identifies himself:

> "I am Cyrus, king of the world, great king, legitimate king, King of Babylon, king of Sumer and Akkad, king of the four rims of the earth, son of Cambyses, great king, king of Anshan, grandson of Cyrus, great king, king of Anshan, descendant of Teispes, great king, king of Anshan, of a family which has always exercised kingship. ..."

The center of the Cylinder script is a statement of purpose and fulfilment that has been born out by history and stands in sharp contrast to the boastings of earlier Middle Eastern kings. Cyrus says that when he entered Babylon as a friend and established the seat of government in the palace (which was and is the seat of government in Iran) that he sought the love of the local inhabitants and that he worshipped daily their great God Marduk.

He states that he did not allow anyone to terrorize any place in the country (Sumer and Akkad) and that he strove for peace in Babylon. "My numerous troops walked around Babylon in peace, I did not allow anyone to terrorize any place." Cyrus states that he lifted the yoke (corvee) which was against the peoples' social standing, brought relief to their dilapidated housing, and put an end to their main complaints. He returned all of the images (local Gods) to the sacred cities of their origin and returned all the foreign inhabitants of the country to their former habitations in the manner of the Jewish decree of 538 B.C., granting a return of all lands to the Jews.

Cyrus states that all the kings of the entire world from the upper (Mediterranean), to the Lower (Persian Gulf) Sea now "brought their heavy tributes and kissed my feet in Babylon."

Finally Cyrus states in closing that he hopes that all of the Gods whom he had resettled in their sacred cities and Marduk in Babylon would give to him and his son a long life.

It is a remarkable Cylinder this. The humanity of Cyrus comes through clearly as does his strength. In thus setting the tone of the Achaemenid dynasty, moreover, Cyrus bequeathed to his successors a model that the world had never seen up to that time.

The conquest of Babylon could well have been the closing chapter of a great career. But it was not in the nature of Cyrus to rest on his laurels. Instead, once again, as he had in his first eastern campaign (545 – 539 B.C.), Cyrus turned his face toward India. The next ten years are really lost to history. All that we know is that this is a period of constant warfare and strife. It is probable that he was occupied in beating back one of those invasions from the East that occurred and re-occurred in the history of the Persian Empire. Some reports indicated that Cyrus was in Parthia. The best known, however, is that of Herodotus who states that Cyrus offered marriage to Tomyris, Queen of the Massagetae, but was refused. He invaded the country of that wild tribe and in the first encounter, killed the Queen's son and heir. The Queen, then, apparently offered to reconsider her position if Cyrus would come for further talks to her. He walked into the trap, and was killed in the battle that ensued. This was in 529 B.C.[13] His son, Cambyses, on hearing of his father's death, marched to the East and destroyed the tribe with a vengefulness that Cyrus had never shown. He recovered his father's body and returned it to Pasargadae in Fars, the land of his ancestors, for burial.

Great commander though he was, the great strength of Cyrus and in fact his place in history, is due not only to his magnificent campaigns, but as well to the man's unusual understanding and his ability to inspire through leadership and proper action rather than through fear.

The character of Cyrus appears in sharpest focus in the accounts of the Old Testament where Cyrus was seen as God's appointed agent, as Yahweh's pledge of the Jewish deliverance. Again and again in the Old Testament[14] we see the prophetical theme repeated of this great hammer of God smashing before it the wicked power of Assyria and Babylon. The characterization of Cyrus continues and moves up on to a very personal plane. His wonderful qualities are much remarked upon and like Saul of old, he wins the ultimate accolade of the Jews, "the Lord's anointed."

Deutero-Isaiah, so concerned with the transcendence of God actually includes Cyrus in its central theme of the "Servant" — a religious signification that moves him close to Messiah, and Yahweh himself reportedly says of Cyrus, "He is my shepherd and shall perform my pleasure."

It was not only the Jews, however, who saw in this man a new vision of rule.

Plato tells us that

> "Cyrus was a great leader and friend of his people. During his reign the Persians ruled numerous peoples. He gave to all of them the rights of free men, and by that he won their hearts and his soldiers stood ready to face any peril to serve him. If, among his subjects, there was someone who could offer just and reasonable advice, he was not angry; rather he gave the subject complete freedom of speech. ... Under his rule, the vast Persian Empire realized an ever increasing well being, profiting from the liberties accorded to it through the wisdom of the king and from the harmony which prevailed throughout the country and from which his successors benefited."[15]

The noted Iranologist Comte de Gobineau said centuries later :

> "Cyrus towers over all other leaders of nations. There has never been one his equal. The world has done well to proclaim him ... to declare that he is a Messiah, a man predestined to be above all others."[16]

The present ruler of Iran is of a like opinion. Not only did he throw the biggest party of the century in his honour, but he sees himself, not only as a successor to the throne of Cyrus, but of a likeness and kinship.

The moral significance of Iran's monarchy is best expressed by the present Monarch himself :

> "A real king in Iran is not so much the political head of the nation as a teacher and a leader. He is not only a person who builds roads, bridges, dams, and canals, but one who leads his people in spirit, thought and heart."[17]

So it is that Cyrus left what the present day Iranians describe as "the legacy of greatness." In his own time he set the pattern for Achaemenid kingship and those in succession after them for the most part strove to match the greatness of Cyrus.

Cambyses, Cyrus' eldest son by Cassandane, the daughter of an Achaemenid, succeeded to his father's throne. Quite understandably, his first task was to consolidate his own position. That there would be some conflict within the realm upon the death of the founder – Emperor is not surprising. This situation involved Cambyses in minor, not major campaigns for perhaps four years. But meanwhile his long range objectives were taking shape in his mind.

Cyrus' rapid conquest of Lydia in 546 precluded any possibility of Egyptian intervention at the time despite the alliance that Croesus had forged. But, the Persians were not unmindful of the potential danger that lay in Egyptian sympathies with a defeated enemy. The consequence of that knowledge meant, of course, that Egypt was marked for conquest in due time. The time came four years after the accession of Cambyses to the throne.

Certain precautions were taken for the campaign. A secured water supply for the Persian army was arranged with the Arabs when the time came for the crossing of the Sinai. A naval base was established at Acre in support of the land army. Finally, overtures were made to dissident forces within Egypt that bore almost instant fruit. One of the leading mercenary officers of the Egyptian army, came over to the Persian side. The Admiral of the Egyptian fleet apparently agreed to keep the Egyptian fleet out of action. The priesthood may even have collaborated. In a final turn of the wheel of fortune, Amasis, Pharoah of Egypt in fact as well as in name, fortutously died before the invasion to be succeeded by an untested son of middle age, Psammetichus.

In a lightning campaign, reminiscent of Cyrus' own, Cambyses led his army by the coast-road from Gaza to the confines of Egypt. At Pelusium, he met the Egyptian army and defeated it. The remaining forces retired to Memphis and underwent siege. Six months later all Egyptian resistance ended and Psammetichus III, who had never known power, capitulated. By the end of May 525, Cambyses was recognized as King of Egypt.

At this point in time, Cambyses was faced with the master problem of Empire — what are the limits of Empire ? The fact that the Persians maintained their suzerainty over Egypt for one hundred years showed that in conquering Egypt, the Persians had not yet reached that point. But the plans of Cambyses were clearly expansive at this point. He was aiming for nothing less than an African Empire as extensive as that already held in Asia. Libya and Cyrene submitted on the Egyptian surrender to avoid attack. This left great Carthage, Ethiopia, and the oasis of Ammon for further conquest. Cambyses took the difficult one — the invasion of Ethiopia. The original thrust was two-fold, one to the west of Thebes, led by Cambyses, and the other to the south following the Nile to be led by one of his generals.

The reports of the success of the expedition to Ethiopia have been subject to various interpretations. One story was to the effect that Cambyses' army was buried under a sandstorm before reaching the oasis of Jupiter Ammon — perhaps ten days march from Thebes. Still another was to the effect that there was not provision made for an adequate supply route but there was later evidence found that the Commissariat of the Persian king reached to four-fifths of the distance from

Thebes to Napata, the sacred city of the Ethiopians. Some say that Meroe, the capital, was actually conquered and the fact that the securing of the southern boundary of Egypt by Cambyses continued for one hundred years would seem to suggest this.

Surely it was a difficult campaign, and Herodotus speaks of it as sheer folly and madness, an epithet later applied to Cambyses himself. But, the Ethiopians paid tribute to Darius, the successor of Cambyses, and elsewhere Herodotus speaks of Cambyses "subduing" the Ethiopians.

In Egypt, Cambyses had at first comported himself precisely as his father, Cyrus, had done on the submission of Babylon. As King of Egypt, he received the name, Re-mesuti, born of Re. He worshipped and made offerings to all the Gods. After his return from the Ethiopian campaign, however, his attitude appears to have changed. He because less tolerant of the Egyptian religion and leaned heavily on the priesthood. Whether this was the result of machinations by the priesthood—after all, they probably collaborated in the overthrow of their own Pharoah — or whether it was the result of a mental breakdown on the part of Cambyses as a result of the exhausting Ethiopian campaign, we shall probably never know. But be that as it may, Cambyses established Persian rule in Egypt with the same thoroughness with which he had initially conquered it. The Egyptians did not rise in revolt against their Persian overlords on Cambyses' death in 522 B.C. when a wide spread revolt broke out that took his successor Darius many months to quell. Indeed, once his position was secure as Shahanshah, Darius came to Egypt, asserted his personal authority over the country, proclaimed his devotion to the great God, Re, and though he held Egypt as a conquered country, he did much to lessen the tensions that had sprung up in the last years of Cambyses' reign.

The next chapter deals with the particulars of the accession of Darius to the throne of Cyrus. But reserving that crucial period, it is possible to continue on here to seek a resolution to the problems of the limits of Empire as it faced a succession of Achaemenid rulers.

The revolts within the inner limits of the Persian Empire against the authority of Darius on his succession to the throne, were, as will be seen later, put down in a series of lightning campaigns. The next few years however, were years in which Darius retraced the campaigns of Cyrus and Cambyses in his efforts to stabilize the great Empire that had been built by his predecessors. If he had not the military genuis of Cyrus, he had a sufficiency for the task before him. His expedition to India, which at that time referred primarily to the Indus Basin, took him over almost the exact route that Cyrus had marched his armies. The success of Darius' expedition is attested by the fact that the Persian province of India thereafter paid to the Achaemenid kings, more tribute than any other of the Imperial provinces.

But what Darius had done had not yet solved the problem of the limits of Empire. He was now holding — and consolidating with great skill — what Cyrus and Cambyses before him had conquered and held.

In or about 516 B.C., Darius faced this problem squarely. He delivered the first attack of Asia upon Europe.[20] Unlike those who followed him — probably because Darius had great prudence and a sense of balance — he did not in the first instance direct his march upon Greece as did the Ottoman Sultans of the 14th century, but rather he chose to move into the Balkan hinterland.

The "Scythian Expedition" as this was called, ended very much as did Cambyses' campaigns into Ethiopia, and indeed as Xerxes' expeditions against Greece which were to follow. There was withdrawal but not in disaster. In this way, it is hard to see how historians can see in Napoleon the sense of appraisal, of pressures, of a real evaluation and accountability, that marked the imperial probes of the Achaemenid kings. Darius' expedition was no defeat, no "1812 campaign," that could be likened to Napoleon's retreat from Moscow. He made an orderly withdrawal with his armies intact and did not attempt it again.

Darius led the expedition in person — common among Persian kings. The size of his army could not have exceeded more than 80,000 men — this was no all-out effort. He possibly had three hundred ships. He crossed the Bosphorus on a floating bridge. He moved north, traversed Thrace to the Danube. As usual, the Persian armies moved with great speed. The natives they encountered capitulated early on and consequently Darius was not required to pause to consolidate his gains. He forced the passage of the Danube by means of a bridge of boats that his fleet had built for him at a distance of two day's sail from the mouth of the river. He probably moved then to the north or northwest through the Moldavian plain, but the line of march has never been clearly defined.[21]

Eventually, Darius moved into the steppe lands of the Scythians, but the latter never closed in battle and Darius found himself pursuing an elusive foe that could not justify a long and protracted campaign. Once having come to this conclusion, Darius doubled back upon his track and recrossed the Danube bridge which the Greeks had held for him, though it is true that he was pressed by the Scythians. He finally crossed back into Asia at Sestos and retired to Sardes.

The expedition against the Scythians saw the capitulation of Thrace and Macedonia and their incorporation into the Persian Empire. So while Darius had not the success against the predatory nomads of the north for which he had hoped, he did make a substantial addition to Empire as a result of the expedition. Since a great portion of the Mediterranean coastline already accepted the Persian rule, the addition of Thrace and Macedonia provided a solid limit in the north. Only after Xerxes' ill-fated expedition against Greece did the Greek provinces on the Asiatic coast and the Thracian possessions break off in a re-definition of the limits of Empire. Yet, this was by no means a major disaster of the dimensions that early schoolboy histories seemed to suggest. Xerxes, who succeeded his father as Shahanshah in 485 B.C., on the latter's death, returned from Greece to Asia with his armies intact. The Achaemenid kings were ever prudent. The accounts that history records of the errors committed by Napoleon or Alexander were not the mistakes of the Achaemenids. Xerxes never threw the full weight of his Empire against Greece, as Greece was not that important to him. Had he done so, it is entirely possible that history would have been written differently. But, that was not the way of the Persian. The limits of Empire, he would explore. But he had an Empire to administer.

Xerxes continued to reign until his death over his vast Empire, holding it intact, neither expanding nor receding. The Persians had reached the limits of Empire.

What was it that drove the Persians. The Greeks said it was their *daimon.* Perhaps it was pure family pride. Or perhaps it was a powerful nobility — the possibility will be explored in the next chapter. But, whatever it was, the Persians —the Achaemenids — delivered.

Some further attention belongs to Darius and Xerxes, but before moving to that subject — which will be placed in only brief focus — it seems important to turn from the hard campaigns of the early Achaemenid kings to their other accomplishments. Arms alone could never have done what the Persians accomplished. The Assyrians had the arms and their armies probed, too, to the limits of Empire. But it was entirely military and hence, like Alexander, their efforts were doomed to failure.

The pattern set by Cyrus the Great and followed by his successors, involved a number of what might almost be described as principles of government.

(1) The treatment of subject races saw a sharp break between the policy of Cyrus and those of his predecessor kings in the Middle East. The Persians, in the first place, conducted their wars with great humanity, if any war can be described in these terms. With only a few exceptions, enemy kings were spared and towns and cities preserved. Never was a scorched earth policy followed. Mutilation, rape and murder was not a hallmark of Persian success in the field. To the contrary, members of the conquered nationalities were welcomed into service. High ranking generals and administrators were given land grants and they served with pride. Troops were both Persian and native. Garrisons were composed of the most varied nationalities. This is not to say that the Achaemenids shared their high position with others because they did not. The inhabitants of Persia proper paid no taxes. Instead they brought gifts to the Shahanshah. But the point is that subject races were not abused and care was taken that their interests should receive due consideration. Subjects of noble rank sat side by side with Persians in the regal and vice-regal courts and served especially effectively within the satraps, the provincial system set up originally by Cyrus.

(2) Persian kings became equally kings of the states they

occupied. Cyrus proclaimed himself King of Babylon, a title held by his successors. Cambyses adopted the full titles of the Pharoahs of Egypt. Every effort was made to maintain the fiction that the old state still remained — that their peoples were not a captive peoples.

(3) Although the orders of the Persian Court were issued in cuneiform script, translations into Elamite and Babylonian were always made in royal inscriptions. In Egypt, one in hieroglyphics was added; in Greek communities, Greek.

Aramaic, which was widely used as the language of commerce in the western half of the Empire, was similarly used by the Persians. Coins issued by the Satrap were in Aramaic. In short unlike the Arabs who imposed their language at the time of the conquest on subject peoples, the Persians left to their subject peoples, their language.

(4) The provincial organization known as the satrapies, provided for sufficient decentralization in government to permit subject races and communities to occupy a reasonably independent position. As a rule they were permitted to decide lawsuits among themselves according to their customs. The Jews were permitted to convene their own assemblies. The great houses of conquered territories for the most part were permitted to keep their estates and pass them from father to son. In fact, Cyrus was extremely careful to address himself to foreign elites and to protect their prerogatives. Within the cities like Babylon, Jerusalem, Sardis, Memphis, the internal affairs were controlled by the officials of the community. Similarly, the priests controlled and administered the temple properties.

(5) In an Empire as vast as the Persian, the problem of maintaining a viable economy was a real one. The Persians solved this problem by accepting what could be described as a "natural economy." Some peoples were paid and in turn paid their taxes in currency, some in kind. In the eastern provinces, it was barter. Only the Shahanshah could coin gold but silver could be coined by satraps, generals, independent communities, etc. However, the Achaemenids themselves dealt mostly in precious metals. At Susa, Persepolis, Pasargadae, and Ecbatana, there were great treasure houses full of gold and silver.

(6) Cyrus gave the Jews permission to return and rebuild Jerusalem. Darius permitted them to restore the Temple. Artaxerxes I made the foundation of Judaism possible. The Persians were on the best of terms with the Greek oracles. And so it went. The Persians were extremely eclectic in their religious temperament. As kings they accepted and if need be, restored the religion and the Gods of the subject peoples. Cyrus could only be said to be above religion. No one would presume to suggest what he believed. The later Achaemenids professed a belief in Ahura Mazda, the Great God of Zoroaster, but there was certainly no fanatacism shown in enforcing his worship. Zoroastrianism, unlike Judaism, was not exclusive and intolerant. Indeed, the world has probably never seen as many cults and creeds and syncretisms existing side by side as were present in the Persian Empire. The early Aryan folk figures mixed gladly with the gorgeous Gods of Civilization. The Shahs even got drunk at the feast of Mithras as this was the ancient practice. For those of us who live in these latter days in the shadow of the one true God, it must have really been a grand time in which to worship.

So much for the internals of Cyrus' great Empire. It seems now as if something further can be said about the Imperial idea as it was shaped into a more cohesive pattern under Darius and Xerxes.

Both these kings, Darius the Great and Xerxes, have left their own inscriptions, the former at Behistun and the latter in an Akkadian version of a foundation tablet from Persepolis.[22]

Darius begins his own accounting by establishing his legitimacy which, as will be seen later, might possibly have been in question. There is a long recital of the line of Achaemenians from which he was descended. "From long ago we have been noble. From long ago our family has been kings." He then lists twenty-three provinces "which came unto me" and constituted his empire in the first instance. This, of course, was organized in classic form under the title, satrapies. This was not only a geographical division of various provinces but it was financial and administrative as well. For the Achaemenid kings, taxation went hand in hand with geographical subdivisions of the Empire.

Darius then devotes considerable space to the account of his coming to the throne which will be reviewed in a later chapter as it involved rather complicated manoeuvers involving other nobility. But, most of the Behistun inscription deals with his campaigns. Revolts against his rule were common when he first ascended the throne and Darius was hard put to it to preserve his crown. He fought nineteen campaigns in one year, one right after the other, and as any soldier knows, this is a lot of campaigns. He captured nine rebellious kings in these campaigns.

Another thing that emerges in the inscription is Darius' own physical strength, although it is interesting that by comparison, Cyrus never spoke of these matters. When Darius says he killed a king or a commander he means that he did it himself. He was a fighter who had been trained professionally as a young man and he carried this great competence as an older man.

On the other hand Darius displays much of the consideration of his predecessor, Cyrus the Great. He tells, for example, that he restored whole kingdoms "re-establishing" them on their original foundations. Like Cyrus, he restored local sanctuaries and lands. "I restored to the people the pastures and the herds, the household slaves and the houses."

Darius also introduces in the Behistun inscription, the great God Ahura Mazda, who was of Zoroastrian origin. Unlike Cyrus, who was quite easy in his relationship with the various Gods he encountered, Darius constantly referred to Ahura Mazda as giving him the battle or doing other good things. "By the favour of Ahura Mazda this I did." "Ahura Mazda bore me aid," etc.

Darius was capable of personal cruelty which seems to have been somewhat uncommon among most of the Achaemenid rulers. He relates how he took one Cicamtakhama, king of the Sagartians, cut off both his nose and ears and put out one eye and kept him chained at the palace entrance for the people to see. He also speaks of flaying some enemy and stuffing their hides with straw and impaling others. There is no doubt in reading the account at Behistun, that there were times when he really felt the pressure and actually feared for his kingdom, particularly in his early reign. In this sense he seems to have lacked the self assurance of Cyrus even though he was a great warrior, a greater administrator, and a master builder.

The "Lie" was an important concept of justice to Darius. He states that he was not a Lie-follower. "I was not a doer of wrong — neither I nor my family." He states that kings who follow him shall not be Lie-followers upon pain of losing their thrones. He states that he conducted himself "according to righteousness" and "neither to the weak nor to the powerful did I do wrong."

As will be described later, Darius mentions his friends by name, particularly those who were loyal to him not only at his accession to the throne but in the campaigns that followed. "Thou who shalt be king hereafter," he says, "protect well the family of these men."

Xerxes, despite his fateful expedition against the Greeks, emerges in history equally as a man of superior qualities. In the tablet recovered from Persepolis he begins by praising Ahura Mazda "the great God who gave us this earth, who gave us that sky, who gave us mankind, who gave to his worshippers prosperity, who made Xerxes the king rule and multitudes the only king, give alone orders to other kings."

Later, Xerxes repeats his statement with a more personal emphasis :

> "I am Xerxes the great king, the only king (i.e., king of kings), the king of all countries which speak all kinds of languages, the king of this entire big and far reaching earth."

He also, as did the other Achaemenids repeat for posterity his lineage : "The son of Darius, the Achaemenian, a Persian, son of a Persian, an Aryan of Aryan descent."

Xerxes then lists the countries — in addition to Persia — over which his power extends. They number twenty-nine and range from Egypt to India, both of which he lists.

Xerxes tells of revolt in several countries and how he "put them again into their former political status." Once again, he gives Ahura Mazda the credit and tells how he destroyed the temples of the "evil Gods."

Xerxes, as did many of the Pharoahs, sees himself at the center of a cosmic order and makes much of the fact that things must be done in the "correct way." Toward the end he again invokes the aid of Ahura Mazda and states that he is the one God and only he shall be worshipped and his laws obeyed. He closes by asking for protection for his family.

Other rulers followed Xerxes in succession as the chart reproduced above shows but in a sense Xerxes' reign represented the apogee of Achaemenid rule. The throne of Cyrus upon which he sat never again attained the greatness and the majesty of monarchy until the rise of the Sassanian dynasty in the 3rd century A.D.

Xerxes ascended the throne in 485 B.C. The last Achaemenid ruler Darius Codommanus was killed by his own followers in 330 B.C., and his body was delivered up to Alexander who had the body buried with all pomp at Persepolis.

With the end of the Achaemenid dynasty, the so-called "parallel history" of Iran described in the first chapter comes to an end. The heroic period of the National Epic makes no mention of the Achaemenids. It is with Alexander that the history begins to fuse. Both Alexander and the Sassanians who eventually rose to power under Ardashir figure in both the *Shahnameh* and in actual history. Naturally enough, the accounts differ.

For example, in the legendary account of the birth of Alexander, it was noted in the first chapter that the *Shahnameh* tells us that Alexander, or Iskander as he was known in Persia, was a scion of the Persian royal family. Dara, the Epic says, who was the son of Bahman, a later Achaemenid Shahanshah, and Khumari, his sister, married the daughter of Philip of Macedon. From this union came Alexander. Later, Dara divorced his wife and married a Persian woman from which union came Darius Codomnaus, the last of the Achaemenid kings and the one whom Alexander finally brought to defeat.

So, the *Shahnameh* tells us, Alexander and Darius were half brothers and Alexander's campaigns in Asia were undertaken to wrest the throne from him. The fact that Alexander thus had Achaemenid blood, just as did Darius, his half brother, was, of course, a necessary adjunct to Alexander's legitimacy in ascending the throne and assuming the title Shahanshah.

The actual history of Alexander runs a bit differently and is too well known to require documentation here. Historians such as Sir Percy Sykes have detailed the Macedonian's history in great detail. What is interesting, though, is how thoroughly the legend of Alexander has coloured the actual career of Alexander. Sir Percy Sykes, for example, makes the flat statement that "Alexander the Great was the most famous man ever born."[23] This takes in a lot of territory, but then so did Alexander. Even today they say when the storms are raging in the Aegean, the mermaids may appear to a vessel in distress and ask "Where is Alexander the Great ?" The captain must shout across the wind, "Alexander the Great lives and rules and keeps the world at peace." The waves will then subside.

But, of course, Alexander never kept the world at peace. He was a merciless destroyer and as St. Augustine said, a brigand as well. He was also a murderer and exploiter. It is doubtful, however, if Alexander saw himself as greater than Cyrus. Indeed Arrian relates the visit of Alexander to Cyrus' tomb and his invocation of Cyrus' *daimon*.[24] Even in his campaigns, he pretty well followed the routes taken by Cyrus.

The resistance to Alexander and his devastation of Persia, will be reviewed at considerable length in the next chapter. Perhaps it would be of more value at this point therefore to return to the Achaemenids and touch further on the contributions of that great dynasty to Persian history, if for no other reason than that Iran has gone back again and again in its long history to this early great period in seeking its own identity and establishing its own worth.

The dynasty reigned for over two hundred years and it can be truthfully said that it changed the face of the earth. Achaemenid kings (so great that the Greeks simply called them Basilius—King) created a concept of monarchy that has been perpetuated to this day. The institutions in support thereof, their concept of an elite, of monarchical architecture, of arms and religious signification, all became conceptual as well as actual. They created a world pattern not only for Iranians, but for others as well — the Jews, Genghis Khan, the Caliphate — so many owed so much to the Achaemenids. It is, of course, a truism in the western world that by repelling the Persian invasion the Greeks saved western civilization from Asiatic barbarism. Actually it is hard to argue this position on any rational grounds. The Achaemenids were a sophisticated, cultured people — at whose courts even the Greeks were welcome and whose laws were a model in the west. (Darius, not Hammurabi, was known to the Greeks as the "lawgiver").

The models supplied by the Achaemenids were of a dignity, worth, and refinement that equalled, if they did not surpass, anything produced by the Greeks. The latter, to be sure, possessed an intellectual discipline that has proved to be most congenial to the western mind. But the problems of the Greek city states paled by comparison with the problems of Empire and when the Greeks tried to deal with these problems, they failed dismally. The legacy of Alexander in Iran can only be seen in actual history as essentially one of darkness, constant warfare, and confusion. It is a great tribute to the Achaemenids that despite the chaos that followed their downfall, Iranian traditions and institutions kept themselves alive for this most difficult period that lasted from 336 B.C., when the last Achaemenid king was killed, until 226 A.D., when Ardashir finally brought the Empire together again after years of struggle and founded the Sassanian dynasty which was a renewal of the old Achaemenid dynasty and which lasted until the Arab conquest.

With the Sassanids, the Persian Empire again became the greatest force in the East and successfully challenged Rome for world mastery. This story will be told in the next chapter.

So it was that the Throne of Cyrus, the Achaemenid, even in defeat was secured to history. The many facets of kingship — Shahanshah — had emerged in clear forms. He was the religious leader. He was the war leader and the defender of the frontiers. He was at the head of the organization of government. He was the seat of justice. He was the most noble of a honed and disciplined aristocracy. He was King of Kings. His was the great office, the great prize in the history of the Middle East.

Within Iran an aura developed around this office known as the Royal Splendour. It is still present today. When the newspapers in Iran speak of the Monarch, there is an added dimension present which is not easy for the Westerner to grasp. The present Shah is seen too often as being himself alone by the Western press. He is not. He is the key element in a mosaic that has been woven for over 2,500 years.

NOTES

1. *Cambridge Ancient History IV*, Cambridge University Press, 1930, p. 2. Hereafter cited as C.A.H.

2. *Iran Tribune*, Vol. VI, No. 85 (Oct., 1971), p. 14.

3. Sykes, *op. cit.*, I, p. 239.

4. *Iran Tribune*, *op. cit.*, pp. 22-23.

5. Quoted in Heeren, A.H.L., *Works I* (London 1886), p. 213.

6. Ghirshman, *op. cit.*, pp. 135-36.

7. *C.A.H.*, *op. cit.*, p. 5.

8. The writer is indebted to the British Museum for furnishing original copies and translations. Also the Behistun inscription.

9. Herodotus I, p. 126. Quoted in Heeren, *op. cit.*, p. 216.

10. Hopkins, E. W., "The Divinity of Kings," *Journal of the American Oriental Society*, Vol. 51, No. 4 (December, 1931), p. 315.

11. Quoted in *C.A.H.*, *op. cit.*, p. 7.

12. *Iran Tribune*, *op. cit.*, p. 14.

13. Sykes, I, *op. cit.*, p. 153.

14. For Biblical citations, see Inlow, *op. cit.*, pp. 402-405.

15. Quoted in *Iran Tribune*, *op. cit.*, p. 15.

16. *Ibid.*, p. 16.

17. *Ibid.*, p. 15.

18. *C.A.H.*, IV, pp. 21-23.

19. *Ibid.*, p. 22.

20. *Ibid.*, pp. 212 ff.

21. *Ibid.*, p. 213. For a detailed account of these campaigns, see Sykes, *op. cit.*, pp. 165 ff.

22. Both texts, in the original and in translation, have been provided to the writer through the courtesy of the British Museum.

23. Sykes, I, *op. cit.*, p. 239.

24. Arrian, *Anabasis* of Alexander, Quoted in Inlow, *op. cit.*, p. 409.

Chapter 3

THE ARISTOCRACY

When Alexander had completed his conquest of Iran, all the princes and descendants of the nobility and the leaders and rulers and provincial aristocracy gathered in his presence. Their splendour and numbers troubled him and he wrote a letter to his old mentor, Aristotle :[1]

> By the grace of great and glorious God, our fortunes have prospered so far. I wish to go to India and China and the farthest East, but fear to leave alive these Persian nobles, lest they create troubles in my absence which will be hard to remedy, and come to Greece to do harm to our land. It seems prudent to me to destroy them all, that I may carry out my purpose with untroubled mind.

Aristotle wrote a long and careful letter to his former pupil. He pointed out to Alexander that the Persians were "pre-eminent for courage and boldness and skill on the day of battle." Further, they form *en aggregate* "one of the mightiest tools of Empire and instruments of power."

"If you destroy them," Aristotle wrote, "you will have overthrown one of the greatest pillars of excellence in the world. Moreover, when the noble among them have gone, you will be forced of necessity to promote the base to the same ranks and stations."

Subsequently, Aristotle advises Alexander to take the heads of their first families and their men of rank and divide the realm of Iran among them. "The best course," Aristotle writes, "is to divide the realm of Iran among your princes, and to bestow throne and crown on whomsoever you appoint to any province; giving none precedence, ascendancy or authority over another, that each may be absolute on the throne of his own domain."

In this way, each ruler would, argued Aristotle, be dependent on Alexander's position and patronage and in addition be so busy in petty rivalries among themselves that they would have "no leisure to seek vengeance upon you."

Alexander adopted the course which Aristotle advised. He divided the land among ninety rulers who became known as "kings of the people," while he himself retained the ancient title Shahanshah — "King of Kings."

The genesis of this group for which Aristotle expressed such admiration lay in (1) the character of the men themselves, (2) the structured arrangement of early Aryan society, and (3) in the particulars of the accession to power of Darius the Great.

The first must of necessity be general. Ammianus Marcellinus draws us the picture : "The Persians were almost all slender, with dark or livid complexions, hard, 'goat-like' eyes, arched eyebrows meeting in the middle, carefully tended beards, and long fuzzy hair. They were incredibly wary and suspicious; in hostile countries they would not touch the fruit on the trees, for fear of poison or spells. They wore golden bangles and necklaces, precious stones, and above all pearls. They always wore swords, even at banquets and entertainments. They were talkative and boastful, stern and ferocious, threatening whether things went well or ill with them, wily, proud, and cruel. Their bearing was easy, their gait ambling. They were the best fighters in the world, cunning rather than dashing, and especially dangerous in long-distance combat, that is, with the bow. On the whole they were brave, and bore the hardship of campaigning easily. They arrogated to themselves the right of disposing of the lives of slaves and common people, and no servant durst open his mouth in their presence. They indulged in sexual debauches without restraint. In brief, the great men divided their time between the exercise of arms, in war or sport, and the joys of love. They were courteous, too, and chivalrous in character."

The word "Aryan" itself carries with it the meaning of "noble". To move immediately to the structure of Aryan society, "Aryan" is a term which is properly applied to Indians and Iranians but not to western Europeans or to the English.[3] The reason for the distinction lay in the requirements of the early Aryan society which have been briefly discussed above, but perhaps deserve elaboration here.

Shortly after 2000 B.C., as we have seen, advance groups of the Aryans penetrated the Zagros Mountains. They were followed by more massive invasions for the next several hundred years. The eastern wing of these invasions went to India where they arrived about 1500 – 1400 B.C. They reduced the ancient Indus Valley civilization and set up the caste system which has endured to our own time.

The western wing of the invaders moved across the Iranian plateau and by 815 B.C. had effectively settled in the land that roughly corresponds to present day Iran.

Aryan expansion on such a massive scale as this, demanded great organizational efficiency and functional specialization. It also required a firm confidence in the importance and the need for the conservation of tradition as a counter to the resisting force of those people whom they conquered. Clearly these requirements pointed up the need for some kind of elite corps which would bear the burden of these multiple responsibilities.

The Iranians were divided into fourfold local units — the family, the clan, the tribe and the nation, and these distinctions were never lost. At Naqsh-i-Rustam where the Royal Achaemenid Tombs can still be seen in all of their splendour, there is inscribed on the tomb of Darius the Great : Son of Vishtaspa (family), an Achaemenid (clan), a Persian (tribe), an Aryan (nation). Socially within these units there was a threefold division. One of them, the *airyaman* represented the ruling class. This comprehended what would seem to us as a rather mixed bag. There was the priest, the chariot-driving noble, the herdsman and the artisan. However, they were all Aryans — the lower classes being recognized as distinct in race, for the name of this group was pishtra (colour).[4]

Both the Medes and the Persians, being Aryans, were organized along the same structural lines. But the Medes, who were organized into six tribes, each inhabiting a number of villages, were the first to rise to pre-eminence. The Persians, or Iranians as they came to be known ultimately, however, prevailed. This was due primarily to the organizing genius and great personal competence of Cyrus II (the Great). A vassal king in Anshan, the story of his birth and his conquests, has already been told. As stated in Chapter 2, Cyrus' family was the Achaemendae, named after an early clan chieftain

Achaemenes. They were Persian, not Media. This family had traditionally provided the rulers for Cyrus' tribe — the Parsagadae. Knowing that he could count on his own tribe, Cyrus enlisted the help in the first instance, of the two other noble Persian tribes[5] — the Maraphii, the Maspii. After the Median Conquest, he gained the support of the nomad herders — — the Dai, Mardi, Dropici, Sagartii; and the agricultural Panthialaei, Derusiaei, Germanii. They were a varied lot. The Mardians occupied the desert around Persepolis and had a reputation among the Greeks as brigands. The Sagartians inhabited the oasis of Yazd and, disdaining defensive armour, fought only with the dagger and lasso. But they all eventually united under Cyrus and ultimately created the great Achaemenid Empire which endured until 329 B.C. This was the earliest true Empire in the world in that it constituted a government of many different peoples under a single ruler. It stretched from Cyrenaica to India and from Ethiopia to the oases of Russian Turkestan. It was divided into provinces or satrapies which reached thirty-one in number by the death of Darius in 486 B.C.

Such a vast Empire could only be maintained by the most vigorous discipline. Some of the organizational and administrative aspects of this imperial scheme have already been dealt with in Chapter 2. What is important to point out here was the key role played by this early elite. Always there was the small core. For example, the royal guard which was organized into three corps, composed of two thousand cavalry and two thousand infantry, were all noblemen — Medes and Persians. Xenophon in his great *Cyropaedia* gives a detailed accounting of how the young noblemen, including the future king, were trained for their future jobs, not only in handling arms but in meting out justice to equals as well as inferiors. Their's was an education in leadership, not simply domination. The young Cyrus was taught to command and to counsel. He was told by his father, "there is no shorter road than really to be wise in those things in which you wish to seem to be wise."[6]

The education of Cyrus and selected sons of the aristocracy became the model for the education of later Shahanshahs. Even after the constitutional crisis of 1906 when strong democratic forces were at work in Iran and when one might have expected some changes in so ancient a pattern, the education of the monarch proceeded in the familiar manner. An "Imperial Class" was organized in Teheran by the regent and the Minister of Court in 1909. A general officer who had been a student at the School of Fine Arts in Paris was named general director. In attendance was the young Sovereign himself, the heir prince, a half brother of the Shahanshah, the young brother of the deposed Shahanshah, the sons of the Minister of Court and the general director, and about a dozen other young people "all sons of important people."

Instruction was given in Persian, Arabic, and Russian originally, but French was added in 1912. Persian literature was taught but without regard for "minute facts" or "useless details" — the references being to the long winded chronicles that were a part of Persian tradition. There was a simplified math program and "a great place was reserved for the experimental sciences." The teaching of geography emphasized its political and economic character.

Apart from the academic aspects of instruction, there was a strong emphasis on horsemanship which was taught by an officer of the guards and gymnastics "following the European Methods." There was also instruction in military tactics.

On June 2, 1913, an examination was given to these young men at "a solemn ceremony in the room of the Great Council of the Gulistan (the imperial palace which is still to be seen today in downtown Teheran) in the presence of the Ministers." One can well imagine that an examination under such auspices would be in itself a test of self control and discipline.[7]

But to return to the early elite. The Greeks, fierce and independent to the last, seemed to have a full comprehension of this new political phenomenon of King and surrounding elite, that came flashing from the East and they wrote much about it. But then so did the Jews as pointed out above. What both these people found in common was a concept of rule that was efficient yet tolerant. Subject populations kept their special organizations, their religion, even their chiefs. In the eyes of his subjects, as pointed out above, Cyrus was never really an alien king. The administration of his Empire was one of high operational efficiency tempered with justice. In fact, Persian justice was famed throughout the world and served as a model. In all of this, Cyrus dealt large through the concept of an elite.

Because of the nature of Cyrus, however, the interplay between conqueror and conquered tended to distil the early Aryan patterns of traditional behaviour within his own lifetime. Cyrus still retained the support of the Aryan clans and tribes but as he grew older he seems to have developed too eclectic a temperament to have relied exclusively upon an immediate Aryan elite. Thus, his proclamations and his actions, are constantly pointed toward the elites of other societies as well. This is shown in his decrees to both the Jews and the Babylonians.

If Cyrus did not identify with a particular elite, his successors did. Particularly Darius is credited with launching the seven great families in their historic role, thus creating a permanent nobility of Persians. With him we move to the third of the bases of Aristotle's expressed admiration — the particulars of Darius's accession to the throne.

Herodotus says they were conspirators. Christensen says the Greek was mistaken — that these men were of noble blood. It is possible both historians are correct. In all likelihood they *were* of noble blood as Christensen says. But the kingship is a great goal that even a noble birthing does not allay. They could have been conspirators. The facts do not come clear, but if tracks had to be covered, Darius was the man to do it. Hence, reconstruction of the actual events leading to Darius' enthronement is a tricky business. When the year 522 B.C. opened, Darius was the king's (Cambyses) spear bearer in Egypt. Before the year was out he was Shahanshah with a father and grandfather still living. Clearly this took some doing.

When the news of Cyrus' death reached his son Cambyses in September, 530 B.C., Cambyses assumed the full titling of his great father. He married his sisters Atossa and Roxana and moved against Egypt, the last of the four great Empires yet to be conquered. In this he attained to great success and Persian domination over Egypt established by Cambyses remained unchallenged for one hundred years. But this story has already been told.

Cambyses died in the eighth year of his reign (i.e., Spring of 522 B.C.), probably by his own hand. Darius tells his story on the Behistun inscription which is still to be seen on the road to Kermanshah.

> "When Cambyses slew Bardiya it was not known to the people that Bardiya was slain; afterwards Cambyses went to Egypt : when Cambyses had departed into Egypt, the people became hostile. ... afterwards there was a certain man, a Magian, Gaumata by name ... he lied to the people (saying), 'I am Bardiya, the son of Cyrus, brother of Cambyses ...' afterwards all the people rose in revolt, and from Cambyses they went over to him both Persia and Media, and the other provinces : he seized on the kingdom ... afterwards Cambyses died."[8]

The sketchy story needs filling in. Cambyses had a brother, Bardiya, "of the same father and mother." Before he went to Egypt on the death of his father, Cambyses apparently killed his younger brother — which was not uncommon — to secure his throne. However, this "was not known to the people."

Cambyses did not return to Persia for eight years and dissatisfaction grew up in his absence centered on the name of the (slain) brother. Gaumata, capitalizing on this — with the people not knowing — passed himself off as the slain Bardiya, raised a revolt against Cambyses, and crowned himself king. Herodotus tells us that Cambyses, on hearing the news, immediately marched for Persia but died on the way. Herodotus ascribes his death to an accident, other chronicles said suicide. Whatever the truth, Darius, the spear bearer, with the legitimate king now dead, moved against Gaumata with the help of six other Achaemenids who had apparently made a pact with him. Whether they knew of Darius' actual lineage was probably at this point immaterial. Later, as pointed out above, Darius boasted of his descent from the early Achaemenid kings. "Eight of my family were formerly kings, I am the ninth; nine are we in two lines." The truth of the matter was that while he had come from an old median (Achaemenid) line Cyrus' early conquest of Media had reduced Darius' line to a common vassalage. The new line of power was Cyrus, Cambyses, Bardiya. When Darius became king his grandfather, Arsames, held a petty kinglet and his father, Hystaspes has been fortunate enough to be made a satrap in distant Parthia. Darius himself, as a poor but effective soldier, had been taken by Cambyses into personal service.

Whatever his status, though, Darius had all of the qualities of kingship and it is not improbable that the other Achaemenids decided for this reason it was best to throw in their lot with him. So the agreement, "conspiracy," was made. They would move against Gaumata and carry the struggle for consolidation of the Empire as it was known that Gaumata had great popular support. In the autumn of 523 Darius killed Gaumata who claimed he was Bardiya. No one but Darius and his wives — two of his wives had been wife to Bardiya — ever probably really knew if the real Bardiya had, in fact, really been slain by Cambyses before he left for Egypt, or whether in fact the man slain in 522 was really Bardiya, the rightful claimant to the throne, or a pretender. But kingship is a great prize and Darius (at first called the "usurper" just as William the Conqueror was known as the "bastard" before he earned his other title) knew what to do with it. The recounting of his battles are not of primary concern here. What is important is that Darius had the support of seven great men who headed great families and he names them in his autobiography which is carved into the great wall at Behistun. The names read unfamiliarly.[9] They are Vindafarna (Intaphrenes), son of Vayaspara; Utana (Otanes), son of Thukhra; Gaubaruva (Gobryas), son of Marduniya (Mardonius); Vidarna (Hydarnes), son of Bagabigna; Bagabukhsha (Megabyzus), son of Datuhya; and Ardumanish, son of Vahauka. Following their naming, as mentioned above, the Behistun inscription says : "You who shall be king hereafter, preserve well the family of these men." Here was the basis for the future aristocracy of Iran — together with their women.

The women of Iran were always an essential aspect of the monarchical-aristocratic arrangement that began to develop with the Achaemenid. Anyone who has travelled in Iran has come across the name Atossa again and again. It was she whom Aeschylus memorialized in the play, "Persae." "O Queen," he wrote, "most exalted of Persia's deep girdled dames, venerable mother of Xerxes, spouse of Darius, hail !

Consort wast thou of the Persian's God and mother art thou likewise of a God."[10]

Not surprisingly, therefore, the women were not excluded in the performance of Darius' historic coup. Apparently it was agreed among these young and conspiring Achaemenids that if Darius won (and it was also apparently agreed that if he should be killed, they would all stand together to secure the throne for one of their own number), he should marry only Achaemenid women. Darius kept his bargain and in swift succession he married Atossa and Artystone, both of whom were daughters of Cyrus. Atossa had also been wife to Cambyses, Darius' father and to Bardiya, the younger brother of Cambyses. Darius then married Phaedyrne, daughter of one of the seven, Otanes, who like Atossa had been wife to Cambyses and then Bardiya. Finally, he married Bardiya's own daughter Parmys. These are impressive statistics and among other things show how the noble women wished to remain close to the throne.

At this point something more should be said of Persians and of their marriage customs. Before Alexander — and indeed after the collapse of his Empire — only an Achaemenid might be king and only a small select circle of the highest nobility might marry into the royal family. Thus, in the course of time, Achaemenid kingship came to be accepted by the aristocracy who immediately surrounded the throne as being an unshakeable principle. From what we know, this principle spoke to the fact that (1) the king's father must be an Achaemenid; (2) his mother must be an Achaemenid, and (3) if she was not of the royal family she must be of the seven great families. While Darius was not in direct descent to the throne, he was an Achaemenid and he did marry Achaemenids. The importance of the Queen's bloodline, then, was of equal importance to the kings. In-breeding was a recognized institution of royalty in most of the Orient and it was no different in Iran. There are known cases where brother and sister marriages were accomplished, as well as mother and son relationships. The important thing was that the claim of the woman should be clear. For example, when a dispute of succession rose after the death of Artaxerxes II, the successor was the one whose wives were closest to the royal family. The winner, Ochos, married Artaxerxes' wife and daughter, his own half sister Atossa.

After Artaxerxes, increasing numbers of Babylonian women became prominent at court and within the ranks of the nobility. A legendary and historic name, Semiramis, was the prototype of these much-admired Babylonian women. Around her personality as much legend has grown as around Atossa, the Achaemenid. Her charms were irresistible and perhaps even her sexual excesses. She is modestly described, however, on a column discovered in 1909 as "a woman of the palace". She might enjoy knowing that today a small but very attractive and well maintained hotel in Teheran bears her name (also in Cairo). Atossa's name, to the writer's knowledge, claims only an excellent jewelry store in Teheran, although perhaps she would have preferred the choice. Despite this relaxing of the old rules, however, the importance of the Queen or the Queen Mother, cannot be overestimated in Iranian history. Only a Persian queen or queen mother could sit at the table with the king until Artaxerxes changed the rules around 400 B.C.

This chapter opened with the correspondence between Alexander and Aristotle regarding the Persian elite. Now that the genesis of this extraordinary group has been explained it now seems important to return to that crucial period in Persian history.

From Alexander's point of view, he gained what he wanted, the title of Shahanshah. But the corollary to this was the destruction of the Persian Empire. Alexander's actions that followed upon the completion of the conquest were strange and disturbed. He saw himself as the successor to Cyrus the Great. (He had invoked his *daimon* before moving to gain his Empire.) But he was no Cyrus. In fact it is difficult to see him as a world statesman of the first rank. A brief review will suffice to make this point.

After Alexander's victory of Gaugamela (1 October 331 B.C.), and the death of the last Darius, Alexander regarded himself as the legitimate head of the Persian Empire and adopted the dress and ceremonial of the Persian kings. It never occurred to him that in doing so he looked ridiculous in the eyes of the nobility. He was neither Aryan, nor Persian, nor Achaemenid (despite the legendary account of the later *Shahnameh*). This may have meant nothing to Alexander but it meant everything to the people he had conquered. Moreover, by burning and sacking the great palace at Persepolis, Alexander showed himself insensitive to what Persepolis stood for. Greeks had studied Persia for years — many of our best sources of the Achaemenid period are Greek. Yet, Alexander and his followers continued to provide Greek substitutes for indigenous Persian concepts and not understand the meaning of it. For example, Alexander ordered a great marriage feast at Susa where ten thousand of his officers and men were married to Persian women. At Alexander's death, his high officers took over the government and these same wives were practically all discarded as the administrators returned to their Greek wives. But Persian women were not Greek women. Their place in history and in their society was well and highly regarded. The damage of such a callous action within Iran cannot be overestimated, there is no doubt that these women contributed fiercely to the collapse of Alexander's empire.

Finally, Greek law was introduced — in a land where even the Greek scholars themselves had called Darius "Lawgiver." The head of Zeus appeared on coinage. In the *Letter of Tansar*, it is written "that Alexander burnt the books of our religion — 1,200 ox hides at Istaxr."[11]

Small wonder that the Greeks, who thought highly of themselves, could be accused on occasion by others of obduracy if not stupidity. Even some present day recountings of the period misread what was really happening.[12]

With Alexander's death, any facade of accommodation that might have existed broke. In death the great Macedonian became the "Evil Invader", the "Anti-King". He was a man without religion and without legitimacy.[13] The elite emerged as the compact leader of the resistance and in shaping the course of this resistance, they returned to the traditions of the Achaemenids as being the only true source of kingly power and grace. During the Civil War of 401 B.C., a young Achaemenid was killed in his bid for the Crown. His followers offered their allegiance to a nobleman not of the blood. Even though this nobleman had back of him Zenophon's undefeated ten thousand Greeks, he would not accept the bid on the grounds he was not Achaemenid.[14] Thus, there began the long and concerted effort toward restoration and legitimacy.

Greek rule lasted from 331 – 129 B.C. Increasingly with the death of Alexander, his generals fell into embittered warfare and Iran began to break apart. By 221 B.C. the historian Polybius saw nothing but vacant thrones and youths without experience. Those Persians, who had held high governorships under Alexander were, with a few exceptions, replaced as the struggle between the Greeks and the Persians went on. But the Greeks, courageous though many of them were, were — even in their greatest victories — always on the defensive. There is a saying — even current in Iran today — "Time is on our side." A patient people who believe this can accomplish much, particularly if they retain their flexibility and their eye for the main chance. It finally came to the Persian elite. In 247 B.C., two brothers revolted against their Greek overlords and founded an independent kingdom in the old Parthian area subdued by Cyrus, located in the north and east of what was once the Persian Empire. Despite the offensive efforts of Greeks, Mongols, Scythians, as well as local Iranians, these Parthian warlords, known as the Arsacids, consolidated and began their expansion. Not that there were consistent gains. Arsacid power collapsed more than once in the face of offensive action and dynastic feuds. But the leadership hung on and eventually under Mithradates II and Phraates III, the Parthian Empire — as it was now known — and which endured from 129 B.C. to 226 A.D., assumed the inheritance of the Achaemenid dynasty. Physically, of course, it was not a true world empire. Only half of what is now Iran was subject to Arsacid rule. But the Arsacids now began to use the old Achaemenid title, Shahanshah or King of Kings which no one had claimed since Alexander. More important was the microcosm created here that previewed the great Sassanian dynasty to come.

There seems little doubt that the thrust of power of the seven great families after the Greek debacle had been in the direction of the creation of something like the Arsacid claim. Not that such a creation was seen to be final and complete. In fact in many ways the Parthian Empire was a half-way house for the elite. It was very loosely organized by comparison with the empire under Darius. This gave the great families who were very much in evidence with their huge country holdings and private armies; their favoured position within the Parthian Empire; their leadership in restoring Persian administration and customs; a consolidated position from which they could eventually move to even greater power. The Arsacid dynasty ruled loosely, then, for four hundred years. But it was an important period; one in which Iranism "was more chaste than that of the Achaemenids."[15] For that reason it seems desirable to examine certain of the basics that identify this period.

The ancient patriarchal regime of the early Aryans had recovered with vigor. The notion of a family tree of descendants of the society — which had been only loosely maintained towards the close of the Achaemenid period and during Greek rule — was re-established and was maintained even after the fall of the Sassanids. It is to be found today in Iran within the Zoroastrian community.

Very early, as has been pointed out, there was a hierarchy of kingship beginning with the king or chief of the house; of the village; of the tribe; and of the country. The last two eventually disappeared with the formation of the Achaemenid Empire and the replacement of the chief of the country with the Shahanshah. The kings of the tribes, at the same time were replaced by the royal satraps. This condition of affairs existed in the Empire of the Arsacids simply because the strength of the Achaemenid organization was such that it was able to survive even the shock of defeat and Greek rule.

This left the two lower ranks of the patriarchal system, however, pretty much as they had always been and in a sense they were the strongest links in the patriarchal system. The chiefs of the family and of the clan never lost their power or their position and in a sense formed the superior class of the aristocracy. They were hereditary land owners and they maintained their armies. They were the "center of gravity of the State" as Christensen puts it.[16] They could raise their subjects either for or against the great king, the Shahanshah. Suren, for example, one of the powerful family chiefs, led an army of ten thousand "cavaliers" who were his "slaves" against Crassus. During the Arsacid dynasty, kingship was attached to the family of Arsacids but it was not necessarily transmitted from father to son. The aristocracy, and more particularly the heads of the great families, decided who would be king. If they were not in agreement, each side would engage in armed combat in this case, each side choosing its Arsacid prince.

Often, but not necessarily always, the heads of these great families were also governors of the provinces. These governorships were smaller than the great satrapies of Achaemenid times, but they also held a more independent position. These governorships, designated as royalty bore the title of Shah (King). There were eighteen of them under the Arsacids. Also members of the royal family were designated as Shah when they held governorships. Overall, of course, was the Shahanshah.

There seems to be no doubt that in the era between Alexander and the rise of Ardashir, the Sassanian, the power lay with the heads of the great families. The Arab historians have designated this period as belonging to the "kings of the tribes." Pahlavi literature uses the term "head of the house" or "the reigning prince."

The political authority of these great men found expression in the aristocratic council which, as will be seen later, played such an important part in Ardashir's rise to power. This council consisted of governors and generals, princes of the royal family and the great lords of the privileged families. During the Arsacid reign, the names of Suren and Karen seem preeminent. Christensen states flatly that this aristocratic council limited the royal power.[17]

Certain important administrative functions were also attached to these families as members of Council and these functions will be discussed in a later chapter.

Limitations of royal power are, however, variables at best, and during this period a strong king could dominate the nobility. The argument that the Shahanshah was always first among equals — an argument often advanced — would similarly seem to be a variable principle rather than a consistent one. At the same time, there are examples from this period where a dying nobleman would himself confer upon his son all his rights and even invest him with his position — normally considered to be the prerogative of the Shahanshah.

Revolts of princes and governors were common enough but to dare to usurp the title of Shahanshah it was necessary to belong to a ruling family. On the occasion that this did happen, if the Shahanshah proved the stronger he would use the opportunity to exterminate the noble families which seemed dangerous to him and if possible he would profit by the occasion by taking their land and serfs and adding them to the royal domain.

Treachery on the part of nobles was often forestalled by giving the great men the command of royal troops which kept them near the throne.

The power of the king was, of course, not limited by any law. If circumstancces permitted, he ruled with all the tyranny of an oriental potentate. He feared above all his own family for with the importance of the principle of legitimacy (i.e., Achaemenid blood) that was a religion with the Iranians, no nobles would dare to risk a war against the Shahanshah without having an Arsacid candidate to oppose him. Even though the Parthian kings thus so often raged against their own blood, there was usually one prince who had escaped the massacre who would form the nucleus for new opposition.

The most prominent characteristic of the Parthian period, in sum, was the continuing tension between the great families, the nobility, on the one hand and the authority of the Shahanshah on the other. Christensen personalizes the political relationship with a marvellous description from Plutarch, the Greek historian, of the case of Suren, already mentioned.[18]

> "The perfect type of great Parthian lord is Suren, the enemy of Crassus, and Plutarch has described him to us. 'In richness, in nobility, and in glory he was supreme after the king. In valour and in his ability to be the first among the Parthians, in stature and in looks he had no equal. When he went into the country, he was accompanied by a thousand camels carrying his baggage, by two hundred chariots for his concubines, by a thousand armoured knights and by a great number of lightly armed soldiers for he had, in total, ten thousand knights partly made up of his vassals, partly of his slaves.' On the day of battle, he would display himself, blessed and

> handsome, at the head of his troops, and 'with a reputation of valour which accorded wrongly with his effeminate beauty; for in the manner of the Medes, he made up his face and wore his hair divided, while the other Parthians wore their hair long and shaggy, in the manner of the Scythians, in order to have a frightening appearance. He took along his harem and while in the country, he spent his nights amusing himself with wine, song, music, and love'."

The period of 549 years which elapsed between the death of Alexander and the rise of the Sassanian dynasty (323 B.C.) was a period, then, that rightly belonged to those noblemen and their descendants who faced Alexander on that memorable occasion when the Macedonian made the assessment that he passed on to Aristotle. They had survived the period of Greek rule (331 – 129 B.C.), where they carried the burden of active resistance. They supported the Aryan nomadic tribe that came from the north to overcome substantial areas of Greek rule to create the Parthian dynasty (129 – 226 A.D.). Here in the northeast pocket of what had once been the great Achaemenid Empire they ruled their small kingdoms and kept the old traditions. It was to them that Ardashir came with his appeal to the kings of the tribes.

The *Letter of Tansar*, mentioned above, is a classic appeal to the aristocracy. It was a fugitive piece of Middle Persian literature "the greater part of which, being Zoroastrian,[19] vanished like snow in the heat of the Islamic summer."[20] It was re-translated a number of times. The work begins with a brief sketch of the history of Iran down to the time of Ardashir, the first Sassanian king who reigned from 224 – 240 A.D. It recounts the death of the last Darius, the division of Iran by Alexander among the local kings, Alexander's death, and finally the rise of Ardashir himself and his conquest of the descendants of those ninety kings. In a sense, as it is with all Iranian literature it is a king's book as it was in all likelihood proposed for Ardashir by his supporters. But it deals with several subjects, all essential to understanding the basic elements of Sassanian society. Its essence is historical, not legendary. The concern here, however, is with Ardashir's relationship to the aristocracy.

"When Ardashir first took to the field, he wrote urgent letters to the kings of the people in which he established his claim and summoned them to obey him."[21] It took him fourteen years to bring them to full support. In some cases he overthrew the local rulers and seized their lands. But for others, Ardashir used the force of argument and advantage. The *Letter* itself, although not written by Ardashir, is an example of how support for Ardashir developed in communications through the elite group. He is seen as constantly labouring to reassure the nobility of his true allegiance to the ancient ways; to true religion "for Church and State were born of one womb";[22] to the many blessings of "Crown and Throne."

There can be no doubt that Ardashir, like Cyrus before him — and to whom he is compared in Iranian history — was much more than a warrior. His close companions were wise men, and men of excellence. On two days of each week he held assembly. On one day at grand audience, he drank wine with the great men of the realm and treated each graciously, behaving to him as was fit. On the other day he drank wine in seclusion with the wise men and men of excellence who were his close companions, and the *Letter* says he profited from them. Throughout his assemblies the talk ran seriously and never turned to jest.

The nobility, Ardashir saw as being very special. The *Letter* specifies that "the working people should salute them and bow before them, and that the fighting men in turn, should show reverence to the nobles."[23]

Many children were seen as fitting for the populace, "but kings and nobles take pride in the smallness of their families. The hedgerow bird has a numerous brood but the falcon contents herself with a small one."[24]

The nobility were to be distinguished from the common people "with regard to horses and clothes, houses and gardens, women and servants." Further, there were to be entrances, sitting places and standing places, ornaments, etc., according to the dignity of rank. "No commoner may share sources of enjoyment of life with the nobles." Alliances and marriages between the groups were forbidden.

A further appeal of Ardashir was his continuing promise to carry the resistance against the Greeks — after all those years !

He promised that he would not rest "till he has avenged Darius against the successors of Alexander, and has replenished the coffers and the treasury of the State, and has restored by the capture of descendants of his soldiers, the cities which Alexander laid waste in Iran."[25] Ardashir, like Cyrus and Darius before him, was a man of genius. Once he had established the Empire, however, the organizational aspects of the society and of the State developed — as they so often do — a continuum of their own. This will be dealt with in a later chapter. Here it is enough to point out the nature of the Sassanian social structure.

There were four estates, which Ardashir was credited with having "restored". "The Shahanshah, through his pure intelligence and surpassing excellence caused these four estates, which had fallen away, to be restored and brought back each to his own place."[26]

> "The first estate is the clergy; and this estate is further divided among judges and priests, temple-guardians and teachers. The second estate is that of the military-cavalry and foot-soldiers. Within them are differences of rank and function. The third estate is that of the scribes and they too are divided into groups and categories such as writers of official communications, accountants, recorders of verdicts and registrations and covenants, and writers of chronicles; physicians, poets and astronomers are numbered among their rank. The fourth estate is known as that of the artisans and comprises tillers of land and herders of cattle and merchants and those who earn their living by trade."[27]

The administrative aspects of this social division — which became so rigid as to approximate in severity the caste system of India — will be dealt with later. The important thing to note here is that this is a new division and one which endured until the Sassanids fell. Each of these estates were subdivided into several classes, each with its leader — who was surrounded by his supporting element. There was a continuing state of tension between the older feudal group and the new bureaucratic absolutists. Both possessed aristocratic elements and this can be seen even today in Iran where the bureaucracy can be just as much of a stepping stone to advancement and preferment to a promising young man as if he inherited large holdings from his father.

The feudal aspects, as mentioned, were the more ancient tradition — the old men, so to speak, holding out against the new — the bureaucracy. The *Letter of Tansar* said : "We shall not take away the title of king from any of those who will come to offer us their submission and will remain on the great path of obedience." The ancient division of the Empire into smaller states was preserved under the Sassanids and the governors of these little states bore the title of Shah (not Shahanshah) or king. Some were of royal blood, some were of the great old families. Interestingly enough, the number seven — the privileged families that were named by Darius — was retained in number in the new empire of Ardashir but only three of them, Karen, Suren, and Aspahbadh dated back[28] before the Parthian dynasty. Thus, it can be seen that over hundreds of years, the same families might not continue as privileged if the line died out, or was destroyed, but the concept remained and was filled in fact by newer blood. Two such new families, Spaniyadh and Mihran, were privileged in the Sassanid period. All of the families held great land holdings — Suren around modern Sistan, Spaniyadh around modern Teheran, etc.

Important though land holding was, it was also true that as the lines of the bureaucracy tightened, the great families found it more and more essential that they remain at Court rather than be out governing their lands. Consequently the character of the nobility during the period took on more and more a professional standing within the high estates, particularly the first estate — clergy and lawyers. Also hereditary responsibilities began to grow up around the Court (i.e., the family called Artabides had the duty of crowning the king). Three of these hereditary responsibilities were military and three were civilian. When there was too much conflict between the Shahanshah and those who held the transmitted posts, the Shahanshah invariably followed the old tradition of having the offending official killed but replacing him with a son. Even in modern times in Iran, it is not unusual to find a prominent figure disappearing only to have the name reappear a few years later in a younger generation figure.

In Sassanid chronicles,[29] one encounters on nearly every page the expression "the lords and nobles". Each time a new Shahanshah was crowned, the "lords and nobles" assembled to render him homage and listen to the speech by which he introduced himself to the people. On the other hand it was the "lords and nobles" that dethroned Ardashir II and killed Shapur III. Sometimes one finds the combination of "the lords and distinguished men." All of these terms mean the highest officials of the Empire, the highest representatives of the bureaucracy. They stand alongside of the land holding nobles who tended more to provide the military nucleus of the fine Sassanian Army. The latter, of course, had very special privileges. Beginning in the 5th century, the title of "knight" came into being. Chivalry, as that term was known in Europe, became a part of the culture of this group. In peacetime the majority of knights lived on their land, cultivating their fields and occupying themselves with their peasants, who formed the common soldiers that they led into service. In war, however, their social and political value was very high — as it is in most countries in such times. But the conduct of true knighthood was observed and gave to the Iranians an honoured place in the archives of chivalric tradition.

The aristocracy, like the rest of Iranian society of the period, was based at the local level on the family and property. Polygamy was usual and in addition to their lawful wives the upper class Persians had concubines, slaves bought or taken in war. As the rigidity of Sassanian society progressed, the wife had less independent status than she had had under the Achaemenids but her place was still a more honoured one than in any other Asiatic society. Betrothals increasingly took place in childhood and young gentlemen normally married around their fifteenth year. Marriages between close relations continued. Marriage between brother and sister partook of the "divine splendour" and having the value of an escorcism. While these unions were considered incestuous in the West, and were looked upon with particular horror by the Christians, Avesta and Pahlavi theological literature recommended the tradition.[30]

Marriage regulations were handed down by tradition. The birth of a boy was attended by the celebration of certain rites. The education of boys up to age seven was the duty of the mother. Afterwards he was moved into the training traditions of the aristocracy that dated back to those described above in the *Cyropaedia*.

To ensure maintenance of the family, the law ordained marriage by substitution. If a man died without male issue, his widow married his nearest kinsman. If there was no widow, this kinsman married the dead man's daughter or nearest female relative. In both cases the child of the new marriage was regarded as the offspring of the deceased.

Adoption, as might be expected, was subject to very strict regulations. He must be of age, of the Mazdean religion, intelligent and must not have committed any mortal sin.[31] Priests closely supervised the requirements of these social traditions including inheritances.

While considerable attention has been paid here to the place of the aristocracy under the Sassanids, it has been necessary to do so for two reasons. One, the great literature and traditions even of present day Iran harken back to the Sassanian period. It was a period of splendour and glory and even today university educated Iranians in Teheran will tell of their great interest in this period. It was truly the golden age and it lives in Firdawsi's great *Shahnameh*.

The second reason for this more detailed consideration is simply that the Sassanian period was of such strict organizational discipline, that as will be seen in a later chapter, it became the model for the imperial structures in the Middle East that were to follow. The aristocracy was dispersed during much of the period that followed, but they appeared and reappeared in various roles — philosophy, religion, administration, law. In times of great crisis, they acted in concert. For example, during the Mongol invasion, Iranian women of the upper classes were sequestered in mountainous caves and other out-of-the-way places to protect them against the ravaging soldiers. Purity of blood-lines were still important to these descendants of the early Aryans.

Today in Iran, the aristocracy still waits in close attendance upon the throne. For the most part today they are urban rather than rural. The families number from perhaps two hundred to one thousand. These are the social leaders of Iran, still looked up to by the common people. Their position, which in the past derived largely from their monopolistic ownership of land and water, now has a different base. In fact, one of the interesting phenomena in Iran is how the elite and the middle class are switching places in the economic sphere. The latter is turning to landowning for its prestige symbol. The elite has turned to commerce and industry, although a core of old land holding families still survive. The ideal combination is where great power and position, coupled with wealth, involves as well investment in large land holdings.

Unlike in the days of the Sassanians, the aristocracy of Iran today is not hereditary. Even land with its related prestige and influence, although inherited, is not necessarily hereditary in the legal sense of the word. In other words, the present aristocracy of Iran does not necessarily date back to earlier times even though the aristocratic pattern is the same. It is possible to enter the elite in Iran and to alter one's position within the group. This can be done by the accumulation of wealth, by promotion within the bureaucratic or army hierarchy; or even, as in one case known to the writer, by writing an excellent book of verse. What all of these do have in common is their relationship to, and their support of, the monarchy.

There is an important dimension to the Iranian elite which should be mentioned here. The writer is referring to its intellectual capabilities. We are accustomed in the West to think of the Greeks as being the thinkers *par excellence* and it is true that Plato and Aristotle — to take two examples— have been translated and have been studied for generations by the Iranians. Particularly Plato is much read, even today, in Iran. But it was Mohammed himself who is credited with the famous statement that the Persians "would journey to the Pleiades after knowledge,"[32] and anyone with any familiarity with Persian intellectual history can enumerate dozens of great minds that have helped Persia to conquer a domain far more extensive than any won by the arms of Cyrus and Darius. This tradition is still a part of the current tradition of the Iranian elite. The writer can recall a conversation a few years ago in Teheran at an embassy party. Two senior officials of the diplomatic corps were discussing a young Iranian junior within the corps, who was being much feted that evening because of the publication of a new volume of poetry. Finally, one of the officials said to the other, "you know it is time to make M.——— (referring to the author) an ambassador." The other agreed and they both moved into conversation with the author and his wife. This would seem most strange in North American circles where the author of a volume of poetry might, in fact, find the publication working to his disadvantage in official circles. But in Iranian circles — including business — it is not at all uncommon to find young men in responsible positions who have been tutors at Oxford and Cambridge. Seniority has little to do in Iran with senior appointments. Most of us can recall any number of young Iranian Ambassadors or others in an equivalent position elsewhere who might well in the West be seen to qualify for a second or third secretaryship.

It is not too often known that the world's first university was Iranian. In a passage in the oldest existing Pahlavi language book, "The Epic of Ardashir" reference is made to the high proficiency reached in academic studies on the part of this founder of the Sassanian dynasty and of his reputation as a scholar and writer. Ardashir is said to have encouraged the translation of over eight hundred books into Pahlavi from Sanskrit, Greek, and Syriac, and al-Tabari, the great Arabic historian, tells us that "not only was he a courageous warrior on the battlefield, but a great contributor to literature as well. Besides his collection of ancient books, more than one thousand scholars gathered at his court, devoting their efforts to research in various fields of science and the arts."[33] It is said that Ardashir devoted a few hours each day in translating books on science and philosophy, then joining in the debates of the scholars.

Being the kind of man he was, it became inevitable that Ardashir should begin to think in terms of a University Center. He sent scholars to India, China, Egypt, Greece, Rome and Mesopotamia in search of rare books and he made no secret of the fact that he intended to build the finest library in the world.

Ardashir never lived to see the fruition of his dream. This was left for his son Shapur I to accomplish. Encouraged by his late father's example, Shapur continued the tradition of gathering at his court great scholars from throughout the world and continuing the work of translating and discussion.

Seven years after his father's death, Shapur created the great

University at Gondi Shahpur in what is now Iran's southern province of Khuzestan. Professors were brought in from many lands and within five years of its founding, the University was attracting students and intellectuals from the then civilized world. At one time almost five thousand of them were gathered in this great center.

No doubt one of the main reasons for the recognition given the University was that Shapur would not permit any interference with its work, or its scholarship — and this included the clergy. "It is my order," Shapur declared, "that any citizen of my realm who desires to acquire greater knowledge, is absolutely free to go to Gondi Shahpur to study and no man shall interfere with him."[34]

Professors were picked with great care. Candidates were interviewed by a selection board of senior officials and senior professors and Shapur himself occasionally attended the proceedings which might last for several days.

Gondi Shahpur was famous for its faculties of mathematics, philosophy, and astronomy but its international fame really rested on its distinguished school of medicine and western medieval accounts credit the Persians with being the best physicians in the world. During the reign of Khosrow (531 - 579) medical congresses were instituted lasting for long periods of time and attracting physicians from all over the world. As well, Khosrow ordered the construction of a large hospital adjacent to the University and a library of two hundred and fifty-nine rooms with books carefully catalogued and stacked according to language and subject. "The like of it has not been seen in the history of civilized man" said the great Cambridge scholar E. G. Browne, whose great four volume "Literary History of Persia" is still the classic in its field.

Although the University survived for some years after the Arab conquest, the anti-intellectual attitude of the Arabs made its demise inevitable. Eventually the Caliphate moved it to Baghdad and then shortly thereafter, ordered it closed. Some books were saved through translation but the great intellectual monument never recovered itself. Eventually, as will be pointed out, individual Persians rose to fame and distinctions within the Muslim Empire and Arab science of well known medieval fame owes much to the presence of these men. But, the best of it was lost. Today the name Shahpur is preserved in a new University at Ahvaz named Jondishapur.

Contributing as well to the aristocratic-intellectual complexion described, is the strong literary tradition of Iran that is such an integral part of the historical and cultural tradition of Iran. This tradition, which forms the subject of a massive four volume study by the late E. G. Browne, already referred to and cited, has been primarily directed toward keeping alive and transmitting the tradition of the institution of monarchy. These literary figures in turn, have been protected and their works preserved for posterity. They are honoured as in no other country and all through Iran, one can find the shrines of the great poets and literary figures. In Shiraz, the tombs of Sa'adi and Hafez are a must on any travel agenda and they are well worth seeing, so well have they been preserved and landscaped. These poets, certainly along with the intellectuals, have formed an integral part of the aristocratic tradition.

The aristocracy of Iran is, then, many faceted even though essentially political. It exists within and encourages the preservation of a class structure in Iran which has been a fact of life since the Achaemenids. The Sassanian dynasty made the structuring even more indelible. Finally the Qur'an itself spoke to the matter : "It is He who has made us the inheritors of the earth, who has elevated us one above the other by degrees, in order to help us experience His gifts." (Chapter VI, Verse 165).

Today, as stated above, the present aristocracy of Iran waits in close attendance on the throne. They are great families — popularly (inaccurately) described in the West as the "thousand families". They may intrigue among themselves as they have always done, but they close ranks against any outsider. Individual members of the families may rise and fall from power. As in older times, prominent names will disappear — only to re-appear in a younger generation. Some of the names within the elite are very old. Some came to prominence and power with Reza Shah in the 1920's and took old, historical names. Many are in the diplomatic corps. In recent years Canada was served by two brothers in succession as ambassador whose name Esfendiary was prominent in the *Shahnameh*; the Afshar brothers — of Turkoman descent — held parallel portfolios at the Court of Saint James and in Washington. As of this writing, two Zahedi brothers hold the rank of Ambassador in Ottawa and in Washington. The aristocracy of Iran seeks personal privacy and it was not until Professors Bill and Leiden published their book in 1974 that actual family names were listed en bloc.[35] As listed and described, they are : "Pahlavi, 'Alam, Diba, Qaraguzlu, Isfandiari, Ardalan, Bayat, Sami'i, Farmanfarmaian, Akbar, Afkhami,' Adl, Amuzigar, Bushihri, Iqbal, Jahanbani, Imami, and Khal'atbari."

"The ties between key members of these families are tight even though there may be changes — even as of the time of writing. Minister of Culture Mihrdad Pahlbud is the husband of Princess Shams, the sister of Muhammad Reza Shah. Major-General Minbashian is the brother of Minister of Culture Pahlbud (formerly 'Izzatullah Minbashian). Influential Senator Bushihri is the father of the husband of powerful Princess Ashraf, the twin sister of the Shah. Former Chief of the Air Force Muhammad Khatami was married to the Shah's sister Fatima. Ardashir Zahedi, Iranian Ambassador to the United States, was formerly married to the Shah's daughter Shahnaz. Two recent prime ministers of Iran married sisters whose mother was herself the daughter of a prime minister and a member of the prominent Vusuq family. The right family connections still remain an important passport in Iran."

The aristocracy also appears in the *Iran Almanac*. The Almanac is, incidentally, worth perusing. Like *Who's Who in America* it lists "only leading men and women in various fields". There are some interesting additions to the American publication. For example, the language capability of each entry is listed in the *Almanac*. So is the family background, rather than just the parents. Social activities rate as much prominence as political activities. Travel is listed. Occasionally when someone holds a special relationship to the Shahanshah, it is noted. Amir Assadollah Alam, former Minister of Court, for example, is described in the *Almanac* as "very close to and highly trusted by his Imperial Majesty the Shahanshah."

Again, unlike the American *Who's Who*, more than one

member of the family listed is quite common. This, of course, is a mark of the aristocracy in Iran. If one man makes it, the chances are his brothers will too.

At the front of the *Iran Almanac*, the Pahlavi Dynasty is listed separately. The Royal Family is also listed in *Iran Today*.[36] The official listing and description of the Family is as follows: "His Imperial Majesty Mohammad Reza Pahlavi, Shahanshah Aryamehr, was born in Teheran on 26th October 1919. At the age of six he was proclaimed Crown Prince at his father's Coronation.

"After attending the elementary military school, where he wore uniform and received a stiff military education, the future Shahanshah was sent to Switzerland at the age of 12 for his secondary education. Back in Iran, he entered the Military Academy, graduating in 1938 as a second Lieutenant. As Inspector of the Army, the young prince then spent three years travelling around Iran, inspecting civil as well as military installations and acquiring a wide knowledge of the country and its problems. He was still only 21 when, as Mohammad Reza Shah Pahlavi, he took the Royal Oath of Office before Parliament.

"In 1959 the Shahanshah Aryamehr married Empress Farah Pahlavi. The Imperial couple have four children — Prince Reza, the Crown Prince, Princess Farahnaz, Prince Ali Reza and Princess Leila. From his earlier marriage to Princess Fawzia, the sister of former King Farouk of Egypt, the Shahanshah Aryamehr has a daughter, Princess Shahnaz. From his second marriage to Princess Sorayya His Imperial Majesty had no children.

"The Shahanshah Aryamehr deliberately postponed his Coronation until the 26th year of his reign, having pledged that he would not formally crown himself until he had transformed Iran into a prosperous and progressive nation. In 1967 the time had come, and in a glittering ceremony in the Golestan Palace, the Coronation finally took place. At the same ceremony the Empress and Crown Prince were officially proclaimed.

"In 1965 Parliament bestowed on the Shahanshah the title Aryamehr, literally 'Light of the Aryans'.

"Empress Farah Pahlavi was born on October 14, 1938, the

only daughter of Sohrab Diba, who died when she was only nine years old. Her father, a graduate of St Cyr and an Iranian Army officer, had a law degree from the University of Paris. Her mother, Mme Farideh Diba, personally supervised her education, first at Teheran's Jeanne d'Arc and Razi schools, and later at the Ecole d'Architecture in Paris, where she was studying up to the time of her marriage to the Shahanshah Aryamehr, which took place on December 20, 1959.

"As Empress she has pursued her interests in social work, sport and art ... and she is patron of 24 educational, health, cultural and charity organizations...

"The Shahanshah Aryamehr has five brothers and three sisters. One brother, Prince Ali Reza Pahlavi, died in a plane crash in 1954.

"His Imperial Majesty's elder-sister, Princess Shams Pahlavi, is President of the Red Lion and Sun Society, Iran's equivalent of the Red Cross.

"Princess Ashraf Pahlavi, the Monarch's twin sister, ... is currently the leader of the Iranian delegation to the United Nations General Assembly.

"The Shahanshah Aryamehr's third sister is Princess Fatimeh Pahlavi, who is closely concerned with higher education.

"Prince Gholam Reza Pahlavi is Inspector-General of the Imperial Iranian Armed Forces and President of Iran's National Olympic Committee.

"Prince Abdorreza Pahlavi is a specialist in economic affairs, and closely concerned with environmental problems at home and abroad. The Monarch's other brothers are Prince Ahmad Reza Pahlavi, Prince Mahmud Reza Pahlavi and Prince Hamid Reza Pahlavi."

The above — to move from the official text — roughly approximates to what is described, in Iran, particularly by Western businessmen, as the "Palace". This group holds a real position of power in Iran. No Shah has ever forgotten Aristotle's further advice to Alexander quoted above, that "there is no wickedness or calamity, no unrest or plague in the world which corrupts so much as the ascending of the base to the station of the nobles." However, it should be pointed out in this connection that the present Shahanshah does not see the aristocracy as a political grouping by itself. Nor is its position forever stabilized vis-a-vis the throne. The Shahanshah relies on individual families and this accounts for the fact that certain names appear and re-appear in different categories of imperial labour.

Occasionally, western scholars seek to formalize information on the Iranian aristocracy. But, invariably they are not granted access to this level. A recent such study purporting to be of the elite could not meet the claim advanced in the introduction.[37] It was, rather, a study at the second and third levels.

The reason for the inaccessibility of the aristocracy is not difficult to understand once the nature of their power is understood. They are truly self-conscious and they are truly exclusive. Even in their social life in Teheran, except for court functions and other special occasions, they are constantly with each other. If foreigners are included, it becomes a "foreign night" — very similar to an embassy party. Otherwise they enjoy their constant social pattern of exclusive intercourse among themselves. Gossip, new expensive clothes, trips, etc., are familiar topics of conversation among the ladies. Paris, particularly, is a frequent destination. While there is (or was) a 10,000 rial tax imposed on Iranians leaving the country, it forms no hardship for the aristocracy. There is great wealth here. One family hires only titled Englishwomen as tutors for the children — thus insuring proper accent and behaviour of their children among westerners from an early age. The homes are lavish, and, of course, there is an abundance of servants. They are still as in the olden days, quite patriarchal.

The writer can recall hearing with amusement, a teenager telling his son in Teheran, five years ago, how it was to visit her grandfather when she was very young. He lived in a great compound with his wives each in their own house — "very impressive," she said. For hours before she was to be received by the old man she was scrubbed and cleaned and decorated. "You would have thought I was going to see the Shah." She was ushered into his presence for a short time only and then ushered out. It was all very formal.

Today, of course, with the new law that permits only one wife in Iran, there tends to be more of a partnership between husband and wife than existed formerly. Fewer children, more education, lots of money, gives the elite wife great flexibility.

Among the men there is still the same awareness of what is going on around the throne that existed two thousand years ago in Iran. Active family members seldom leave Teheran without having their interests covered. The normal pattern is to keep an important male member in Teheran when others go abroad. There is extreme sensitivity to what the Palace is doing.

The term "Palace" is frequently used in conversation rather than the Shahanshah. It is no more a "family" encomium. There is a reason for this distinction. Forces around the Shah within the family, must be taken into consideration in the power struggle for position and money. The Shah's twin sister has, in the past, been a formidable contender for power. The mother of the present Empress, Madame Diba, is likewise a strong and forceful participant in the life of the Palace. The Empress herself has not only given the Shah the children necessary for the continuation of the dynasty, but has emerged in her own right as a leading spokeswoman for the women of Iran. So the Palace becomes extended and is comprehensive. But, the Monarchy, within its "Palace" context, (as contrasted with the Monarch) is constantly a variable as individuals rise to assert power. Like the aristocracy, the Palace reaches out into the key areas of national life. For example, since Plan Development has become such an important aspect of Iran's growth and modernization, many leading figures from the elite and from royalty are involved in liaison with the West. If a foreign firm wants a major contract in Iran, it is essential that an Iranian representative be contracted at a sufficiently high level to insure success. One of the favourite pastimes of the foreign community in Teheran is to guess who is involved with whom. For example, does a member of the Palace represent General Motors, and if so, what does this royal person get paid to represent the western corporation? It is not always understood that the use of the middle man broker is as old as the Middle East itself and that its use now is not a deviation from the general historical practice. Ten per cent to the broker has been the traditional figure. There is, of course, always speculation that it moves higher in some circumstances. However, officials in the World Bank have told this writer that this is not the case — that the ten per cent figure still generally obtains.

Needless to say the oil industry has produced its large share of prominent men who sit close to the throne. The late NIOC Chairman and Managing Director, Dr Manuchehr Eghbal was such a person. The present Prime Minister, Dr Jamshid Amouzegar, first came to prominence during the winter of 1970, as an oil man. He was Minister of Finance in Iran when he dropped into the London office of the Western Oil Corporation, three days before Christmas, to announce that the Organization of Petroleum Exporting Countries would shortly announce demands for huge increases in tax and royalty payments. The western companies were stunned but the days of western ultimatums to Iran are over and the twenty-three international oil companies finally signed with Dr Amouzegar skilfully carrying the ball as chairman of the negotiating teams for the producer companies. (At that point in time, of course, the oil crisis three years later became inevitable as the oil companies turned to new methods of keeping their profits up.)

The case of this tenacious Iranian negotiator, who was sophisticated enough to host his guests on a luxurious trip to Isfahan, in a very real way demonstrates the nature of the aristocratic relationships to the Shahanshah. The throne relationship is first in importance. It is generally agreed that the Shahanshah outlined the settlement himself and influenced the negotiations with his own diplomacy. Dr Amouzegar was decorated by His Imperial Majesty for seeing that the plan was accomplished with finesse and cordiality. Second in importance is Dr Amouzegar's own relationship with the West. Here is an increasingly important avenue by which members of the elite consolidate their positions in Iran. The case in point is not untypical. Dr Amouzegar took his doctorate from Cornell in 1951. He was lecturer at that distinguished University for four years. He married a German woman whom he met there as a student. Clearly here is a man who understands the western mentality and how to deal with it. The third aspect of this aristocratic network lies in Dr Amouzegar's own situation. He was born into a distinguished Iranian family in 1923 and he was given a distinguished name. His father was an historian and philologist, a former Health Minister and a

Senator. He has three brothers, all highly placed in Iran and all important. His example, singled out here merely as a case in point, shows clearly the type of elite human resources upon which Iran presently builds.

The secret of power, then, for members of the aristocracy, is to maintain a correct level of importance vis-a-vis the Throne and the Palace. In other words, the great families must remain great but must not rival the Throne. There have been powerful and important men falling from power in Iran because of a failure to observe this principle. Above all, they must remain active in the service of the Throne. They are power people, good administrators, good liaison, excellent representatives of their country and their Shahanshah. While they are well educated, they are not all necessarily intellectuals. Distinguished professors have come from the Farman-farmaian and Afshar families, but, generally speaking, the Iranian ideal is the intellectual in the service of his country and not in the role of critic. Thus political scientists or sociologists, as such, do not do as well as do poets or engineers. The concept of service to one's country in Iran is entirely comprehensive and there are rewards for this. But meanwhile what is required is loyalty and dedication — as well as capability.

The deployment of the Iranian aristocracy gives a clue to the matter of capability.[38] Professor Bill distinguishes between national elite families and provincial elite families. The latter have as their strongholds smaller cities such as Rezaiyen (Afshar), Sari (Sang, Kasemi, Mokri), Darab (Sarfarraz, Baharlu), Qazvin (Yar Afshar, Amirshahi, Haj Seyyid Javadi, Shadman), etc. These — the traditional aristocracy — are especially strong in the areas of wealth and finance.

The national elite families — many of whom are named above by Bill — tend toward the larger cities — and number some 40, although 10 form the core. These 10 are Pahlavi, 'Alam, Diba, Qaragozlu, Esfandiari, Ardalan, Samii, Farman-farmaian, Mahdavi, and Bushihri. Family member deployment (in 1973-74) was divided between the Majlis and Senate (90); High Business. Professional and Quasi-Governmental Personnel (100); Military Security leaders (50); Ministers and Deputy Ministers (75); Courtiers and Confidants (40).

The aristocracy in all countries is under constant challenge. In England, Jack Jones, Companion of Honour, proclaims publicly that 3/4 of the aristocracy of his native land are descended from "cattle robbers, land thieves, and court prostitutes".[39] In Iran, some of the political elite admittedly are the sons of "servants, mule drivers, and pedlars". Perhaps it was ever thus. Even in Aristotle's time, the aristocracy was under virulent attack. The point, however, boils down to the matter of survival. The writer is more optimistic than most, that the traditional Iranian elite will survive—and well. The Iranian aristocrat has a tenacity and a boldness that is not often seen —certainly not in the West. He moves to the attack with great strength and expertise. He is today, as in the day of Alcxander, pre-eminent in the field of his endeavour. He is a professional. The great families are professional.

NOTES

1. *The Letter of Tansar* (trans. by M. Boyce), Rome, 1968, p. 27. I use the words "aristocracy" and "elite" interchangeably here.

2. xxiii 6, 75-84, quoted in Huart, C., *Ancient Persian and Iranian Civilizations,* New York, 1927, p. 166.

3. *Encyclopaedia Britannica,* 1960 II, pp. 496-97.

4. Olmstead, A. T., *History of the Persian Empire,* University of Chicago Press, 1966, p. 23.

5. *Ibid.,* pp. 34-35.

6. Xenophon, *Cyropaedia,* I, vi 7 (I, p. 91). Quoted in Inlow, *op. cit.,* p. 407.

7. Bouvat, L., "L'Administration de la Perse," *Revue du Monde Musulman, XXIV* (1913), pp. 219-21.

8. C.A.H., IV, *op. cit.,* p. 17.3

9. Olmstead, *op. cit.,* p. 108.

10. Quoted in Inlow, *op. cit.,* p. 405.

11. *The Letter of Tansar, op. cit.,* p. 37.

12. *Encyclopaedia Britannica,* 1960, XVII, p. 557.

13. Eddy, S. K., *The King is Dead,* University of Nebraska Press, 1961, pp. 58-59, Chapter II is an excellent recounting of the resistance.

14. *Ibid.,* p. 61.

15. Christensen, A., *L'Iran sous les Sassanids* (Copenhagen, 1944), p. 51.

16. *Ibid.,* p. 16.

17. *Ibid.,* p. 17.

18. As quoted in Christensen, *op. cit.,* p. 23 ff.

19. This quotation has reference to the fact that with the coming of Islam and the Arab conquest, Zoroastrianism was proscribed as heretical and most of its literature was destroyed.

20. *The Letter of Tansar, op. cit.,* p. 1. Middle Persian was the language of Persia from about the 3rd century B.C. to the 9th century A.D.

21. *Ibid.,* p. 16.

22. *Ibid.,* p. 33.

23. *Ibid.,* p. 49.

24. *Ibid.,* p. 49.

25. *Ibid.,* p. 65.

26. *Ibid.,* p. 39.

27. *Ibid.,* p. 38.

28. Christensen, *op. cit.,* p. 98.

29. Recounted in Christensen, *op. cit.,* p. 105.

30. Huart, C., *Ancient Persian and Iranian Civilizations,* New York, 1927, p. 161.

31. *Ibid.,* p. 163.

32. Quoted in Rice, Cyrian, *The Persian Sufis,* London, 1964, p. 21.

33. *Iran Tribune, op. cit.,* p. 20.

34. *Ibid.,* p. 20.

35. Bill, J. A., Leiden, C., *The Middle East, Politics and Power,* Boston, 1974.

36. Published by the Imperial Ministry of Foreign Affairs, Teheran, 1976. As this is official, it is quoted exactly.

37. Zonis, M., *The Political Elite of Iran*, Princeton University Press, 1971. See the writer's review in *Middle East Forum* Vol. XLVIII (1972), pp. 158-60. In this chapter, I have used the words elite and aristocracy interchangeably.

38. Lenczowski, G. (ed.), *Political Elites in the Middle East*, Washington, D.C., pp. 17-40 "The Patterns of Elite Politics in Iran" by J. A. Bill.

39. *The Guardian*, January 8, 1978, p. 3.

CHAPTER 4

THE IMAMATE

It was a canon of the Zoroastrian faith that church and state were one. Firdawsi writes in the *Shahnameh* that the dying words of the great Ardashir to his son Shapur were : "Consider the altar and the throne as inseparable; they must always sustain one another. A sovereign without religion is a tyrant."[1]

In *The Letter of Tansar*, that remarkable piece of Middle Persian literature already remarked above, the same statement occurs in slightly different language. "For Church and State were born of the one womb, joined together and never to be sundered."[2] So reads the early Pahlavi text, showing that by this time Iran's parallel history of the National Epic and the reality of the period were closely drawing together.

Although the texts cited are Zoroastrian in essence, (which became the canonical truth of the Sassanids) they nevertheless represent a statement of tradition that both precedes and follows the period of the Sassanian dynasty. It is the purpose of this chapter to establish this continuity in a tradition that has come to be peculiarly Iranian rather than Moslem. In other words while present day Islam would generally regard itself as representing a unity of church and state, the position of the Kings of Saudi Arabia, for example, is much different within this context than is the Shah of Iran. The difference is explained in the first instance as being one of kingly divinity. The Arab has no such tradition. In fact, in the strong egalitarian traditions of the Arab peoples, such a concept would be anathema. But the tradition is very much a part of Iranian history. As a leading authority puts it :

> "In the course of the 2500 years of Persian history, the power of the Persian kings has from time to time rested on other additional bases ... but the original basis of their authority, the only pre-Islamic basis, is the theory of kingly divinity."[3]

A special hymn composed for the 2500th anniversary celebrations points up its present day application. The hymn contains the words "our everlasting happiness and prosperity derive from your kingly glory, O King." This is an historic concept, clearly stated. Further examples of "the Kingly Glory" have been given and will be given later, but at this point it is necessary to go back again to the Aryan traditions for the earliest explanation of the concept.

The division of society into social classes with distinctive functions may be traced back to the ancient hymn of the *Rigveda* and continues forward to the Sassanian period. This doctrine of the creation of these classes is found in Aryan sources and explained in terms of divine ordination. In the *Atharvaveda*, for example, society is described as having been formed of the respective limbs of primitive man when he was sacrificed by the Gods. The signification of this is that society is a divine institution owing its origin, not to any human, but to a divine agency.[4] In this society, the king was central. In the *Rigveda*, the King is referred to as a demi-god "like Indra" and the election hymns contain many analogies with the gods. There is, in further support of the concept of divine ordination, a Rigvedic verse quoted in an *Atharvaveda* text which boldly moves the address to the God Indra to the human king. Also the King in this text is twice greeted as "Indra's companion." King Parikshit is acclaimed in *Atharvaveda* as "one who succeeds mortals like a god."[5]

The King, we are told in *Satapatha Brahmana* "is Indra for two reasons, namely because he is noble and because he is a sacrificer." This is interesting because it is commonly believed that the Brahmins, as the priestly caste in India, would be the sacrificers. But this was not true in the ancient tradition. The King, who was of the warrior caste, the *Kshatriya*, one step below the Brahmins, though he, too, was noble, became, at the sacrifice, the religious leader as well. "The King is master of all and the Brahmin is placed below the *Kshatriya* at the sacrifice."[6]

There was no Brahmin caste in ancient Persia but the King still was the sacrificer. Herodotus noted very early the Achaemenids had no images of the Gods but rather sacrificed to the sun and the moon, to the earth, to fire, to water, and to the winds — brothers of the King. This was, of course, Vedic in its origins, as was the great horse sacrifice performed by the Shah. Zenophon elaborates further in his account of the priestly sacrifice. On the eve of battle, the servants brought to the staff officers the holy offerings. The Shah stood separate, dressed in his vestments (purple trousers, saffron shoes for a start). As priest, he took the holy meat and cakes and first presented them to the Gods. He himself ate, then breaking and giving to his officers. Next he took the *haoma* (wine), mixed it with water, poured a libation, prayed and drank. His officers then followed his example. Strabo, who was something of a gossip interpreted this as meaning the Persian staff never undertook serious discussion when sober.[7]

Further to the Aryan origins of the King's divinity, there are two quotations from the famous Code of Manu which should be noted :[8]

> (1) "The Lord created the King for the protection of this world, having taken immortal particles from Indra, the wind, Yama, the sun, and Fire and Varuna, the Moon, and the Lord of Wealth. Insomuch as the King is formed of these particles of these chiefs of the Gods, he surpasses all beings in brightness. Like the sun he burns the eyes and minds, nor can any so-ever on earth behold him (note below the invisibility of the Sassanian kings). He is fire, and wind, he is the sun, the King of law."
>
> (2) "The sovereign has a body composed of Soma (the Moon), Fire, Sun, the Wind and Indra, of the two Lords of Wealth (Kubera) and Water (Varuna) and Yama, the eight guardians of the world."

The King was, of course, man. Much of his authority was of a secular nature and the King, in Aryan tradition, was in a sense always elected — at least the great noble families and the high ranking officials could impose a veto on anyone they felt ignoble or unworthy.

On the other hand, the early descriptions of the King's antecedents, and of his power and personal magnitude point up certain characteristics of the King and his power upon which there seems to be general agreement. They can be described as follows :[9]

(1) The King's own person was holy and inviolable. In support of this, Widengren cites cases where the King, even though defeated in battle was not killed. Cyrus the Great apparently never killed Croesus of Lydia but accepted him as an honoured guest. Alexander was horrified that Darius' own followers would kill the Persian king and leave his body abandoned. True, kings were killed, but the action was regarded as sacrilege.

(2) The King was holy because of his descent from the Gods. His person was of a divine nature. He was the brother of the sun and moon (a phrase of address used by the Sassanian kings) and his real home was among the stars. His real nature was fire and this fire-nature was always symbolized by the nimbus of fire surrounding his head.

(3) The King's divine nature was reflected in court ceremonial and in the insignia of royalty. It is significant that the Code of Manu[10] states that the radiance of the King turns the eye like the sun, so the custom developed early in Iran of the Shahanshah always having his face veiled when ascending the throne.

(4) The King's divine origin was reflected in the stories and the circumstances surrounding the birth legend of great figures like Faridun, in the heroic period, of Cyrus and Ardashir in the historical period, of Zarathustra, the great Iranian prophet, and of Jesus. Indeed the three wise men who travelled to Bethlehem from Persia were acting in this prophetic tradition that was known for centuries preceding the Christian era. There was always talk of the "Great King." In the Aryan tradition this was Mithra whose human reincarnation the Iranians believed would bring salvation. A Saviour-King was as much a part of the early Iranian mystique as it was of the Judeo-Christian tradition.

(5) The King was the cosmic ruler, the Lord of the seven climes. The King saw himself in this role as well as did the people. The language of Cyrus on the Cylinder in the British Museum remarked above states this clearly. "I am Cyrus, King of the World, the great king, the powerful king ... King of the four quarters of the world."

It can be seen from the above then, that the Iranian concept of kingship at a very early period in time took on a nature that distinguished it from other kingships. The King's charisma was a personal thing but it was also derived from long tradition, from the nobility of his family (for this nobility was essential), and from his power as first among warriors. The term Shah itself means warrior and is derived from the ancient *Kshatriya* or warrior caste. It was a capital offense to sit on the Shah's throne. His person was sacred. On the day of his coronation he was "re-born" and assumed a new throne name and put on a garment symbolizing his position as a cosmic ruler. At his death his "personal fire" was extinguished and mourning on the part of his family took on extreme forms of suffering.

Very often there appears to the observer an apparent contradiction between the position of the King of Kings (Shahanshah) as one among many and the sacred divine nature of early Persian kingship. But there was never any doubt in Persia that Shahanshah meant supremacy. In fact, during the Parthian period after Alexander's death, no king used the title Shahanshah for almost four hundred years, so sacred was its nature. Kings there were but as the Greeks put it, there was really only one — Basilius-King, Shahanshah.

So in Persia, kingship became divine and this was the essence of the King's legitimacy. This divinity was often seen in what is best described as the Royal Splendour. The case of Ardashir has been cited above. Two other historic examples have been chosen by Professor Browne in his great Literary History as excellent and slightly contrasting examples.[11]

> "Now Kisra (Chosroes) used to sit in his audience-hall where was his crown, like unto a mighty cask. ... set with rubies, emeralds, and pearls, with gold from the top of an arch in this, his audience-hall; and his neck could not support the Crown, but he was veiled by draperies till he had taken his seat in this, his audience-hall, and had introduced his head within the Crown, and had settled himself in his place, whereupon the draperies were withdrawn. And no one who had not previously seen him looked upon him without kneeling in reverence before him."

The second instance relates to an anecdote told of the flight of Bahram Chubin after his defeat by Khusraw Parwiz :

> "And Bahram fled headlong, and on his way he passed by a hamlet, where he halted, and he and Mardan-Sina and Yazdan-Gushnasp alighted at the dwelling of an old woman. Then they produced some food which they had with them, and supped, and gave what was left over to the old woman. Then they produced wine; and Bahram said to the old woman, 'Hast thou nothing wherewith we can drink?' 'I have a little gourd,' replied she; and she brought it to them, and they cut off the top and began to drink from it. Then they produced dessert; and they said to the old woman, 'Hast thou nothing wherein we can put the dessert?' So she brought them a winnowing-shovel, into which they poured the dessert. So Bahram ordered that wine should be given to the old woman, and then he said to her, 'What news hast thou, old lady?' 'The news with us,' answered she, 'is that Kisra hath advanced with an army of Greeks and fought Bahram, and overcome him, and recovered from him his kingdom.' 'And what say'st thou,' asked Bahram, 'concerning Bahram?' 'A silly fool,' replied she, 'who claims the kingdom, not being a member of the Royal House.' Said Bahram, 'Therefore, it is that he drinks out of gourds and eats his dessert out of winnowing-fans.' And this became a saying amongst the Persians, which they are wont to cite as a proverb."

The full meaning and implications of the divine right theory of Persian kingship probably reached its apogee under the Sassanian dynasty which fell before the Arab conquest. For the four hundred years of Sassanian rule, their kings called themselves "Pahlavi bagh", connoting divinity. In Pahlavi literature, the king, as in Aryan literature, is still the lord of the world. He is the cosmic ruler. He is Lord of the Seven Climes. He was a ritual person and he functioned as a priest. In language that must have appeared astounding even to a Roman Emperor, Shapur II, the Sassanian ruler, wrote to the Emperor Constantius : "I Shapur, King of Kings, partner with the stars, brother of the sun and moon." Indeed the Romans — and after all it should never be forgotten that Shapur's great forebear, Shapur I, was the first man up to the history of that time to take a Roman Emperor as prisoner of war — were impressed by the Persians as the earlier Greeks had been impressed and fascinated before them. Ammianus Marcellinus relates of the Shahanshah :

> "... and nobles and commons rivalling each other in agreement, he was placed among the stars according to the sacral custom of the country ... (and) to this very day the over-boastful kings of that race suffer themselves to be called brothers of the Sun and Moon and they venerate and worship (them) as a god."[12]

The sacrifice, under the Sassanians as in Achaemenid times, remained the primary responsibility of this cosmic ruler. The finest Nisaean horses were brought to the royal palace for the great horse sacrifice of Aryan origin. White bulls and bucks were brought to the God of Fire for sacrifice. At the No Ruz (New Year) festival, the king functioned as the dragon killer, slaying the mythical monster as Rustum did before him, thus assuring the fertility of the world.

So it was that the Sassanian rulers during the period known as the Pahlavi period, ruled as divine beings, secure in the belief that they alone dominated the universe. It is not without significance that the present dynasty in Iran — succeeding the Qajars — took as its dynastic name Pahlavi. The present Shahanshah is second in this present dynastic line and this has caused, some embarrassment in circles of Western royalty. There has also been a certain amount of condescension expressed in print about the present Shah's background and/or pretensions,[13] but clearly his historic position is in a much more ancient and royal tradition than is the English who were still climbing out of the reeds during the Achaemenid period. But forces were gathering that were to destroy this belief and these concepts as they were then understood. Perhaps it was that the rigid social arrangements imposed under the Sassanians that became more and more like the caste system of the Indian Aryans separated the Shahanshah from his people in a manner never understood by Cyrus or Darius or even Ardashir. Perhaps it was the continuing struggle against Byzantium that, after the Battle of Nineveh in 627 A.D., began to sap the strength and manhood of the Empire. But the determinant force, it would appear, in the decline of the royal power of Persia was the rise of Islam.

About the time that the Emperor Heraclius was in Jerusalem re-installing the true Cross recovered from the Persians after the Battle of Nineveh, his troops beyond the Jordan reported an attack by an Arab band which was repelled with little difficulty. While only thus briefly noted, it marked the beginning of a great struggle that was not to cease until 1453 when the name of Mohammed would be substituted for that of Christ on the walls of the magnificent basilica of St Sophia in the capital of the Byzantine Empire. But this was yet some eight hundred years away. What was more immediate was the conquest of Persia, Syria, Iraq and the lands beyond by the Arabs, a rapid conquest that was accomplished within a generation.

Eight years after the Persian defeat at Nineveh, by the Emperor Heraclius in 627 A.D., with Yazdigird III, the last of the Sassanian kings, still on the run, the Arab forces came to the Tigris River on a dark and wind-blown day to face the Persian army. The leader of the Arabs was Sa'd, one of the companions promised paradise by Mohammed himself and now serving under the Caliph Umar (Omar). Facing him across the river was Rustum, last administrator of the Persian Empire whose namesake had crowned the heroic period, holding together the last effective fighting forces of the Sassanian army. (Indeed it is possible that Firdawsi confused the two in his own mind and assigned place to this historic figure within the heroic pantheon). However, it was on this day in June 637, an aging Rustum faced for the last time the enemies of his people. It was hot, and the dust was like the shadow of locusts. And Rustum was killed and he lay on the battle-field with his army fleeing in panic. And Sa'd rode forward to claim the fertile lowlands west of the Tigris. Fourteen years later, Yazdigird III, carrying his crown and a few treasures, accompanied by only a handful of followers, was killed by his own people near Merv. With his death, there came to an end an Empire of great antiquity that would not rise again in imperial form for some eight hundred years. But curiously enough the conquest by the Arabs did not come entirely without warning to Persia. The decline and fall of the House of Sasan was the subject of tales of portent that had been around for at least a century. In the reign of Nushirwan (A.D. 531 – 578), which was famous in Iran history for its great length and achievement, there was no year so important as the 42nd (A.D. 572 – 73) called by the Arabs the "Year of the Elephant." In that year two things happened. First, the Sassanian Empire reached to further glory. The rich and ancient kingdom of Yaman was annexed by Persia. It was a master stroke and one highly regarded by the imperial court and the elite as presaging an even greater future. Second, in that same year, there was born in distant Mecca, the man who was destined to overthrow the House of Sasan and the religion of Zoroaster and to bring to destruction the greatest Empire then existing in Asia.

On the night Mohammed was born, the legend tells us that the palace of the Shahanshah was shaken by an earthquake so great that fourteen battlements fell to the ground. The Sacred fire, which had burned continuously for a thousand years was suddenly extinguished. The Lake of Sawa dried up. The chief priest in a dream saw camels and horse troops crossing the Tigris. Nushirwan was greatly disturbed by these portents and even more so when his uncle who dwelt on the borders of the Syrian desert sent him a courier with a message in which these same things were recounted.[14]

The great king died six years thence and with his death the rapid decline of the House of Sasan began. It was a period of strife, intrigue and murder. Regicide and parricide was practiced, with sons revolting against their kingly fathers. Nushirwan, who had finally interpreted the fall of the fourteen battlements from his castle as meaning that fourteen kings would rule after him could not have seen that between Khusraw Parviz (590 – 627 A.D.) and Yazdigird III, the last Sassanian king (killed in 632 A.D.), eleven Shahanshahs would reign less than five years total. The Arab conquest of Persia took roughly a decade. Islam became the religion of Iran imposed by the sword and a scorched earth policy. Subsequently the Arabs made separate treaties across Persia with the many feudal overlords and princes and whatever loyalty had once clung to the Shah began to be gradually transferred to the Caliphs who were the successors to Mohammed.

The Shah was dead and there were no heirs. Consequently the Persians found themselves grappling with a new search for identity within a new political structure that was as foreign to them as the concept of divine kingship was to the fiercely egalitarian Arabs. They were eventually to find this and when the Safavids came to power in the 16th century, these new concepts of authority would be added to the older restored Persian traditions that really never died — in fact that have endured to this day. It was a brilliant recovery that showed once again in history the tenacity of the Persian in search of an ideal that was, in fact, his reality. Further comment on this will be made later.

The Caliphs, as successors to Mohammed, were, of course, Arab. Further the Arab holding that office was, in the first instance to be a member of the tribe of Quraysh, upon election by the qualified members of the community. Further it was generally assumed that he would also act as the religious leader of the community. As will be pointed out below in further elaboration, this was known to the Moslems as the office of *Imam* or the *Imamate*.

There were three important corollaries that accompanied the office of *Caliph* (meaning successor). They were, first, that there could be no fruitful tension deriving from a separation of church and state. Second, it was believed that orthodoxy in the faith would assure political stability. The third corollary was that although differences in functions were recognized — as between say the *Caliph* who was secular and the *Imam* who was religious — since all power emanated from the same source, there was no requirement for an exact balance between the various powers. While this gave flexibility to the offices, it also opened the way for dissent and interpretations that would ultimately destroy the importance of both the first and second corollaries.

To the Sunni or Orthodox Moslem, the Caliph was also known as *Amir el-Muminin* or the Prince of the Commander of the Faithful. He was the head of the government and administration of the Muslim Empire and the Commander-in-Chief of its armies — at least in theory. The title *Amir*, of course, is still common in the Middle East and the former Prime Minister of Iran, Hoveyda, is usually referred to in the press as *Amir*.

During these years of Sunni rule, many Persians gravitated to the Caliphate as chief administrators and advisers and eventually reintroduced into that office many of the trappings, customs, and ways of doing things that had been characteristically Sassanian despite the early preferences of the Caliphs to a simple life more characteristic of the desert than the court.

From 632 A.D. to 1258 A.D., 626 years, successive Caliphs succeeded one another in Arabia, in Syria, in Iraq, in Egypt, and in Spain. In the last mentioned year, Baghdad was sacked by the Mongols and the Caliphate was destroyed.

Over a period of time, however, the office of the Caliphate as a power force had been steadily losing ground even before the Mongol invasion. By 1186 A.D., or some ninety years before the destruction of Baghdad, when the last Ghaznavid was killed, the authority of the Caliphate for all intents and purposes had ceased to exist.

In secular terms, the power replacement was to be found in the office of the *Sultan* and even during the Mongol invasion, this office continued to exist. Mahmud (999 – 1030 A.D.) is credited with being the first ruler in Islam to be designated Sultan. He was a strong ruler, a patron, as pointed out in the first chapter, and a superior commander in the field. Gradually the Sultans, many of whom were Turks, acquired *de jure* recognition, and as the Caliphate became more and more remote from reality, the Sultans began to arrogate to themselves the titles and prerogatives formerly reserved to the Caliphs.

The word Sultan signifies dominion and it represented a definite trend toward absolutism that was lacking in the theory of the Caliphate. The power of the Sultan, originally represented temporal authority delegated by the Caliph who represented the spiritual power and interpreter of the *Sharia*, or the law of Islam. But, as the Caliph increasingly ceased to function as the intermediary power between the law and the ruled, the Sultan assumed a more direct role. While theoretically, kingship and religion were still complimentary, in fact the documents of the time[15] make it clear that the duty of the Sultan was to rule and the duty of his subjects was to obey and pray for him. In other words the idea of the community that existed in the first century of Islam ceased to exist and what took its place was an obligation, not unlike that of the Shahanshah of earlier times, on the part of the ruler to rule so that the various classes of society would be able to fulfil their different functions. The Sultan came to see himself as being appointed directly by God and directly responsible to Him. He was, however, secular. He was to properly order the temporal affairs of his kingdom, to protect his people, but also to judge them. Equal they may have been before the law, but the differences in function between them was also to be maintained.

Religious matters were left to the *ulama* or holy men, whom the Sultan saw as "heirs to the Prophet."

In short, the Sultan was a temporal ruler, a law giver, a judge, and a preserver of the ordered society. No distributive justice here. Just straight rule.

The Sultanate of course, was a concept much more congenial to the Persian than the Caliphate. In Persian literature, the Sultan held a much more central position, although little of the literature reflects an attitude of prayer. Rather the concept is that Sultans come and go and the best thing for the common man to do is to avoid him if he can.

"Tis but a tent where takes his one day's rest
A Sultan to the realm of Death addrest;
The Sultan rises, and the dark Ferrash
Strikes, and prepares it for another guest."[16]

Where the Sultanate really joined with Persian tradition, however, was in the rule of the more secular minded Shahs. For example, the theory of the ruler as the Shadow of God upon earth was very much a part of the thinking of the Afshars, the Zands, and the Qajars, rulers immediately preceding the present Pahlavi dynasty.

Nevertheless the Sultanate was not enough at this point in time. In the thinking of most Persians there had to be religious authority as well. If the Church and State are one, as has been believed over the centuries in Iran, then the secular rule of the Sultan was still deficient, no matter how direct and efficient it might be.

So it was that the Iranians came to a new concept which demonstrated their creative best as thinkers and speculators and eventually as rulers, once again, of a mighty Empire — the Safavid.

As in the case of the Parthian period that bridged the gap between the Achaemenid and Sassanian dynasties, the time of Arab rule was a period of germination in which Persian tenacity, intelligence and skill worked for a new definition of authority that would be peculiarly Iranian and would bring about the restoration of the Empire that had existed in the Persian mind since the days of Cyrus the Great. Today we would call this action a brilliant display of counter intelligence as the Persians slowly but surely undermined Arab authority against the day of final collapse and the restoration of Iranian rule.

The key to the attack was the Imamate. The strategy has its origins in the struggles of Mohammed's successors. The tactical aspects included :

1. the concept of divine kingship;
2. the principle of legitimacy;
3. the principle of infallibility;
4. the reunion of religious and political power.

As stated above, the concept of divine kingship was foreign to the more democratic Arabs. An example of their fierce egalitarian tradition is to be found in a story told of Omar, the second Caliph.

He once received several lengths of cloth as a gift from a neighbouring ruler. He divided it equally among the Moslems, retaining one length as his share. He had it tailored, donned it, and ascended the pulpit to preach. A Moslem came up to him and said "we neither listen or obey."

"Why so," he replied.

"Because you have preferred yourself to us," the man answered, "when you divided the cloth, each Moslem received one and so you too. But one length would not make you a whole shirt because you are a tall man."

Omar turned to his son and said, "reply."

The son stood up and said : "When the Commander of the Faithful (Omar) wished to tailor his length of cloth it was insufficient and I gave him enough of my length to complete it."

Upon hearing this, the Moslem said, "Now we listen and obey."[17]

The first Caliph, following the death of Mohammed was Abu Bekr. He was an older man, one of the original companions, and was elected in 632 A.D. While he faced several rebellions from various tribes in his short reign — one of them Al-Katif which had forty thousand fighting men and whose resistance resulted in a terrible slaughter of the Moslems, including thirty-nine warriors who were original Companions of the Prophet — he managed to bring peace and unity to Arabia in the end.

Abu Bekr reigned two years and appointed Omar (Umar) as his successor in 634. Omar masterminded the great campaigns of the Moslems that moved beyond the borders of Arabia and it was during his reign that Persia was conquered with the result that to this day in Iran the name Omar is execrated. In fact the anniversary of his death is usually marked by rejoicing by the Iranians.

Omar was assassinated by a Persian slave in 644. He was succeeded by Othman who himself was murdered in 656.

Ali was the fourth Caliph. As a boy he had been one of the early converts to Islam and during the Prophet's life had shown great heroism and conspicuous ability on the battle-field. He was the cousin of the Prophet and the husband of Mohammed's only daughter, Fatima. None of the first three Caliphs had founded a dynasty. But Ali had two sons and it was hoped, particularly by the Persians who thought in terms of dynastic succession, that such a dynasty was now possible. But the blood-letting was not to stop. Ali was faced by close rivals who continually tested him in battle and particularly by the Umayyads under Mu'awiyah, governor of Syria. It is not clear what happened along the Euphrates River but in January 661, Ali was killed by a poisoned sabre and the Umayyads seized the Caliphate. Mu'awiyah was proclaimed Caliph in Jerusalem although Damascus became the capital of the Moslem Empire. Mu'awiyah did found a dynasty, thus introducing the hereditary principle into the Caliphate. His son Yazid succeeded him as Caliph at his death.

Several dissenting sects now began to take form with the Umayyad succession. The Kharijites, once the supporters of Ali but later his bitter enemies, arose in armed opposition to the prerogative conferred on the Quraysh tribe that the Caliph should always be one of their number. The Murjites were another sect who were more tolerant but who nevertheless believed that all Moslems were servants of God including Ali.

In many ways the most important sect, however, were the Shi'a who saw in Ali a canonized martyr. Most of this sect were Persians and to them Ali became the paragon of Moslem nobility. The site of the tomb of Ali, Najaf in Iraq, is one of the great centres of pilgrimage in Islam, almost rivalling Mecca as a centre of devotion. Every tenth year, on the tenth of Muhurram, a passion play is enacted testifying to the messihanic beliefs of Ali's followers.

The Abbasids, descendants of the uncle of the Prophet and later to succeed to power, held common cause with the followers of Ali but emphasized the rights of the house of Hashim, from whom the present Hashimite Kingdom of Jordan claims legitimacy.

Basically the non-Arabian Moslems and the Persian Moslems were the most dissatisfied with the new Caliphate. But the Persians had the edge in opposition because of their long and prominent history and they proceeded to make the most of it through the Shi'a doctrine that began to take shape.

After the first four Caliphs mentioned above, the office became increasingly secular — the highest in Islam to be sure — but with none of the religious authority enjoyed by Mohammed. Religious authority, or perhaps one should say the religious leader of the community, was known as the Imam — "one who follows" is the meaning in the Arabic tongue.

The Imam and the Caliph could be the same person and, generally, under the first four Caliphs, they were. But after Ali's death the nature of the Caliphate became increasingly subject to religious argumentation and discussion. Several interpretative books were written dealing with the problem. The most authoritative were by a Persian, al-Bukhari and they stand next to the Koran itself in importance. An oath taken on them is valid.

Six of these authoritative books came to be known as the Shari'a and they recognized but one supreme authority, the Imam. He, in turn, could delegate all or part of his authority to his appointed ministers, governors and generals.

The Umayyads and those who followed the Caliphate assumed this authority was one. This group which were the forerunners of today's Sunnis — which comprise the greater part of the Moslem world — continued then, to treat the Caliph as the religious leader and as remarked earlier, this role became so primary that with the rise of the Sultanate, the religious power became increasingly lofty, detached, and impotent ending finally in the demise of the Caliphate as such.

The Shi'a, the followers of Ali — and it should be remembered that Ali served as a useful, common ground for dissent — saw the matter in a different way. To them the Imam, as religious leader, stood as the intermediary between God and man. In theological terms, this meant rejecting the idea of the conquering Caliphate which imposed authority on its own terms. Being Persians, always the most subtle of philosophers as well as enemies of the conquering Arabs (the Sunnis) they proceeded to espouse a concept of the Imamate completely at variance with that of their conquerors. By the 10th century, this concept had been worked out in detail and to this day, it generally obtains.

Before considering the Shi'a doctrine as expounded, a footnote to history — "the Iranian intermezzo" as Minorsky called it — should be added here.[18]

In the third century of Islam, the Buwayhid (Buyid) tyrant-princes from the Caspian slopes of the Alborz mountains, seized power over much of what is now Iran. They were a lawless bunch — the encyclopaedist describes them as "rough fellows without education". Their conquering forces swept down into Fars, over the Kerman and eventually into Baghdad. They rejected the tribal customs of the Arabs and denied the elective principle of power. They revived the title "Shahanshah" and used it for over 100 years. They were also enthusiastic Shi'ites.

Older traditions were important to the Buwayhids and they were helped in the formulation of them by the "more cultured indigenous aristocracy of Iran" with whom they apparently closely worked.

The theory of the Caliphate was, of course, doctrine to the Abbasids who presumably were the rulers of the Moslem world during this time. When the Buwayhids seized Baghdad — and continued to hold it in occupation — they set up what has been described as an "Abbasid-Shi'a condominium" which preserved the Caliphate but which freed the Shi'ites from Sunni (Caliphate) domination. The Caliphate really got the worst of the bargain. The Caliphs themselves were kept in a position of utter humility. Even the mention of the Caliph's name was withheld. The office of the Vizierate was suspended and that high personage became the Caliph's secretary. The ancient office of Commander was revived and became substitute for that of Vizier. Most important — from the standpoint of Iranian tradition — the hereditary principle of succession was revived along with the great office of Shahanshah.

In turn, the office of Caliph was not abolished. The Buwayhids had no pretensions to spiritual authority other than being "Partisans of Ali". The Hidden Imam — in practical terms — was of no great concern to them just as the Caliphate had no real meaning for them. They did, however, encourage Shi'ite traditions and many of the forms contained in present-day Shi'ite worship — for example the lamentations of the Ashura date from this period. Some intellectuals emerged during this interregnum. Babuya, a distinguished theologian, was among those who challenged the traditional, orthodox four schools of Sunni thought and proposed a fifth to include Shi'a doctrine.

Eventually the Buwayhids suffered the splitting of power. Trade with the West from India was directed to the Red Sea causing economic loss. The mastery of the Gulf slipped from their hands. When the Ghaznawids occupied Rey (near Teheran), massacred the Shi'ites in that sacred city and destroyed the treasures of the great library, it was the end of the Buwayhid rule. The Seljuks, a Turkish tribe, were waiting in the wings to seize power. They had different plans of Empire — a Sunni Empire which would free the Caliphate and substitute the title Sultan for Shahanshah. To return now to the Imamate. The Shi'a accepted the leading role of the Caliph-Imam, then, and saw it as a divinely designated office. But, the Persians argued, because of the latter requirement, only a descendant of Mohammed could thus properly be described as legitimate. The Imam, in other words, must be a lineal descendant of Mohammed. Ali, Mohammed's first cousin, was therefore to the Shi'as the first Imam and by his marriage to Fatima, Mohammed's daughter, their sons Hasan and Hussein followed in succession as Imams. The last nine of the twelve Imams to whom the Shi'a swore allegiance were all descendants of Hussein. Of the nine, four met death by poison, the others at the hands of the Caliphs or their executioners because, of course, representing a challenge to the Caliphate, this line would be ruthlessly hunted down.

The twelfth Imam disappeared in 873–874 A.D., in the cave of the great mosque of Samarra without leaving offspring. But Shi'a doctrine holds that he is immune from death and will come again as the Mahdi (i.e., the guided light) who will restore true Islam, conquer the world, and usher in the millennium. Though hidden, this Imam is the "master of time", a concept to which we will return later.

Because the Caliphate, under the Umayyads, denied the hereditary principle which had always been espoused by the Persians, it was necessary for the Persians, within the Shi'a doctrine, to find a more total concept of legitimacy if they were to break from orthodoxy. They did this by means of three principles :

(1) Ali's nature is magnified until it assumes a divine nature. This, of course, is the older Persian doctrine of the Divine Right of Kings in new clothes.

(2) The line of succession is Fatima's. It is she who is the daughter of Mohammed despite the exalted-position held by her husband and, hence, she gives legitimacy. It is the woman, too, who brings to the Imamate of the Shi'a the ancient kingly line of Persia. The mother of the fourth Imam was a princess of the old Royal House of Sasan.

(3) The line of succession, being hereditary, passes from father to son. Each Imam, therefore, chooses his son as successor. It is on this point that dissent arose within the Shi'a doctrine — a dissent that can be simply described as between the "Twelvers" and the "Seveners." This is explained in terms of schismatic division.

This schism within the Shi'a sect took the form of a division between the Twelvers (Ithna-ashariya) and the Seveners (Sabiya). The former constituted the larger number of followers and they eventually won the day. They held to the legitimacy of all Twelve of the Imams as well as the magnifying of Ali's nature.

The Seveners accepted Ali as Imam but tended to play down his divinity. However, they did go along. Where they broke with the Twelvers, however, was over the succession after the sixth Imam.

Ja'far as-Sadiq, the sixth Imam, was a man of great learning and profound insight. Theologically he holds a position not unlike that of Thomas Aquinas in the Roman Catholic Church. The Iranian Constitution of 1906, for example, binds the Shah to protect the Ja'fari doctrine of Shi'a. This is the origin of that phrase.

The sixth Imam apparently had trouble with his sons as so many fathers do. Ismail, his oldest son, is recognized by the Seveners as being the last Imam because they feel the principle of legitimacy broke down at this point. Because, in fact, the Imam named a younger brother, Musa, to succeed him for reasons of "honour," or so the Twelvers believe. It is from Musa's descendants, therefore, that the line goes on to the Twelfth or Imam Mahdi who disappeared from the earth, eventually to emerge "to fill the world with justice."

The Seveners, or the Ismailis, as they came to be called, became, eventually, the famed "Assassins," a major heretical sect of Islam. The "Valley of Assassins," is still a place of pilgrimage in Iran for the adventurous minded and the stories revolving around this group are numerous. In the 13th century, Marcó Polo wrote about them and about the blind obedience tendered to their leader, the so-called "Old Man of the Mountain" who maintained a discipline that is reported not only by Marco Polo but by the Crusaders as well — who were in this area at this time. One brief account states that when Henry, Count of Champagne, was on a visit to the "Old Man" they walked together one day and saw some lads in white sitting on top of a high tower. The Old Man, turning to the Count, asked if he had any subjects as obedient as his own and without waiting for a reply, made a sign to two of the boys who immediately leaped from the tower to their death.

Assassination was the theme of this heretical group and they were feared even into Europe. The Assassins were finally destroyed and their great strongholds taken by the Mongols at the same time they extinguished the Caliphate of Baghdad.

It is not important here to explain either the heresy or the methods applied. Many distinguished rulers were killed by them and all, until the Mongols, held them in fear. The use of hashish, which gave the order its name and the promise of Paradise — in this world or the next — a promise made only by Mohammed, was strong meat for capable young men who enjoyed the habitual use of hashish, and the endless "dallying" with damsels to their hearts content — when they were not killing — in a garden scene that Marco Polo describes as "the largest and most beautiful that was ever seen."

So this description must rather reluctantly be cut short but the special properties of hashish recalls a story told this writer years ago in Isfahan. Three men came to the city by night (it was once a walled city) and found the gates closed. One was a drunkard, another was an opium smoker, and the third a hashish eater. The first said : "Let us break down the gates and go in." The second said : "Let us lie down and sleep until morning." The third said : "No, let us pass through the keyhole."

Today, of course, the contentions between the Seveners and Twelvers are almost gone. In fact, the present Shahanshah and the Agha Khan who is the spiritual head of the Ismailis are good friends. The writer can recall one day at the Mehrabad airport in Teheran seeing the Shah drive up to the airport to meet the young Harvard educated Agha Khan in person. The two greeted each other in brotherly fashion and drove away together.

It is now necessary to return to the concept of "the matter of time," a term attributed by the Shi'ites to the twelfth Imam, and to relate the concept to the reunion of religious and political power accomplished by the Safavid dynasty. It begins quite understandably with the doctrine of infallibility.

In Shi'ite terms, this doctrine can be described as follows : From the Creation of Adam onward, a divine light has passed into the substance of one chosen descendant in each generation. It was present in Ali and in each of the Imams after him. By virtue of this light, only the Imam has secret knowledge and immunity from sin. His decisions are decisive and final.

When the twelfth Imam disappeared, this divine light was

placed in abeyance, so to speak. Political authority still existed and was exercised but under the guidance of agents of the hidden Imam. Some thought this to be found in the collective decision of the leading *mujtahids*, the most learned theologians and lawyers (as contrasted with the *ulama* or general body of holy men in Islam). This concept has in fact come down to the present day but for reasons which will be explained, has lost most of its power in fact.

The countervailing theory is that the political power moved to the temporal authority just as the theory of the Caliphate moved to the theory of the Sultanate. The infallibility of the Imam thus became an assumption of perfection in the temporal ruler. This, of course, could only lead to absolute rule and no justification of power was needed. The ruler ruled by divine right and his rule was absolute. As far as he was concerned, the *mujtahids* could enjoy the representation of the Hidden Imam. What these rulers and their apologists wanted was the temporal rule in the tradition of the Sultan.

But between these extremes lay a more central doctrine of the Hidden Imam that welded the two concepts together. And this was the creation of the Safavids.

The Persian ideal of kingship as the sister of religion has been remarked on a number of times previously. In a very real sense it was lost at the Arab conquest — simply because of its many ramifications — but the slow restoration of Iran to the point of final merger with a separated religious doctrine finally came within Islam, dictated on Persian terms. In 1502 A.D., Shaykh Ismail, a descendant in the fifth generation of a celebrated saint of Ardabil named Safi al-Din (died 1334 A.D.), combining the role of warrior with the profession of Grand Master of the mystical Dervish Order of Sufis, entered Tabriz after numerous campaigns against the prevailing Turkoman order to be crowned, after many centuries, once again Shahanshah. The dynasty that he founded — the Safavid — endured until 1722.

It was fortunate for Iran that such a man as Shaykh Ismail rose to power. The combination of forces that had moulded him provided an unusual amalgam. His family was an illustrious one. They had been settled at Ardabil for many generations. Safi-al-Din, his ancestor, after whom the dynasty was named — Safavid — translated as "Purity of the Faith". Safi's son was honoured by a visit from Tamerlane himself. Another ancestor, Khoja Ali, was known in Jerusalem as the "Shaykh of Persia." On the female side, there was Greek blood. Martha, Shaykh Ismail's mother, herself the daughter of a Greek princess, gave birth to three illustrious sons, Sultan Ali, Ibrahim *Mirza* and Shah Ismail. The Sultan was killed. Ibrahim *Mirza* died shortly afterwards and only Shaykh Ismail remained to be crowned Shahanshah.

But most important was the fact that Shah Ismail claimed direct descent from Musa al-Kazin, the seventh Imam. Consequently it is not surprising that one of his first acts of state after being crowned was to declare the Ja'fari doctrine of the Shi'a faith to be the official state religion and the only tolerated creed in his dominion. This has continued as the official state religion of Iran to this day and as remarked above, it is so stated in the Iranian constitution.

So it was that the office of Shahanshah was restored after centuries of intrigue, maneuver, power and prayer to its native land. Cyrus the Great would have approved of the office. For now, the Shah was not only Shahanshah in the ancient tradition, but he was as well :

(1) the Shadow of God sweeping the earth;
(2) the representative of Mohammed;
(3) the direct descendant of the Hidden Imam;
(4) and the commander of a religious order

that in its day matched the Jesuits of the west in discipline, militancy, learning, and prayer. The Sufis today are not seen in Iran as they were banned by the father of the present Shah. But there is no doubt that they provided the framework within which the complicated theological and political concepts of the Safavid rulers were worked out and given the form that to a very large extent exist to this day.

This order, although mystical in nature, was extremely well organized and has been compared in a classic Iranian commentary as being very similar to the single party of a modern totalitarian state.[19] It was the Sufis who promoted "the new secret doctrine" that elevated the successors of Shaykh Safi to the position of living embodiments of the Godhead.[20] It was the Sufis who gave absolute obedience to the Safavid kings. It was the Sufi's who, when internal crisis arose within the government's provided the discipline of a single party within which the political problem could be settled. Sufi's also acted, at least in the early days, as a corps similar to the Ottoman Janissaries, for guarding strategic places as well as providing intelligence to the Shah through its far flung network.

It is important, then, to understand more fully the nature of this mystical order that provided the party apparatus to the Safavid Shahs.

The Sufi's were surprisingly eclectic, drawing many of their ideas from other religions. Buddhism was perhaps most influential and a large number of notable Sufi leaders came from Khorosan, in the north eastern corner of Iran where Buddhism had flourished. When Sufi's came to India they were always welcomed by the gurus and swamis as true co-religionists who had the same mystical preoccupations as themselves.

The element of mysticism, of course, was at the heart of the Sufi movement. Self abandonment to the divine beloved. This was the theme of the writings of the Sufi's, including two of the most famed poets in Iranian history — Rumi and Hafiz. Reason was quite secondary. Hafiz wrote in one place, "Oh thou who art trying to learn the marvel of love from the copy-book of reason, I am very much afraid that you will never really see the point." and again he wrote : "Rub out everything you have copied into your exercise book, if you would be my fellow learner, for the science of love is not to be found in books."[21]

So it was with the Sufi's that they sought a higher form of knowledge, that divine reality which transcends the sphere of the senses and of concepts based on sense perception. It was, in fact, what any true mystic seeks — a direct vision of reality. When the dervish (the so-called "whirling dervishes" were Sufi's) came to perform his central gyration within the circle of his confraternity, he turned as the sun amid the planets having no other meaning than the love of God.

Politically the Sufi's had adopted an early position of total other-worldliness in reaction against the Moslem conquests, but by 750 A.D., during the Abbasid Caliphate, they had moved to a pro-Ali Shi'a position. Some of the writers began to see in kingship the main force that sustained existing things — an equipoise, so to speak, of the wholeness of society as found in the kingdom. Since men by nature needed other men, some arrangement had to be made for the proper functioning of their relationship. At the same time, there had to be a proper union of this society with the Supreme Being. Kingship thus became the organizing principle and the function of the king was to cause those who were worthy of wholeness to achieve it.[22] The ideal king was thus a philosopher king — there is strong evidence that the Sufi's were familiar with Greek thought and particularly the neoplatonists — and one who was the true vice-regent of God. The highest good was obtained when the kingship of faith and the kingship of the world were united in one person. Thus the Sufi's found themselves returning to the Zoroastrian tenet that religion and government are complementary.

As the Caliphate declined, the Sufi's turned more and more toward the historic imamate as providing the political solution. Consequently it was almost inevitable that when Shaykh Ismail, a Sufi himself, established the Safavid dynasty, he should declare the union of the divine right of kings and the historic imamate.

If the Sufi's were important theologically and politically for Iran, they were also important historically. Islam proscribed the drinking of wine and spirits. Yet in Persia from ancient times grapes were grown and wine drunk and the vineyards around Shiraz were famous. Wine for the Sufi stood for the joys of divine ecstacy and self-forgetfulness, proscribed by what they considered to be the narrow minded Moslem moralists. As the function of the heart was to mirror or reflect God, and in Him and through Him, the whole of creation, so the heart to the Sufi's became identified in their literature with a cup, or a mirror, or a globe, even. This God-revealing mirror of the human heart was described by the Sufi's as *jam i jam* or "Jamshid's mirror or cup," hearkening back to the heroic period described in the first chapter. Jamshid, according to the Avesta was a prolific inventor, and this mirror was one of them. When he succumbed to the temptation of pride, it was taken from him and it became, to the Persian, a kind of Holy Grail for which man must eternally seek anew. Omar Khayyam, who was probably a Sufi, has many quatrains in the Rubaiyat where he glories in the drinking of wine and this has often been misunderstood as suggesting he was a bit of a sop. Actually, of course, he was a distinguished astronomer and mathematician. But in one quatrain he specifically speaks to these matters:

> Iran is gone with all his rose
> and Jamshid's 7-ringed cup where no one knows
> But still a Ruby kindles in the Vine
> and many a Garden by the water blows.

Again, Omar Khayyam writes much of taverns and tavern keepers. Standing before the tavern, he shouts "Open then the door. You know how little while we have to stay and once departed, may return no more." Or the voice within the tavern cries of the temple being prepared within. The nightingale cries to the Rose in "high piping Pahlavi" 'wine, wine, wine, red wine,' so he tells us to "fill the cup that clears today of past regrets and future fears." Interestingly enough, to the Sufi's, a priest (Piri mughan) could be either a Magian or a Christian priest or a tavern keeper who was defying Moslem law by dispensing wine.

The chief film on the inner mirror of Jamshid is the film of self. Rumi, the great poet admonishes men to accept discipline of the soul "like a mirror without rust" and he tells in illustration a marvellous story about a king who wanted to have his palace decorated. He called in a group of Chinese artists and another of Anatolians. Each claimed superiority in their art. So the king, to test them, gave them two rooms facing each other and a curtain was drawn across the entrance. The Chinese called for a great variety of paints and they set to work painting. The Anatolians said they would do nothing but remove rust. When the Chinese finished, they called the king to see their work and he was ravished at the sight of the magnificent colours and designs that fairly leaped at him from the wall. Then he visited the Anatolians. They drew the curtain aside and the Chinese painting reflected on the burnished wall, was transformed into something far more beautiful.[23]

So, Rumi, says, is the way of the Sufi's. They must burnish their breasts and make themselves pure of greed and avarice and hatred because the purity of the mirror is the heart which receives images innumerable.

There is a footnote to this that also belongs to Persian history. Alexander the Great, who sought so hard to be great, but who really never understood its meaning, had Aristotle built for him in Alexandria a world revealing mirror that he felt would rival Jamshid's. But Alexander died in a rage at thirty-four, never having learning the secret of the mirror that Aristotle had built for him.

With the restoration of the great office of Shahanshah, the ancient Persian ideal of religion as the sister of kingship was once again realized. However, there were complications that had developed as the result of the long period of time elapsing between the disappearance of the twelfth Imam in 873 A.D., and the accession to the throne of Shah Ismail in 1501–02 A.D.

As pointed out above there were essentially two views held as to the nature of authority during this period, one holding that the Hidden Imam ruled as "Master of Time" through the *mujtahids* or learned theologians; the other that, power moved to the temporal ruler. These two quite different beliefs set up a tension that has existed even today in the thinking of some. The logic of the first point of view is tied in with Ali's martyrdom and the relentless pursuit and destruction of the Imams after Ali. It leads to the conclusion that the state is unjust and even illegitimate. This accounts for the important role played by the *ulama* in the opposition to Qajar rule that led to the Constitutional Crisis of 1906. The tyranny of the Qajars was compared in this period to that of the Umayyads and it was even stated by leading *ulama* that the Qajars were descended from the Umayyads. The demands of the *ulama* for a "House of Justice," only emphasized the fact that they believed the Qajar government was illegitimate and was ruling unjustly.[24]

This, however, was a long way in the future even though it does point up the persistence of the theory that religious leadership in Shi'a Islam can be at odds with temporal rule.

To return to the Safavid State, Shah Ismail, in declaring Shi'ism to be the official religion of his new state in fact claimed for his kingship, and that of his descendants, the prerogatives of the *mujtahids* who had during the previous centuries acted as agents to the Hidden Imam. When he added to this, the ancient absolutist theory of Divine Right, he in fact had the whole package, so to speak. What clearly emerges in the Safavid state is that the Shahanshah now became the *locum tenens* of the Hidden Imam and he exercised power in the Imam's name. The *mujtahids* were reduced to being religious spokesmen and intermediaries between the Shah and the people.

Today in Iran, it would not be prudent to ask regarding the Imamate as it relates to the exercise of power. There are people still living who remember the bitterness of this debate during the constitutional crisis of 1906 and the fact that men were killed over the issue. Nevertheless, in Shi'a Iran, it is important who controls the Imamate. The fact that it is not a subject for discussion — the constitutional period is not studied in the Universities and, in fact, the Journals of the Convention have all but disappeared in Iran — does not mean that the matter is no longer important. It merely means that the exercise of power is seen in a different perspective. The constitution — this will be considered in the last chapter in greater detail — states that the Shah is charged with promoting the Ja'fari doctrine of the Twelve Imams and he is to "seek help from the holy spirits of the Saints of Islam."[25] On the other hand there sits in the Majlis (Parliament) a constitutionally ordained committee of five of the most learned *ulama* which has, as its function, the scrutiny of all laws promulgated by the Majlis to see that they are in accordance with Islamic law. Further, the constitution provides that this particular article cannot be modified until the reappearance of the Mahdi — the twelfth Imam. This is a clear constitutional restraint although it is apparently not being exercised — which in itself is significant.[26]

As of this writing, the present Shah is without any real opposition to claims on the Imamate in Iran. There are perhaps a dozen *Mujtahids* left in Iran, 6 in Q'um. One hears certain names — Shariat-Maderi, Malati, Taleghani, Qomi, Tabatabai — but they are quiet men. The fiery Abolghassem Kashani who openly bragged that he had ordered the assassination of Premier Ali Razmara in 1951 — a worthy successor to the assassins — died in 1962.[27] Burujerdi who was the acknowledged leader of the Iranian Shi'ites, an eminent *mujtahid*, died after breaking with the Shah in 1958. Khomeini is in exile. Others were sent or went into exile, most of them to Iraq. Ayatollah

Seyed Mohsen Hakim, formerly of Tabriz, was one of these. The stature of this man is so great in the Shi'ite world that when he underwent a prostate gland operation in London in 1970, Iranian Embassy officials regularly visited him on behalf of the Shahanshah.[28] It is interesting, too, that in 1974, Ayatollah Musavi, another leading *mujtahid* in Iraq appealed to the Shah for protection of the Shi'ites in Iraq against Baathist persecution. The Shahanshah, in a return cable, pledged to "take any measures necessary" to prevent such persecution and further assured the religious leader that he would spare no effort to help Shi'ites throughout the world when they requested assistance.[29]

No, the present Shah is too wise to state a claim regarding the Imamate. But his actions are those of a ruler who is assuming this. He repealed his father's ban on religious demonstrations during the period of Muharram, when the Shi'ites mourn the assassination of Hussein, son of Fatima. The writer can recall that when he was in Iran in 1970, No Ruz, easily the most important of Iranian festivals, coincided with the Days of Ashura which mark the martyrdom of Imam Hussein and seventy-one members of his family and associates of Karbala, the following statement issued by the Imperial Court appeared in all information media :

> Since this year, the ancient No Ruz coincides with the days of Ashura, H.I.M. the Shahanshah Arya-mehr have willed to spend the beginning of the New Year at the side of the Holy Shrine of Imam Ali Ibn Musa al-Reza at Mashad. For this reason the No Ruz Salaam ceremonies will not take place in Teheran this year. The Cabinet and the heads of the two houses of Parliament will be accompanying the Shahanshah.

The statement was signed by Minister of Court Assadollah Alam.

Not only has the present Shah appropriated large sums of money to restore shrines and mosques, he sees himself as well as his office in a largely mystical way. In his autobiography, for example, he claims divine intervention on his own behalf.[30] A single example of several offered is the time, as a boy, when he was riding along a rocky mountain path and he fell from his horse only to be lifted up and held from danger by the sainted Abbas. Abbas was Hussein's brother and the Shi'ites believe that while he was not one of the twelve, that he is sacred and has been given the title *Hazrat* Abbas. An amusing aspect of this story is that Abbas is said to have lost his arms in battle and so became a water carrier who carried the water skin in his teeth to the troops in the thick of the fray. As one Iranian waggishly remarked to me : "Did he catch the Shah in his teeth ?" Clearly this story would not bear repeating at court. Finally the Shah has stated that he intends to "rebuild the faith in the way the Prophet really meant the religion to be."[31] What else could be *locum tenens* of the Hidden Imam do or say ?

If it is an article of faith with the Shi'ites that the Mahdi will return, it is important to realize that in terms of this world's exercise of power, he must not return. On this point both the Shah and the *ulama* would agree.

To illustrate : Among Christians, while perhaps not an article of faith solidly held by the whole community, there is general agreement upon the second coming of Christ. But, whenever anyone or any sect has announced this coming, the orthodox have denounced this as being false and unwarranted. It is a standing joke among Christians that if He were to come again, Christianity would neither recognize nor accept Him.

It is no different with the Mahdi. In the course of history, men have declared themselves as the Mahdi but their worldly success has been of limited duration. In Iran, the Bah'ais — now held in high regard by adherents throughout the world — were once brutally and bloodily exorcised. Not that the leaders of the movement claimed the title of Mahdi, but they were moving dangerously close to it. The story has been told in detail, but it might bear repeating in brief focus.

On the 8th of July 1850, a young man of thirty-one was dragged before a firing squad in Tabriz and executed. His corpse was dragged through the streets of the city and cast out beyond the gates to be devoured by dogs and jackals. Friends with ready money recovered the body, however, wrapped it in white silk, and transported it to Teheran. For a number of years, the body lay in a small shrine outside Teheran on the Hamadan road. It was later removed to an unknown site as a precaution against defilement and sacrilege. Today, the body of the young man is enshrined on Mt. Carmel, the chief centre of the Bahai pilgrimage.

The Bahai faith, which has several hundred adherents scattered throughout the world, from Iran to the Black Forest, to the Pentagon, and claims twenty thousand martyrs, is based on a belief in successive progressive revelations of God, none of which is final. It claims to restore to mankind the power to achieve unity through love. The troubles of this present time are but a prelude to the necessary and inevitable unification of the human race. Like the Christian Scientists, the Bahai encourage the establishment of reading rooms and Americans may occasionally notice them in communities as diverse as the Quaker village of West Chester and Los Angeles.

There have been a succession of leaders of the Bahai faith, perhaps the most famous being Bahau'llah, a Persian nobleman, who took the name "the Glory of God" as the one foretold by the Bab — the young man whose death has just been recounted. He wrote widely and was banished in succession to Baghdad, Constantinople, Adrianople and the prison city of Acre. He died in 1892. Professor Browne, in his index, tells the story of this great religious story simply by title : "regarded as a man perfect in humanity;" as "He whom God shall manifest;" as "Christ returned;" as "the Comforter or Paraclete;" as the "Lord of the vineyard;" as "Shah Bahram, the Zoroastrian Messiah;" as the "Father;" as "God."

This is quite a succession and there were others who followed Bahau'allah or Mirza Huseyn Ali to use his real name. But none has ever captured the imagination of the world as the Bab himself.

Mirza Ali Mohammed was born at Shiraz on the 9th of October 1820. His father was a cloth merchant of that city who died while the boy was still young. For a few years he was in the care of his uncle but at the age of seventeen, he was sent to the Persian Gulf where he was engaged in business. It was here that he first began to attract the attention of his contemporaries by the sweetness of his disposition and the austerity of his morals. Clearly here was a young man more inclined to religious meditation than to commercial pursuits.

Just when the young Shirazi undertook the pilgrimage to Mecca is not certain, but it must have been in his twentieth year. He also visited the shrines of the Imams at Nojef and Karbela. It was at the latter place that he became the pupil of Hajji Seyyid Kazim of Resht, a distinguished theologian who had already begun to exert a considerable influence on Persian thought (albeit incurring the opposition of the orthodox Shi'ite clergy). Not surprisingly, before long the teacher fell under the spell of the student. Apparently none could look upon the countenance of the young man from Shiraz without yielding to his charms and an increasing number of learned and devout men began to be drawn into the circle of his authority.

On the 23rd of May 1844, the young man proclaimed himself to the world as the Bab or Gate whereby men might win to the sacred mysteries and spiritual truths of which he had become the recipient. Disciples, many of whom were pupils of his old teacher from Resht who had recently died, gathered themselves around him. They eagerly adopted the new doctrines of the Bab and began to preach them openly throughout the land. Everywhere men began to say that the Imam Mahdi had come at last for the deliverance of the nations and the establishment of universal justice and peace.

By the fall of, 1845, the orthodox clergy as well as certain officials of the government had become alarmed at the rapid spread of the teachings of the Bab and subsequently he was brought to Shiraz and placed in confinement. He escaped, however, to Isfahan where the governor of that city made him welcome. Early in 1847, the governor died. His successor, no doubt disturbed by the presence of this provocative personality, seized him and sent him, under escort, to Teheran.

Everywhere, though, it seemed as if popular uprisings accompanied the journey and finally the Shah, fearful of the possible effect of the Bab's presence in the capital city, had him conveyed to Maku, a fortress on the north west frontier of Iran. The imprisonment served no other purpose than to inflame the followers of the Bab, however, and the conflict between them, the government, and the Shi'ite *ulama* became bitter and contentious. When the Shah died on the 5th of October, 1848, the factions came into armed conflict. Formidable insurrections were raised in several cities throughout the country and a revolt, which threatened to defy the united efforts of the army itself, broke out at Zanjan, Mazanderan and Niriz. Not surprisingly, it was at this point in time that the decision was made by the young Shah — upon the advice of his prime minister— to publicly execute the Bab. Accordingly, orders were dispatched to Tabriz to bring the Bab to trial and to death. When the word went out as to the intentions of the government, a vast assemblage gathered in the city and through this crowd, the Bab was dragged for many hours until he was finally brought to the place of execution near the citadel. Cords were passed under his arms, suspending him a few feet from the ground. A disciple was suspended along side him. After a false start, the firing party received the command to fire, a volley rang out and the bleeding corpses of the two men were cut down to be dragged to the outer gates. The Bahai faith had begun its road to martyrdom.

So it is with the life of those who come into bitter conflict and confrontation — "Life, mission and martyrdom."[32] To-day the Bahais while not exactly acceptable in Iran, are no longer persecuted although it would not be wise to send a Bahai to Iran on any delicate mission. The Hidden Imam remains hidden and as has been true for centuries, it is unlikely that he will appear in recognizable form. Meanwhile his agent, or his regent rules. That the Shahanshah is the *locum tenens* of the Hidden Imam would seem evident from the information that we have. To make any other kind of a case, would be to ignore the facts as they are.

NOTES

1. Quoted in Sykes, I, *op. cit.*, p. 398.
2. *The Letter of Tansar, op. cit.*, p. 33.
3. Savory, R. M., "Iran, a 2500 year historical and cultural tradition" in *Iranian Civilization and Culture* (ed. Charles Adams) McGill University Press, 1973, p. 78.
4. Ghoshal, U. N., *A History of Indian Political Ideas*, Oxford University Press, 1959, p. 20.
5. All quotations are cited in Inlow, *op. cit.*, pp. 410 ff.
6. Gautama Dharmasutra XI, quoted in Drekmeier, C., *Kingship and Community in Early India*, Stanford University Press, 1962, p. 87.
7. Strabo, *Geography*, XV, 20 (Loeb Classical Library (trans. H. L. Jones), VII, p. 183. Quoted in Inlow, *op. cit.*, p. 407.
8. *Ibid.*, p. 411.
9. Widengren, G., "The Sacred Kingship of Iran," *Numen*, Suppl. 4, 1959, pp. 442 ff.
10. VIII 9, For a further explanation of this code, Inlow, E. Burke, "Manu and Hammurabi, a study in legal theory" in *Journal of Indian History*, Golden Jubilee Volume, 1973.
11. Browne, *op. cit.*, I, pp. 128-29.
12. Quoted in Widengren, *op. cit.*, p. 146.
13. See the article on the Shah in October 14, 1974, *Time*, pp. 55 ff.
14. Browne, *op. cit.*, I, p. 173.
15. Lambton, A. K. S., "Quis Custodiet Custodes", *Studia Islamica* V(1956), p. 137.
16. *Rubaiyat*. Quatrain 45.
17. These and other incidents are related in Browne, *op. cit.*, II, pp. 207 ff.
18. *Encyclopaedia of Islam*, London, 1960, pp. 1350–1357.
19. *Tadhkirat al-Muluk* (Trans. by V. Minorsky). London, 1943, p. 125.
20. *Ibid.*, p. 125.
21. Quoted in Rice, *op. cit.*, pp. 28-29.
22. Lambton, *op. cit.*, p. 138.
23. Recounted in Rice, *op. cit.*, p. 71.
24. Algar, Hamid, *Religion and State in Iran*, 1785 - 1906, University of California Press, 1969, for a detailed study of the period.
25. Supplementary Fundamental Law of Persia, Art. 39.
26. Bayne, E. A., *Persian Kingship in Transition*, American Universities Field Staff, 1968, p. 51.
27. *New York Times*, March 15, 1962. Obituary column.
28. *The Teheran Journal*, March 25, 1970, p. 3.
29. *Kayhan*, December 7, 1974, p. 1.
30. Shah of Iran, *Mission For My Country*, New York, 1961.
31. Bayne, *op. cit.*, p. 50.
32. For the whole story, see Browne, E. G., *A Year Amongst the Persians*, London, 1893, See Index.

CHAPTER 5

SECURITY FORCES

Iran is in one of the world's great military traditions. Much of the literature of the country deals with martial monarchs and elaborate accounts of their campaigns. The concept of a warrior caste has never completely died in Iran and the founder of the present dynasty, Reza Shah the Great, was himself a career officer before crowning himself Shah. From Cyrus the Great to Nadir Shah who conquered India in 1738 – 1739, who took spoils estimated at 87,500,000 pounds not including the Peacock throne which now rests in the Gulistan Palace in Teheran, and who was finally killed by assassins, Iran has claimed its full share of great commanders. Nadir Shah himself is described by another general officer of distinction :

> "Endowed with splendid physique, a fine appearance, a voice of thunder, dauntless courage and resolution, he was a born leader of men and with his battle axe, he hewed his way to fame."[1]

After taking Delhi, the defeated Moghul Emperor gave his daughter in marriage to the son of Nadir Shah. When asked for a pedigree of seven generations of his son by the prospective father-in-law, Nadir-Shah's grim reply was : "He is the son of Nadir Shah, the son of the sword, the grandson of the sword; and so on to seventy instead of seven generations."

This last reference to seventy generations is a part of the continuity in concept if not of actual blood descent that the Shahs of Iran have always held with regard to their great office, which, as pointed out above, is essentially of military origin.

To return briefly to this military tradition. Sheer strength was never the answer. The Persians, over the centuries showed a tremendous adaptability and very seldom on the battlefield did their forces outnumber those of the enemy. For example, as far back as the Achaemenids, Cyrus in building a war machine that conquered an area five thousand miles from East to West and half as much from North to South, used a combination of what were then considered to be revolutionary weapons deployed and used with studied sophistication. The key lay in the special use of the bow accompanied by short lances and short daggers. On the battlefield, the bowmen overwhelmed the enemy under a hail of arrows, thus denying to them engagement at close quarters until the Persian infantry was ready to follow through with dagger and lance. But the secret was always to avoid close contact as much as possible and permit the archers mobility to use their bows unhampered. Students of English military history will recall a similar use centuries later of the English long bow.

The Persian Army of the early Achaemenids thus wore little armour and became vulnerable only when their lines were pierced by heavily-armed hoplites of the type that Alexander perfected.

Practical aspects of battle were not neglected by the flexible leadership by the Persian commanders. Every schoolboy remembers the famed battle of Cyrus' field when the Persians pushed his camel baggage trains into the carefully aligned rows of Lydian spearmen as reported above. This type of opposition was clearly disruptive of the lines of spearmen, and was eventually effective in the conquering of Croesus.

Single examples such as this are replete in the early histories and in the course of the hundreds of campaigns waged. For those who enjoy reading in this specialized interest, there are similar, if always different, other examples to demonstrate the flexibility of the Persian command.

If the Achaemenids established an early tradition of martial arms, the second great dynasty, the Sassanians, carried the tradition on. Here, interestingly enough the campaigns are apt to be depicted more in art than in literary accounts. This is probably because the Roman historians were not as fascinated by the Persians as were Greeks like Herodotus, Zenophon, Arrian, Ctesias, etc., who all wrote about Persian arms.

Nevertheless there are interesting records of Sassanian military accomplishments.

The Sassanians were great carvers of rocks and there is still to be seen in Iran today marvellous depictions of Sassanian military prowess. Shapur I commemorated his victories over Rome in narrative scenes that are really quite comprehensive. On the walls of the K'aba-i-Zardusht, an ancient fire temple at Naqsh'i-Rustum which has been much photographed in recent years, the Sassanian Shahanshah gives a tri-lingual account of the great struggle between Rome and Persia that in its own way rivals Herodotus' account in his great history of the earlier struggle between Greece and Persia.

The text of Shapur's accounting is accompanied by extensive illustrations on five bas-reliefs carved on the rock face and in the gorge of Bishapur, a city founded in the province of Fars — the original homeland of Cyrus the Great — by Shapur and used as his capital.

One of the two reliefs on the left bank of the river of Bishapur commemorates the triple triumph of Shapur over the Roman Emperors Gordian III, Philip the Arab, and Valerian. In the centre, the Sassanian king is depicted on horseback trampling the prostrate body of Gordian III. Before him, bowing the knee, is Philip suing for peace. The Emperor Valerian stands behind his conqueror, who holds him by the wrist. This gesture is important and it can be seen with great clarity on a cameo in the Bibliotheque National, Paris. This marvellous example of Sassanian art (the best collection in the world, however, is in the Hermitage in Leningrad) shows the two Emperors riding toward each other. Valerian is brandishing his sword while Shapur does not even draw his from the sheath. Instead he has seized Valerian hard by the wrist. According to tradition, the two monarchs fought in single combat with the victory, of course, going to Shapur.

On the opposite bank of the river at Bishapur is another relief reproducing the triple victory of Shapur but on a more massive scale, showing rows of mounted nobility, Roman prisoners, and the Persians carrying booty.

In a third of the great Bishapur bas-reliefs, two themes are combined in a single picture. It was probably carved around 244 A.D., the year that Rome made peace with the Persians, as Valerian is not depicted. It does, however, show Gordian III pinned down on the ground by the legs of Shapur's great charger. Philip the Arab is pleading for peace before the "master of the world." On two other reliefs, Valerian is shown again. They would have been carved after 260, the year Valerian was captured and brought to Bishapur for imprisonment.

A few miles from Bishapur, high in the mountains, at the mouth of a natural cave, there is a colossal statue of Shapur I. The statue has been described as being "at once an embodiment of the 'imperial idea' and invested with a super human grandeur."[2] It conveys an authority of absolute power that demands unqualified obedience. It fits Shapur's own description of himself, "Lord of Iran and non-Iran."

Probably because of its close proximity to Persepolis, the reliefs most visited by western tourists are the ones, however, at Naqsh-i-Rustum. Below the Tomb of Darius, here on the side of that great flat-surfaced mountain, Shapur's victories are again depicted, the site chosen no doubt deliberately as demonstrating Shapur's desire to make clear that his feats of arms matched those of his illustrious ancestors.

There are other notable carvings at Naqshi-Rustam depicting investitures, triumphs, hunting and fighting and even a family scene (Bahram II). As one stands down on the plain before this magnificent display looking upward, it becomes more awesome as the hours pass. The huge war horses become monstrous in the sun (there is an old tradition that King Arthur of England travelled to the East and brought back some of these horses with him). There is great action — Hormizd II charging and unseating his adversary in a duel. There is splendour, and dignity, magnificent heads, the sweeping gestures of the Gods — all these are a part of the display of the pride and greatness of Iranian arms in the 3rd century A.D.

The Safavid dynasty (1511 – 1736) took its name from the Arabic *safi-ud-din* meaning purity of religion. As pointed out above, the consolidation of Safavid power in Iran was built upon a combination of arms and religious zeal. Shah Ismail believed in his own divinity and his followers believed him to be a Saint. The Shah also believed in his horses — the cavalry forming the backbone of his army. For years, the numerous campaigns of the Shah — the conquest of Fars, ancient cradle land of the Persians; of Mazanderan, traditional home of the Deevs; of Yazd and Diyar Bakr; of southwest Persia and the western frontiers of Khurasan, etc., were conducted with displays of magnificent horsemanship and feats of arms. When Shah Ismail, for example, moved into the province of Khorosan which was in the hands of the Uzbegs, seventeen thousand Persians rode against a combined enemy force of twenty-eight thousand and defeated them. The Uzbeg chieftain was killed while trying to jump his horse over a wall. His head was cut off and presented to Shah Ismail who had it mounted in gold and set with jewels to serve as a goblet.

Shah Ismail died in 1524. He was succeeded by his young son Tahmasp. Tahmasp is largely remembered for having been on the throne when Anthony Jenkinson, Captain General of the newly founded Muscovy Company (1555) became the first Englishman to visit Iran. It was a fateful meeting. Jenkinson had calculated on the Shah's hatred of the Turks — which was of course very real — and was of course reciprocated. (In fact the creation of the Shi'a state by Shah Ismail aroused the passions of the Sunni Turks to the point where for almost one hundred and fifty years there was unremitting warfare between the two countries).

But Jenkinson had not counted on the Shah's equal hatred of the Christians. He was given an audience but felt mortified by the way he was treated. When he was dismissed from the Shah's presence "after me followed a man with a basanet of sand, sifting all the way that I had gone within the said palace" (i.e., in other words covering up the uncleanness).[3]

With the coming of the English and the continuing campaigns against the Turks, the two themes that were to dominate the life of the Safavids were set. For better or worse, the fortunes of the Persians and the English were joined inextricably — a relationship that has existed into our own time.

Shah Abbas the Great (1587 – 1629) was without doubt the chief figure of the Safavid dynasty as well as being one of the greatest in Persian history. He took Isfahan as his capital and built it into a city so famous that it became known as "half the world." Panegyrists lauded it in even greater dimension, "If the world had no Isfahan, the Creator of the World would have no world." And again, "Isfahan is the meaning of the word 'world'." "World is the word and Isfahan the meaning." Actually the word Isfahan had its origin in the word *cpadhana* "army camp" or *acpadhana* "horse station," bespeaking the great age of the city. Originally it was called Sepahan, however, the word "sepah" meaning an army in Persian. Shah Abbas therefore in making his choice of a capital obviously had in mind in the first instance, its strategic location, which made it an ideal garrison city. The fact that it became a great and luxurious court city is merely an added tribute to the dimensions of this man who welcomed foreigners and Christians alike and who was the subject of considerable attention in English literature and on the stage.[4]

In 1598, Sir Anthony Sherley, already distinguished as the leader of an expedition to the Spanish Main and his brother Sir Robert Sherley, accompanied by twenty-six followers, reached Kazvin within the domain of Shah Abbas, and presented themselves to the young ruler. They exchanged rich gifts and the Sherleys requested that they be allowed to enter the Shah's service.

For the Iranians, it was a fine stroke of fortune. For included among the English was a cannon founder.

In the years immediately preceeding Shah Abbas' ascent to the throne of Cyrus, the noted cavalry of the Safavids had begun suffering serious reverses at the hands of the Turks. The reason for this was that the Turks possessed artillery units — the first to be used in the Middle East — as well as several regiments of musketeers. By the simple device of chaining the cannon together in rows behind which stood the musketeers, the Turks were able to place the Persian cavalry at a distinct disadvantage. Shah Abbas understood the problem and one of the first acts of his rule was to begin the reorganization of his army. A cannon founder was precisely what he needed. It took him fifteen years from the time of his succession to the throne to do the job. This seems a long time today, but in the early 17th century it was really quite an accomplishment.

Originally the force at the disposal of the youthful Shah Abbas consisted of sixty thousand Kizilbash horsemen who would obey none but their chiefs. This, of course, meant that the real power lay with others than the Shah. Shah Abbas met this problem by halving the number of the tribal contingents and organizing a body of ten thousand cavalry and twelve thousand infantry paid and officered by the Crown. Most of the riflemen were recruited from Georgian and Armenian converts to Islam. The Shah made a further wise decision in naming as his commander-in-chief, the celebrated Allah Verdi Khan who not only worked well with the Shah but who seems to have not been resentful of the presence of the Sherleys when their services were accepted by the Monarch. And, finally, Shah Abbas invited members of all the tribes to enroll themselves as Shah Savan or "Friends of the Shah." This stroke of policy was entirely successful and thousands of men joined. The Shah was well on his way. Once sufficient cannon were cast, he would be ready to move against the Turkish Sultan.

The great test of strength against the Turks came in 1604 at Lake Urumia. The Turks had forces of one hundred thousand. The Persians had sixty-two thousand. In this battle Sir Robert Sherley, who was to be appointed Master-General of the Persian Army for his great distinction here, was wounded three times. At the end of the battle twenty thousand Turkish heads were laid at the feet of Shah Abbas the Great. Azerbaijan, Kurdistan, Baghdad, Mosul and Diarbekr now fell to the Persians. The Turk was contained. Shah Abbas, in his new capital in Isfahan, was now the leading figure in the Moslem world. His court glittered with notable personages. More and more travellers from Europe came to the beautiful city on the Zayandeh Rud (the life-giving river) and even today to fly into Isfahan is a splendid sight. Broad avenues — the main one is named after Shah Abbas — lovely bridges, superb mosques and public buildings are all there. A recent addition is the luxurious Shah Abbas Hotel, certainly one of the finest hotels in the world.

An old English book of travels reports of the subduing of the Turks in the following language :

> "The mighty Ottoman, terror of the Christian world, quaketh of a Sherley fever and gives hopes of approaching fates: the prevailing Persian hath learned Sherleian arts of war; and he which before knew not the use of ordnance, hath now 500 pieces of brass and 60,000 musketeers: so that they, which at hand with the sword were before dreadful to the Turks, now also, in remoter blows and sulfurian arts, are growne terrible."[5]

That the Sherleys contributed much to the fortunes of Iran, there can be little doubt. But, their own fortunes never fared as well Sir Anthony served for a time as the Shah's Ambassador to the Courts of Europe and finally settled in Spain after many singular adventures including time in various prisons of Europe, attempts upon his life, being generally discredited in England and even being forbidden to re-enter his native land. He died in Spain "extremely poor in purse and reputation."[6]

Sir Robert Sherley seems to have done better. He also returned as the Shah's Ambassador to Europe. In England, King James who at first saw him as a close associate of his brother — actually they had quarrelled and were separated for years — and as an outlaw, finally forgave him and seems to have held him in some regard. The Prince of Wales, for example, consented to stand godfather to Sir Robert and Lady Sherley's infant son. Sir Robert eventually returned to Isfahan and was returned to Europe as an Iranian Ambassador. But the death of King James (1625) and the accession of Charles, plus the fact that the Shah had sent another Ambassador — a Persian — to England, apparently to undercut Sherley's authority, resulted in Sir Robert's world crashing about him as well. The Lords in Council decided to send both envoys back to Shah Abbas. In the summer of 1628, Sherley reached the Shah's summer retreat on the shores of the Caspian. It was a bitter time for both men. The aged monarch had clouded his great career by having his oldest son killed and two other sons blinded. He was bitter and vengeful and he turned on Sir Robert Sherley and bade him "to depart his kingdom as old and troublesome."[7] Sir Robert died at Kazvin on 13 July 1628 on his way out of the country he had served for thirty years "sucked and empty." Lady Sherley took refuge with the Carmelite fathers in Isfahan. She was eventually smuggled out of Iran to Rome where she devoted the rest of her life to good works. Eventually she was able to get Sir Robert's bones out of Iran to Rome where they were reburied. As a general epitaph on the Sherley brothers, Archbishop Abbott's comment may serve: "All venture on great things and come to beggary."[8]

Shah Abbas died only a few months after Sir Robert Sherley. "When this great Prince ceased to live, Persia ceased to prosper."[9] So wrote Chardin, the great French traveller, whose drawings of Isfahan are still to be seen but the writer cannot any longer remember where he saw them.

The modern military history of Iran has been a combination of tragedy, defeat, and yet, eventual triumph. Caught between Russia and Great Britain in their great competition for Empire beginning in the 18th century and continuing through the 19th, Iran suffered staggering blows from the outside, being forced to give up much of its territory and being reduced to almost the role of a protectorate. Unfortunately the situation was not improved by the struggles for power within the country. The accession of Aga Mohammed Khan, Qajar, to the Persian throne in 1796 after a series of campaigns against the rival Zand dynasty, campaigns of unbelievable cruelty on the part of the Qajar eunuch King, brought no great glory to Iran. Kerman, for example, has really never recovered from the cruelty visited upon it by the Qajar ruler. It was here that the last Zand chieftain had taken his final stand. And it was here that he was finally betrayed and captured. After blinding his rival with his own hands and then sending him to Teheran to be strangled, Aga Mohammed ordered the male population blinded and twenty thousand pairs of eyes delivered to him. He then turned the women of Kerman over to his soldiers with orders to rape and murder. With this beginning, a united Iran was a very remote possibility — and it remained so.

Under the Qajars, themselves a tribal people, tribal units remained strong, stronger even than under previous dynasties who had the power to contain them. All of them — the Bakhtiaris, Kurds, Lurs, and Turkomans of Khorasan to name the most important — possessed a strong spirit of independence and delighted in any provocation that could call them into action. A Persian proverb summarized their outlook : "I and my tribe against the nation. I and my cousins against the tribe. I and my brothers against my cousins. I against my brothers."

As a consequence of this singular deployment of fighting forces, the Qajar rule of the 19th century was one in which the armies of the Shah failed to attain or maintain any real status. The army was described by one British observer as "more terrible to their friends than their enemies" and as "probably, with the exception of the Chinese, the worse so-called standing army on anything like a large scale in the world."[10]

Probably the most efficient military unit in the country was the Cossack Brigade which was established by contract with Russia in 1879. They were stationed in Teheran and presumably acted as the Shah's bodyguard. But its commander took his orders directly from the Minister of War in St Petersburg and, hence, the unit in which Reza Shah, founder of the present Pahlavi dynasty served as a Colonel, was seen by most Iranians, as well as by foreign observers, as being a prime source of Russian influence in Iran.

The English were also involved. They saw Iran as the "outer glacis of an extreme bastion." The Shah's domain served as outworks in Indian defense. Between Great Britain and Russia, therefore, Iran held place only as a buffer state. From the English point of view, the primary consideration was always India. This accounts for the apparent inconsistencies in British policy toward Persia. They offered their cooperation to the Shah, then made war on him. They urged reforms for the Shah's country and then blocked those reforms. Always this was high policy. Lord Salisbury put it this way, "were it not for our possessing India, we should trouble ourselves little about Persia."[11]

So it was, that for several decades — actually until the reestablishment of an Iranian Army by Reza Shah after his accession to the throne in 1925 — Great Britain and Russia for all intents and purposes divided Iran between themselves. The division was finally stabilized by the terms of the Anglo Russian agreement of 1907. This agreement, while holding the "independence and integrity of Persia" to be the fundamental principle defined the division between the two rival powers :

> "Starting from Kasr-i-Shirin, the Russian line crosses and includes Isfahan, Yezd and Kakh, ending at that point on the Persian frontier where the Russian and Afghan frontiers intersect. Going from the Afghan frontier via Gazik, Birjand, Kirman, the British line ends at Bandar Abbas."[12]

This agreement was presented to the Persian government, not signed by it.

After World War I, not counting the tribal fighting forces

which were strictly local, the forces in existence in Iran were the South Persian Rifles, six thousand strong (British), the Cossack Division, eight thousand strong (Russian), and the Swedish Gendarmerie, eighty-four hundred strong. They attempted to restrain the tribes and keep some kind of internal order. It is small wonder that when Reza Shah was crowned in 1926, one of his first acts was to re-enlist the officers and men of the Cossack Division and the South Persian Rifles into a national army and to enlarge its size to forty thousand. He also began the move to disarm the tribes and re-establish the central authority.

In 1911, W. Morgan Shuster arrived in Iran to accept an invitation delivered through the United States government, to reorganize Iranian finances. As an employee, he thought he was dealing with the Iranian government. He found himself in error. Neither Russia nor Britain were sympathetic to the work of the American with the result that after eight months, the Russians gave the Iranian government forty-eight hours to get rid of Shuster and sent a regiment of Cossacks into Teheran to enforce it. Though Shuster's mission was a failure, Iran had discovered the possibility of receiving help from a third party which hopefully might break the British-Russian stranglehold. So it was that here began a long and important association with the United States that was, by the 1970's to lift the effectiveness of the Iranian armed forces to its highest level — in a comparative sense — in well over two centuries.

In World War I, Iranian neutrality was violated when British, Russian and Turkish troops fought on Iranian soil. In 1941, Soviet and British troops again arrived on Iranian soil. For several years, of course, Reza Shah had become increasingly dictatorial and tending to his own way of doing things. The Germans appeared to offer him not only a countervailing force to British and Russian influence but to offer the kind of technical assistance that he felt he needed. The Americans were not yet ready to offer aid other than financial. Advisers, of whom Dr. Arthur Millspaugh was the most distinguished (he served as Director-General of Iranian finances from 1922 to 1927) succeeded in strengthening Iranian finances sufficiently to provide the necessary funds for the building of the

Iranian State Railway which proved such an allied asset in World War II.

German aid and influence in Iran reached dangerous propaganda proportions on the eve of World War II. For example, the swastika adorned the grand new railway station in Teheran. There were youth groups organized under German guidance as well. The arrival, then of the Soviet and British troops in 1941 was not, then, surprising. Over two thousand Germans were run to ground and taken into charge. Reza Shah was forced to abdicate in favour of his son, the present Shah, and was taken into exile by a British intelligence officer of great distinction. For the duration of the War, there was no real central authority in Iran. It was an occupied country. Small wonder that the present Shahanshah makes frequent speeches announcing that never again will Iran's frontiers be violated.

As World War II was being fought, Iran obviously needed a friend. The first real break came when Iran was declared eligible for American lend-lease aid in March 1942. When that declaration came, the new government of Iran was ready to direct American attention to pressing Iranian needs. Specifically this meant (1) strengthening and reinforcing the demoralized and vastly weakened Iranian forces, down from the great days of Reza Shah, and (2) obtaining direct access to the fountainhead of lend-lease supply.[13]

The problems were, of course, overwhelming for a young, green ruler, and one has only to compare the self-confident monarch of today with the young man of yesterday to realize that men can grow and become great in the face of real adversity.

One month after Iran was declared eligible for lend-lease aid, Iran expressed its desire for an American officer to serve as Intendant General to reorganize the finance and army supplies of the Iranian War Department. The next year Dr. Millspaugh returned as Administrator General of Finances. Other Americans served in various administrative and advisory capacities of senior rank. The State Department explained the position of the United States government. The United States, it stated, was prepared to take on this responsibility "because both Great Britain and the Soviet Union are handicapped in their relations with Iran by the inevitable dislikes and distrust of the Iranians for the powers which are in occupation of their country."[14]

It would not be accurate to suggest, however, that American actions in Iran always went unchallenged — even by Iran. Early in World War II, American representation in what was then known as the "Corridor" (i.e., the supply route in the USSR), consisted only of a few hundred officers and men of the United States Army and the civilians engaged in construction and assembly projects. When, however, five thousand American service troops set foot on Iranian soil late in 1942 without any previous notification to the Government of Iran — the Americans used the rather lame excuse that the troops were there at British request — Iran informed the United States government that they considered this an infringement of Iranian sovereignty. There followed a long period of correspondence between all of the allied governments and Iran regarding the matter; but the simple truth was that Iran could not do anything about it until the United States Department of State itself set about trying to redress the balance. When the British proposed that the Allies should declare themselves as having the power to modify the Iranian cabinet at will, the American Secretary of State refused to go along and even issued a memorandum suggesting that the United States should assume the responsibility for building-up Iran "to the point at which it will stand in need of neither British nor Russian assistance to maintain order in its own house."[15]

The meeting of the Allied leaders in Teheran in November 1943, was, among other things then, an effort by the United States to place the problem of Iran within the expressed intent of the Atlantic Charter : self government for Iran, a respect for Iran's integrity, proposals for strengthening Iran's economy along lines of a free enterprise system, etc.

From lease-lend assistance, American advisory elements expanded into four separate Military Missions in Iran under contractual agreements between Iran and the United States government. These missions as they came into being were :

1. The United States Military Mission with the Imperial Iranian Army, known as ARMISH.

2. The Military Assistance Advisory Group to Iran, known as MAAG.

3. The United States Military Mission with the Imperial Iranian Gendarmerie, known as GENMISH.

4. The Gulf District Corps of Engineers, United States Army.

The first officers representing ARMISH arrived in Iran in October 1942. A formal contract specifying ARMISH organization and mission was signed between the two governments in November 1943. It was revised in October 1947, and thereafter at periodic intervals. The assigned mission of ARMISH was to advise and assist the Iranian Minister of War, the Imperial Iranian General Staff and subordinate elements of the Iranian Armed Forces in matters pertaining to plans, organization, administration and training. Members of ARMISH, unlike earlier British advisers, had neither command nor operating staff responsibility in the Iranian Army. They were authorized to make official inspections and investigations for performance of their duties.

The mission of MAAG was to carry out the objectives and insure the effective implementation of the Mutual Assistance Program for Iran.

ARMISH was originally composed of an Army group of thirty-eight officers and eighty enlisted men.

MAAG, Iran, was composed of an Army Section of seventy-eight officers and one hundred and sixty enlisted men, an Air Force Section of five officers and six airmen, and a Navy Section of two officers and two enlisted men.

In 1954 ARMISH and MAAG were consolidated and was thereafter known as ARMISH-MAAG. Their headquarters were located in Teheran. Field training teams operated mostly out of various Corps Headquarters. Team # 1 was in Teheran; Team # 2 in Zanjan; Team # 3 Mahabad; Team # 4 at Kermanshah; Team # 5 at Shiraz, Team # 6 in Torbat-E-Heyariyeh; Team # 7 at Ahwaz. There were also sub-teams in other cities.

American personnel were well provided for both in Teheran and in the field. Direct contact, of course, with Iranian soldiers took place largely in the field. The writer recalls with some amusement that in the early days there were some problems in connection with getting Iranian enlisted men to actively work under the direction of some of the Americans. This matter was partially solved — without malice on the part of the United States — by sending in a few replacement NCOs of oriental lineage. So great was the fear inspired by the Mongols during their invasions of Persia in the 13th century (Mothers in the rural areas were said to still quiet their children by telling them the Mongols were coming) that Oriental type American soldiers were said to have gotten a better response.

The Military Assistance Program of the United States was a well prepared, and in terms of personnel, well assembled force of advisers. Most of them received a thorough orientation of several weeks on Iran at the Military Assistance Institute in Arlington, Virginia, before going over. Technical assistance programs accompanied the military program and hundreds of millions of dollars of equipment were poured into the country by the Americans. By 1969 – 1970, however, Iran had reached the point where it was buying its planes, tanks, etc., and the team stations were being closed down. Even the officer's Club in Teheran was sold.

So it was that within twenty years, Iran had moved from a position of great dependence upon the United States to one of real independence. With oil revenues mounting, Iran was now able to purchase her planes and her hardware. Officers were still sent to the United States for training at great centers like Fort Benning (Infantry), (some Iranian officers were sent to the Military University of France) but even here Iran was building her own competence. The country had come a long way in winning back her historic position of being free of foreign domination.

The present military establishment in Iran numbers over 300,000. Ten years ago, the official figures were 160,000. This is out of a total population of 32,250,000 (approximately) represents a substantial percentage. By western standards it is small but nevertheless it is large enough for Iran to control a large segment of the Middle East. By comparison with its neighbour Iraq, (now on friendly terms but being watched) for example, whose total armed forces are roughly one-third of the Iranian figures, Iran has not only a distinct numerical advantage, but for years the Shah has been procuring only the most advanced weaponry with the result that no one seriously questions Iran's present capability. One would not wish to speculate on any comparison with the powerful USSR to the north, however, for clearly Iran is in no position to challenge a force of this size. But Iran is infinitely better off vis-a-vis her northern neighbour than she was seventy-five yeas ago.

The military establishment of Iran breaks down as follows. The Army consists of about 175,000 men and reserves of 300,000. The Air Force is 50,000 men; the Navy 13,000. The Imperial Iranian Gendarmerie is a para-military force of some 35,000 men. There is also a National Police Organization of about 25,000 men but it has neither the weapons or the training of the Gendarmerie and probably could not shift to military operations. There is also a Civil Defense Organization and a National Resistance Force. The former was organized in 1957 to plan and direct the protection of lives and property arising from enemy actions or natural disasters. To date with the help of the Red Lion and Sun Society, it has provided valuable services for disaster relief. It was also believed to be aimed at the tribes. The announced object of the organization is to train every citizen who reach 16 for civil defense (use of light arms only). It is voluntary and has branches in all the districts of the country. It operates under the Ministry of Interior and has a Supreme Council, reporting to the Shah, consisting of selected Cabinet Ministers, Chief of the General Staff, Chief of Police and Chief of Gendarmerie.

A Cabinet Decree of May 1953 established the National Resistance Forces. These forces do not engage in military training except on annual manoeuvres with the Armed Forces. Its members are not expected to use arms. Its function is to train Iranians for the defense of home and villages. The Government of Iran states that about $8 billion a year (27% of the Government Budget) is spent on defense.[16]

Internal security is a primary responsibility of SAVAK (Sazeman Ettelaat va Amniyat Kashvar), a civilian national intelligence and security organization. Like most security forces, little is actually known of its operation. It is, however, a constant presence in Iran and to reside there for any length of time is to bring the foreigner into a reasonably knowledgeable understanding of its effectiveness of that, more later. Suffice it to say here that there are those of us who sense that internal security in Iran is a more pervasive force than it is in the USSR, but this is a matter on which others might easily disagree.

It seems useful at this point to provide a more detailed account of the Iranian Security Forces and their mission. What follows, then, breaks down into (1) Armed Forces; (2) Gendarmerie; (3) Security and Intelligence; (4) The Securing of the Gulf.

One additional note : It is important in Iran not to overlook important observance relating to the Forces. Tey are : Army day 21st Azar (12 December); Air Force Day 26th Mehr (18 October); Navy Day 14th Aban (5 November). These are also irregularly scheduled "Important Military Manoeuvres" usually in August where the Shah and important personages are in attendance.

Armed Forces

There is a martial air about Iran. By contrast to the USSR where the uniform is seldom seen by the visitor except at airports, Iran is glittering with military display. The officers are a privileged group. They drive good cars, wear uniforms that must surely be the envy of every low profile in the North American military establishment, and, in general, comport themselves with elan. Most of them are from good families. While the military college imposes no social or economic barriers to admission, all candidates for a commission must have a character reference from a member of the Majlis (parliament) or from a general officer attesting to the candidate's reputation and that of his family.

There is universal subscription. Every man does two years of compulsory service at very low pay. Exceptional soldiers in special categories are kept on even, sometimes, against their own wishes. The combat portion of the Army is divided into three field armies to which a total of eight divisions and various independent units are assigned. These forces are supplied and assisted by the important Logistics Support Command, one of the largest organizations in the Army.

The deployment of troops is generally divided between the north (Soviet border area) and the Iraqi border. However, there are sizeable numbers in the west and the southwest and there is a strong military presence in all major cities with cantonments centrally located. In Teheran, for example, there is one located between the central city and South Teheran (a poor and potentially explosive area) and another between the central city and Shemiran to the north (an exclusive suburban area which also includes the Shah's new palace). The deployment is a constant reminder that armies have their domestic potentialities as well as their foreign uses.

Under Article 50 of the Supplementary Law of 1907, the Shah is the Commander-in-Chief of the Armed Forces and is empowered to confer military ranks. It is an educated guess that the Shah personally selects all officers from the field grade up. However, the Shah of Iran is not merely a constitutional Commander-in Chief. Through history, as has been seen above, many Iranian monarchs have been formidable warriors and, hence, there is a strong military tradition in Iran that is an integral part of the society and of the state. Everywhere the Shah is seen in uniform — statues, portraits, newspaper pictures. This image is not projected outside of the country where the Shah usually appears in the tailored suits. But, once again, this seeming dichotomy is so characteristic of Iranian separateness.

The word Shah itself is military. As pointed out above, it derives from the words *Kshatra* as used in the Veda, which means ruler or rule. The *Kshatriya* was the ancient Aryan warrior caste who filled the governing and military roles of Aryan society. Kings who were not of this lineage sought legitimization by forging Kshatriya descent, or as in the case of the Great Darius, by establishing a network of marriages and forgeries that accomplished the same end.

In short, the present Shah — son of a great military man who did so much to restore a sense of history (he gave his imperial bodyguard the title "Javidan" — the Immortals, reminiscent, of course, of the Achaemenid title) to the present Armed Forces of Iran — carries on a great tradition. When he moves through the capital city (Teheran) on important occasions, it is quite reminiscent of a military manoeuvre — the point, the outriders, the closely packed cycles, jeeps and trucks moving at great speed through the streets. It gives the definite impression of power and is intended to do so. Unlike the warlike, but egalitarian Arabs, the Iranians constantly present such displays of strength to its people as a manifestation of monarchy. The same is true when the planes fly over Teheran every morning at dawn, on guard. The same is true in the statements that issue from the Shah. He never lets the people forget the humiliation of foreign occupation during World Wars I and II. He constantly reaffirms the national resolve that Iran will meet foreign aggression with an armed reply. There are a large number of military observances during the year that help to maintain the aura of strength. One of the most important is the anniversary of the liberation of Azerbaijan from communist-backed separatist rule that is celebrated in December of each year with full military pomp. In Teheran, the Shah — on horseback — first reviews the units selected to make the march past. The parade starts after the Monarch joins top military and civilian officials in the Imperial stand. In the provincial centers, armed forces units march past large portraits of the Shahanshah before thousands of spectators.

As would be expected, very senior officers are often of the royal family. The Shah's brother, Gholem Reza is a general officer in charge of the I-G (Inspector-General), thus closely tied in with security. The chief of the Air Force is, was for several years until killed in an accident, the Shah's son-in-law. He was the officer pilot who took the Shah and his Queen into exile in the fateful days of 1953. Other high ranking officers, however, are apt to be turned over on a fairly regular basis. Given the nature of the Monarchy, it is improbable that any officer would ever rise to challenge the historic role of the Shah.

The Imperial Armed Forces is, for a country of Iran's size, a powerful and well organized force. It is equipped with the latest weapons systems with great emphasis on mobility and fire power. The ground forces, consisting of 8 divisions, is supported by training establishments and combined army centres throughout the country. There are infantry and armoured divisions; airborne infantry; special force units backed by artillery, engineering and heliborne units, and three armoured divisions equipped with the English manufactured *Chieftain*, generally considered to be the best tank in the world. The central terrain in Iran lends itself easily to tank warfare. Whether or not future military engagement will see much of this is, of course, a moot question. However, tanks still are much in the thinking of the Iranian high command. A more sophisticated version of the Chieftain that is going into production in England is the *Shir Iran* or Persian Lion. It has a new hull and turret incorporating the expensive Chobham armour, a new 1200 h.p. Rolls Royce engine to replace the notorious multi-fuel L60 a new David Brown transmission and a new suspension. There is one SAM Battalion with HAWK. The IISS lists a complete rundown for those who are familiar with the terminology.[17]

Between 1974 – 1975 the United States committed itself to selling Iran more than $6 billion worth of arms, including some of the newest weapons that were just beginning to enter the inventory of American Forces. Along with this — even though the older military assistance program has been phased out — at least eight hundred official American technical and military personnel are in Iran. Another one thousand Americans are in Iran on private defense-related missions and there are about two thousand Iranians in military training in the United States.[18]

While American congressmen argue that the United States is sacrificing too much to Iran in the way of weaponry and technicians, American Foreign policy is clearly betting on the Shah to maintain the balance of the Middle East. So the United States continues to send F-14S and Phantom F-4S planes; to supply communications systems; an air defense network; anti-tank missiles; surface to air missiles; helicopters and electronically guided air to surface missiles. Eight Hundred additional Chieftains have been ordered from Great Britain along with highly mobile Hovercraft. Itemized lists could be extended indefinitely but these facts are available elsewhere.

Suffice it to say, that the best guess is that while not military, it would certainly function as a major support element and of course, the possibility of future conversion gives it additional importance. Iran has already begun construction of the first of possibly 25 nuclear power plants that it believes it will need. This is a 1,200 megawatt plant being built with West German assistance near the town of Bushire on the Persian Gulf. It is the first of two contracted for with Bonn, each to cost about

$1 billion. It is scheduled for completion in 1981. 149 of Iran's GNP at least, is going into arms as against 5.5% in the United States. Unlike the other oil-rich nations, Iran started its development long enough ago that when the oil boom hit, there was already in Iran an infrastructure that could handle a much larger proportion of the incoming wealth than could a backward nation like Saudi-Arabia, for example.

So it is that the Armed Forces in Iran stand in continued support of the Monarchy. The Shah devotes a great deal of time to conferences with the service chiefs and other key officers from units throughout the country, keeping abreast of conditions within the armed forces. It is hard to visualize a military coup overthrowing his regime as has happened so often in other countries in the Middle East.

Gendarmerie

Iran's Gendarmerie represents, perhaps even more than the Army, a glamourized peacetime version of Iran's great military tradition. Anyone who has travelled throughout Iran is not apt to forget the familiar depiction of the crouching soldier holding his bayonet which is painted along the sides of the occasional compounds flanking the main highway.

A prototype of the present State Gendarmerie which was officially established in 1922, dates from the constitutional period. In 1911 a mission of Swedish officers was engaged by the new constitutional government to create a para-military force in Iran with two objectives. The first was to balance and in a sense challenge, the traditional — and by this time corrupt — role of the military. Historically, the army belonged to the Shah. It was led by him or his Commanders. It owed its allegiance to him. Its organization, numbers, budget, and deployment were matters for his determination alone. When the constitutional movement challenged this traditional arrangement — and allegiance of power — clearly a new focus of armed power was required. The Gendarmerie, dating from the 16th century, had earlier served a similar function, particularly in France. It was well regarded in Europe. The employment of soldiers in police duties served many useful functions and it was only natural that the leaders of the constitutional movement should turn to this new device utilizing armed force for their answer to the naked power of the Shah. The Swedish officers did their job as well as could be expected under the circumstances and the Gendarmerie continued a rather chequered existence until 1922 when Reza Khan—seen at that early date in his rise to power as a defender of the constitutional movement—was able to stabilize the Gendarmerie as an active para-military force. "Gendarmerie Day" is observed therefore in Iran in February of each year as tribute to this important segment of Iranian life.

In addition to affording some kind of check and balance to the traditional army, the Gendarmerie, as created, utilized the very real need in Iran, for some kind of body in force that would have the expertize and organization necessary to maintain much needed internal security. To a large extent this role is the creature of the Americans.

In the decade following World War II, Iran was—to use a western expression—a "wide open" country. Those of us who travelled in Iran as late as the '50s knew very well the dangers of independent travel within the realm in that period. Bandits, tribesmen, brigands of all sorts, showed an independence of spirit and action that would startle a western traveller used to the security of his free transit. Tribesmen, of course, were not bandits in the ordinary sense of the word as they were subject to the will of their Khan and consequently, at the personal level, there tended to be more security for the individual than was provided by small forces of robbers and predators. But on a larger scale, the tribesmen did carry their warlike energies into the very face of governmental efforts to stabilize the countryside. I can remember in the late '50s an entire army garrison being wiped out by a well armed force of tribesmen in an area that one would have thought would have been secure. Clearly, a greater effort was required if Iran were to be domestically free from such local harassment.

When the American advisers came to Iran in the early '50s, therefore, their mission included close advice on the re-training of the Imperial Iranian Gendarmerie. As pointed out above, this was the work of the group known as GENMISH. The assignment was a difficult one—more difficult than the army in a sense. Many of the Iranian army officers had had contact with officers of other countries and had, on occasion, been trained in foreign countries. Militarily then, they could be said to be more sophisticated than the local models of para-military strength. But the American advisers were a highly selected group. For some years the chief adviser in the field, for example, an extremely able career officer with a Ph.D. from Yale, could only be said to have represented the finest American military tradition. His knowledge of Iranian history and literature was a credit to both Iran and the United States.

Today, Iran's Gendarmerie, often described in Teheran's newspapers as "the Crime Smashers", has become a glamourized version (Iranians are devoted to American movies) of the epic American "Gang Busters", the publicity surrounding its activities would have done credit to the late J. Edgar Hoover. The Nemesis of outlaws and smugglers, this latter day Goddess of Retribution is ever on the alert for transgressors of the orderliness of the Realm. "Shoot-outs" are not uncommon and the reports of the organization's "day and night activities" make heady reading for the interested public. In 1975 — a typical year — The Gendarmerie confiscated 35,825 firearms and arrested 2,975 drug smugglers.[19] 8,729 kilos of opium were impounded, 1,255 kilos of hashish and 9.5 kilos of heroin. The force also apprehended 10,163 smugglers carrying 12 million packs of cigarettes and "hundreds" of tons of smuggled tea and other goods. Over 40,000 electronic devices including T.V. sets and sound systems were also seized. The Gendarmerie also arrested 67,614 border infiltrators and 2,674 people trying to leave the country illegally. 39 forgery rings were cracked. The presently constituted Gendarmerie is concerned with the maintenance of law and order outside city limits and with the prevention of smuggling. It is a highly mobile force of well equipped units grouped in twelve districts, four of which are of brigade strength and eight of regimental strength. Most officers are seconded from the Army.

The Commander of the Gendarmerie is a general officer — at the time of this writing it was Abbas Qarabaghi. There are more than a dozen educational training centres throughout the country. There is a new computerized centre and data collection centre which are modern and up-to-date, furnishing information to the various Gendarmerie stations throughout the country.

In addition, the Gendarmerie control the roads and borders. There are over 5,000 motorcycles at the disposal of Gendarmerie stations and several thousand patrol cars (about 400 are added each year to the fleet to keep up with the 30% per annum increase in the number of vehicles on the roads). In addition the Gendarmerie has fast motor boats for the coastguard and a "large number" of helicopters and planes, particularly in support of the patrolling of the Persian Gulf and the Oman Sea by the Armed Forces.

Checkpoints are used throughout Iran as they are in most of the countries of Asia. While this can be of help to the inexperienced traveller in protecting him from violence, it can also be a useful device for the control of access. This is most noticeable in the gulf area. This area is always, of course, a potential problem as the resource value is such as to encourage local problems. Oil men have been known to complain that when trucks have finally, after long delays, gotten material cleared through customs and are on their way north, that they have stopped along the route and subjected to petty annoyances — papers out of order, lack of proper clearance, etc. — that really ended up with only one answer — the payoff. Such information is always difficult to assess but of course it does happen in other countries as well. On the positive side, there is no doubt but what the roads and highways for the traveller are much safer in the 70's than they were in the 50's. Incidents only very rarely occur now that occurred twenty years ago.

The Gendarmerie also keep track of air and bus travel and are familiar sights at all such terminals. It is really pretty hard to move in Iran without the Gendarmerie knowing.

Security and Intelligence

The "eyes and ears of Darius" were famous in ancient times even to the dissembling Greeks. The title "Eyes of the King" was given in old Persian to the official who reported on the activity of provincial governors. These informers of the King were chosen because they were "trustworthy, obedient, pure, devout, learned, religious and abstinent in worldly things."[20] Throughout the centuries, intelligence and security operations have formed an integral part of the Iranian monarchy. Few

Shahs have died comfortably of old age in their beds. While the Monarchy is sacred to Iran, individual Shahs are not always so considered. And so, a strong tradition has been maintained of not only protecting the frontiers of the country but maintaining internal security as well.

SAVAK, the present intelligence and security organization was established in 1957. The chief of SAVAK is appointed by the Shah and holds the portfolio of an assistant to the Prime Minister. Ten years ago, little was known of the organization's activity and a foreign visitor would in all likelihood not be aware of its presence. Recently publicity has changed all that. SAVAK together is almost as well publicized as the CIA. The Shah has even been asked questions about it on television interviews.

That the activities of SAVAK are so well known may or may not eventually result in important changes being made. But at this writing, certain generalities can be noted.

SAVAK activities include the necessary task of protecting the Shah's life. They do, in fact, tend to muzzle public — and even private — criticism, to a very large degree. There is once again in Iran a large American presence, this time technical people rather than military advisers. Anti-American feeling is strong among many segments of the Iranian populace. Criticism is not heard, though, as it is known that they are there on the invitation of the Shah.

In terms of personal freedom, there has been divided opinion as to what it means in Iran. Stories circulate about police-state repression involving night visits, torture, lengthy imprisonment, even death. Less dramatic measures of control may involve a lost opportunity to bid on a contract, a promotion withheld, restrictions on free travel.

SAVAK cannot, however, be blamed for all the wrongs in Iran that foreign observers and more recently, aggressive North American T.V. types, feel should be put right. There is censorship of the press but this is not necessarily SAVAK's doing. As shown elsewhere, there is an Information agency. Probably, however, caricatures of important officials, in whatever guise, would be of concern to SAVAK. It goes without saying that the Shah himself would never be attacked or depicted in an unfavourable light.

Similarly, violence in Iran, particularly that involving opposition extremists, may prompt SAVAK's response but it might also involve the activities of some of the Para-Military organizations of Iran, or even the Army.

It is difficult for North Americans to realize that Iran's common border with the U.S.S.R. is a fact of life and Iran has been under the big gun, so to speak, for as many years as most of us can remember. The term "Marxist" is a common epithet applied to guerillas. This doesn't necessarily mean that the entire business is a hoax and a cover-up. Russian infiltration has occurred and sympathetic behaviour — that is toward the Russian cause — has been present. Americans who remember the McCarthy period should not be unaware of how distorted the whole security problem involving world-wide communism can be.

Having said that, it is a fact that the International Commission of Jurists sitting in Geneva — consisting of 36 law experts from 30 countries — is on record as noting the failure of the government in Iran of according fundamental civil and political rights to the citizens of that country. SAVAK has been singled out by the Commission as being instrumental in this repression.

As one would expect of such an organization, SAVAK employees are carefully selected and highly trustworthy. While ostensibly it is a civilian organization it has normally been headed by a general officer. Its duties are the normal duties of security — gathering data on all parties, groups and individuals having a subversive potential, reporting on anti-government activity, counter espionage, collecting information pertaining to the security of the country and anti-regime activities. There is no doubt but what SAVAK is highly efficient. Some of the stories border, however, on the humorous. One was related to the writer by a foreign business executive of a somewhat explosive nature who in the midst of a very trying day — and days can be trying in Iran — grumbled something about "giving the country back to the Russians." Four months later he was invited to a royal levee. Shortly thereafter — but before the levee — he was contacted by telephone and that sentence among other things, was quoted back to him. He accepted the call as a chastisement and a warning.

Western spy chiefs give SAVAK exceptionally high marks.

for their intelligence-gathering operations. These operations are extremely efficient, even by standards which the West thinks belongs to it alone.

The size and scope of SAVAK is difficult to assess but the full time employees are said to number, perhaps sixty thousand. This is only the skeleton, however, It is a good guess that no fewer than three million Iranians are occasional informers, one out of eight. As a result SAVAK can be assumed to be everywhere. As the ancient proverb says : "The King has many ears and many eyes."

Exiled opposition groups say that more than fifty thousand political prisoners are languishing in Iranian prisons. Although the Shah hotly denies it, it is said that torture is used in Iran.

SAVAK is believed to have close ties with the CIA and Israel's crack intelligence agency, the MOSSAD. Officials of both deny it. However, the presence of SAVAK is a real one. As one Iranian put it to me: "In speaking of the Shah, you do not raise your voice. SAVAK may be listening."

There is no doubt but what foreigners as well as Iranians are under a good deal of surveillence. Academic freedom, for example, and the example is chosen primarily because the writer is a professor, poses real problems to the Monarchy. As the Shah says, "I am completely in favour of academic freedom if the students and faculty are not guilty of treason."[21]

After the attempt on the Shah's life in 1963, later Court Minister Alam installed an elaborate security system in the University of Teheran. There is now a well-manned security office right on campus. Moreover, some of the key administrative personnel is described (behind their backs of course) as being security men rather than academics. Certainly they do hold — and use — the power to keep the academic staff in line. The comings and goings of professors, as well as students, is carefully observed by attendants stationed in all corridors. No one has keys. Offices are opened and closed by the attendant. The University was closed three times during the year that the writer was in Iran last. Student unrest broke out in March 1970, when bus rates were raised. Although the police were out in great numbers, they did not bring in tanks — which had been done on a previous occasion

— nor was there bloodshed. However, student rioters are commonly jailed and it is said that they are often held without trial for several months. Students, of course, are a problem most places but the security problems surrounding the University of Teheran are unique in that a large under-privileged section (South Teheran) is not too far from the University and thus provides an open invitation to student agitators. Keeping students and South Teheran separated is an important task of SAVAK.

Security, however, in Iran does maintain a reasonable amount of flexibility with regard to the whole problem of academic freedom. Archaeologists, engineers, medical doctors, quite naturally have fewer problems. Sociologists, anthropologists and political scientists have more. While the writer personally encountered annoyances, he had no great problems during his sabbatical year and he did encounter many kindnesses. He knew of cases, however, where foreign professors felt themselves to be completely and deliberately isolated, where on other occasions permission to act was delayed until past the point of usefulness and even where in at least one case, a professor was given twenty-four hours to leave the country. In many of these cases, and particularly in the last one, there is not too much that can be said in defense of imprudence. Western academics are often inclined to think things are as they appear to be To give off-the-cuff interviews to enthusiastic reporters who are a part of a controlled press is gauche to say the least. Even in a classroom situation where local speculation suggests that one out of six — higher even than outside — students may well be police informers, the asking of questions suggests a prudent answer. In Iran, as elsewhere, success, if not survival, requires a certain amount of private ingenuity. In the immortal words of that intrepid mountain man, Kit Carson: "It pays to be shifty in a new country."

For the Iranians, of course, it is not a new country. It is an old country. And it is a country in which security has always been a fact of life. If the Monarchy were to go, security would still be there. Revolutions in the Middle East do not offer ideological alternatives to the problem of security. And so today in Iran all cities, towns, and rural areas are divided by SAVAK into districts, each under the supervision of a chief who is responsible for uncovering all anti-regime-activities within his jurisdiction. In this manner every important target is protected. It is highly improbable that the present successful mode of operation will be changed.

The Securing of the Gulf

The Persian Gulf, for one hundred and fifty years, was the private lake of Great Britain. There were no foreign representatives in the area except for British Political Agents and American Consuls at Dahran and Kuwait. The British resident at Bushire was the umpire to whom all parties appealed. Treaties were signed with the nine Sheikhs of what is now known as the Trucial Coast. The foreign relations of Qatar, Bahrain, and Kuwait lay in the hands of the British. Because of its weak position throughout the 19th century and the early part of the 20th, Iran was not a factor in the administration of the area — what British statesmen described as "the pacification of the Persian Gulf and the preservation of the peace of the waters." Journalists were not welcome in the area anymore than were idle travellers. What all of this amounted to was that few people in the world knew anything about the Persian Gulf.

In 1971, two events occurred which changed all this. One was the announcement in March that Great Britain would terminate by the end of the year its treaties with the Gulf Sheikhs and withdraw their armed forces stationed there by virtue of those treaties. The second was the confrontation in January and February between the Organization of Petroleum Exporting Countries (OPEC) and the oil companies. The oil companies, as we know, lost the confrontation and as far as oil was concerned, the balance of power shifted to the producing countries from the consuming countries.

Iran is unquestionably the main Gulf power today though the fact that Iran is a non-Arab country no doubt makes it difficult for some to accept this fact. On the other hand, Iran can point to the fact that as far back as the Achaemenid and Sassanian dynasties, the Persian Gulf was considered in the Persian domain. Further, Iran has no pipeline to the Mediterranean. All of its oil, therefore, has to be shipped via the Persian Gulf. Most of the key imports come in through the same route. Iran cannot afford to have an unfriendly power in control of the area. It is no secret that as far back as 1959, the Shah suffered disillusionment with CENTO. That organization — the Central Treaty Organization — was established in August 1959, and consisted of Iran, Pakistan, Turkey, and the United Kingdom. Its aims were mutual security and economic development. Rail, road, and radio links as well as harbours are included in the treaty arrangements. But, almost from the beginning the Shah mistrusted it and in fact in January 1959, he embarked on secret negotiations with the Soviet Union for a non-aggression pact. He has visited the USSR three times since 1965.

In October 1972 the Shah was able to get a statement out of the USSR issued as a joint communique to the effect that Iran and the Soviet Union expressed their firm belief that matters concerning the Persian Gulf region should be dealt with by the countries of the region on the basis of the U.N. Charter and without any outside interference. In April 1973, speaking to the Foreign Press Association in London, Emir Abbas Hoveyda, then Iranian Prime Minister clarified Iran's Gulf Policy:[22]

> "Let me in this respect explain Iran's policy in the Persian Gulf. Two considerations of paramount significance have governed and will continue to govern that policy. Firstly, that the Persian Gulf and the Sea of Oman constitute our southern borders; and secondly that they form the artery through which daily over 5,000,000 barrels pass today and more than 10,000,000 will pass by the 1980s. No one, and least of all Iran, would deny the littoral states of the Persian Gulf their legitimate interest in the waterway. This includes Iraq which, with some forty kilometers of coastline on the Persian Gulf, is one of its littoral states and must be treated as such to the extent that its natural presence warrants. But we cannot and we will not tolerate any subversive activity that would endanger the security of the Straits of Hormuz or the freedom of navigation in the Persian Gulf. This artery must remain open to international commerce and we in Iran have the determination and capacity to see that it does. The Indian Ocean which borders the Sea of Oman is also of vital importance to Iran."

Having early on made it clear that with Great Britain's withdrawal from the Gulf, Iran intended to fill the power vacuum, she took steps toward doing this by increasing her defense budget by a third in 1971 - 1972. From then on the budget rose rapidly to the present figure of $3,225 million. Much of the expenditure has been for re-equipping and modernizing. In fact with the order of the eight hundred Chieftains from Great Britain (the most powerful tank in the world), Iran began to step up the modernization of all the services at a very fast rate. When existing aircraft orders are completed, for example, the Iranian Air Force will possess some 355 modern fighter bombers and thirty of the very advanced F-14 naval fighters. When outstanding deliveries are made, Iran will have 660 helicopters. Iran is also in the process of acquiring from the United States, precision guided air to ground missiles and the latest anti-tank weapon, the TOW.

She is also procuring maritime surveillance and anti-submarine warfare aircraft. A recent study by the IISS gives an indication of how superior Iran's capability is vis-a-vis that of her neighbours :[23]

	Iran	*Saudi Arabia*	*Iraq*
Fighter Aircraft	30 F-14A	10 BAC-167	10 MiG-17
	108 F-4	50 F-5E/B	35 MiG-21
	131 F-5E	38 Mirage III	34 Sa-7
Helicopters			
	22 CH-47C	30 Commando	15 Mi-4
	46 AB-205A	6 Sea King	12 MI-8
	287 Huey Plus		16 Alouette III
	202 AH-1J		
	10 SH-3D		
Maritime Aircraft			
	1 P-3F Orion		
Long Range Transport			
	50 C-130	4 KC-130	2 AN-12
	6 Boeing 707-370	10 C-130E	
Armed Fighting Vehicles			
	800 Chieftain	30 AMX-30	350T-54/55
	250 Scorpion	? Scorpion	140 PT-76
	300 Fox	? Fox	

It can be assumed that with the increased oil revenues since 1973, that Iran will continue to maintain its superior position and, in fact, may even increase its lead due to the fact that Iran is in a much better position to absorb sophisticated weaponry into her armed forces complex than are her neighbours. In a sense, Iran can be described as having a thirty year lead on her nearest neighbour primarily due to the assistance program of the United States after World War II.

Iran's navy was described in the Iran Almanac, 1967 – 68 as "in the making." In a sense, it still belongs in this category. Although officially it was established in 1972. There is no history of sailing in Iran. What fleets were assembled in very early times were largely Greek manned and more recently, until the present era, very little, if anything was heard of Iranian sea prowess. An ancient calumny was that Persians were afraid of the sea. They well may have been. As a rule, even in our own culture, infantry and cavalry do not choose the sea-faring life. Be that as it may, while Iran's navy is still small, it is growing with her enlarged responsibilities in the Gulf. As pointed out above, at last count it consisted of thirteen thousand personnel. There are three destroyers, four frigates with MK Seakiller SSM and Seacat SAM, four Corvettes, ten patrol boats (the Gendarmerie has forty in addition), six mine-sweepers, four landing craft, and approximately fifty Hovereraft of various types (12 are the world's lattest) with others on order.[24] A key addition to Iran's naval arm will be a squadron of 6 missile equipped destroyers ordered from the United States at a cost of some $700 million. Iran is constructing a network of naval bases along its coast in keeping with its maritime might. Bandar Abbas has been designated as the headquarters of the growing fleet (Southern Command). There is also a small naval force in the Caspian (Northern Command) with a few gun boats and mine-sweepers.

Iran, of course, will depend heavily on her Air Force in the control of the Persian Gulf. The Air Force which was founded in the thirties, as already stated consists of fifty thousand officers and men and approximately two hundred and sixteen combat aircraft. Iraq has an air force of only ten thousand, five hundred personnel and Saudi Arabia fifty-five hundred. Iran's capability breakdown shows six fighter bomber squadrons with Sidewinder and Sparrow AAM; two reconnaissance squadrons; eight transport squadrons; twelve Huskie, several trainers, Rapier and Tigercat SAM; eight F-14 Tomcat, seventy F-4E, 141 F-5E; five F-28, six 707-320C tankers, twenty-two CH47C, two hundred and eighty-seven UH-1H/214A Huey Plus, Blindfire SAM radar.

Iran's build up in the Persian Gulf is seen as a stabilizing influence by both the United States and Great Britain. There is, however, a certain amount of tension between Iran and her immediate Arab neighbours. When Iran took over the three small islands at the southern end of the Gulf in 1971, Iraq tried hard to rally Arab opposition to the move, but was unable to bring it off. When Iraq attacked Kuwait territory in March 1973, the Shah offered military aid to the latter even though it was refused. Similarly the Shah gave considerable assistance, including troops, to the Sultan of Oman in his war against the Shofar rebels. As long as the dispute over the Shatt-el-Arab continues with Iraq, it can be expected that other tensions will from time to time erupt. Iran, however, has displayed a good deal of finesse in her dealings and as a rule handles her problems with firmness and apparent fairness. After all there is in relatively close geographical juxtaposition, not only a Shahanshah, but a King, a Sultan, ten Sheikhs, and a radical Baathist President (Iraq). This is a real assortment of prima donnas and it behooves Iran, if it is to continue its leadership role, to handle problems with care. The recent rapprochement with Iraq is an example of Iranian skill.

There is a certain segment of North American society that looks upon Iran as being a trigger-happy pretentious minor power. This is born out by some of the discussion revolving around that elegant airborne system called AWACS (airborne warning and control system). Iran wants 7, at a cost of $1.2 billion. Jimmy Carter has decried profligate U.S. arms sales. He views such sales "as an exceptional foreign policy implement to be used only in instances where it can be clearly demonstrated that the transfer contributes to our national security interests." On these grounds he decided not to sell the F-18 to Iran. But there are very strong pressures both for and against selling the AWACS to Iran. The matter at this writing had not yet been resolved, but a negative answer, as far as Iran is concerned, would be unfortunate. The Shah has been under great pressure to join the Arabs in the war against Israel, but this the Shah will not do. When he visited Cairo in January 1975, he reiterated his position that while Iran's sympathies were with the Arabs, "there is no question, of course, of Iran participating in the fighting."[25] Yet, at the same time that he accuses Israel of blocking progress toward a Middle Eastern settlement, he states that Iran would replace any oil Israel would lose as a result of returning the Abu Rudeis oil fields to Egypt. This is not inconsistent with the oil shipments to Israel from Iran in the past. In fact, the Shah professes a disinterest that must surely irritate the Arabs. "Once the tankers are loaded, we don't mind where the oil goes" is the way the Shah puts it.[26]

In a sense this essentially neutral position permeates an even enlarged foreign policy. The Shah has made it clear on more than one occasion that he is opposed to military alliances in the Middle East. "We must work for the day when this area should see the establisment of close regional cooperation which would enable us to tell the Big Powers 'there is no role for you in the military sense.' We are capable of fully protecting peaceful shipping ... when agreement among the countries of the area on safeguarding its sea and freedom of shipping ... happens we can ask the Big Powers not to come to us with their fleets."[27]

Foreign policy is not the concern of this book. However it is clear — to note in passing — that the Shah fully understands that he sits on a powder keg. With the great oil boom, the political aspirations of so many of the local peoples in the area are beginning to mount. As arms become more widespread, political violence is made easier. But the Shah is seen by many as representing a balancing force who intends to keep the lid on in the Middle East. Iran has not hesitated to move to serve its own interests. However, the Popular Front for the Liberation of Oman and the Arab Gulf is an example of the kind of problem with which the Shah must deal. The declared aim of this Popular Front to overthrow all the rulers of the Arab littoral states, except Iraq, and replace them with revolutionary regimes. If the insurgency in Oman were to succeed, there would be clear trouble in store for the present ruling heads of the area. The Shahanshah intends to keep his throne. Outside of a major upheaval involving the major powers of the world, the Security Forces of Iran should be able to manage that.

NOTES

1. Sykes II, *op. cit.*, p. 273.

2. Ghirshman, R., *Iran*, London, 1962, p. 162.

3. Quoted in Chew, Samuel, *The Crescent and the Rose*, New York, 1965, p. 211.

4. *Ibid.*, pp. 234 ff. The English called the Shah "The Great Sophy" which in Persian means "the Great Beggar."

5. Quoted in Sykes II, *op. cit.*, p. 176.

6. Chew, *op. cit.*, p. 293, 208.

7. *Ibid.*, p. 334.

8. *Ibid.*, p. 338.

9. Quoted in Sykes II, *op. cit.*, p. 183.

10. Quoted in Greaves, R., *Persia and the Defense of India*, University of London Press, 1959, p.9.

11. *Ibid.*, p. 25.

12. Sykes II, *op. cit.*, p. 411.

13. Motter, T. H. Vail, *The Persian Corridor and Aid to Russia*, Washington, D.C., 1952, p. 162 ff.

14. *Ibid.*, p. 163.

15. *Ibid.*, p. 443.

16. *Iran Today*, Teheran, 1976, p. 50.

17. International Institute for Strategic Studies, *The Military Balance*, 1974-75; London, 1974, p. 33

18. *Calgary Herald* (column of Marilyn Berger in the Washington Post) Jan. 31, 1975.

19. See the article in *Kayhan International*, October 26, 1974, p. 4.

20. Nizam al-Mulk, *Siyasat-nama*, Chaps. 11-14.

21. Bayne, *op. cit.*, p. 84.

22. Wright, Denis, "The Changed Balance of Power in the Persian Gulf," *Asian Affairs*, Vol. 60, Part III (October 1973, pp. 259-60). Sir Denis was formerly Ambassador to Iran.

23. International Institute for Strategic Studies, *Strategic Survey*, 1973, London, p. 42.

24. IISS, Military Balance, *op, cit.*, p. 33.

25. Interview, *Kayhan*, Jan. 4, 1975, p. 1.

26. *Ibid.*, p. 1.

27. *Iran Today*, *op. cit.*, p. 50.

CHAPTER 6

THE GOVERNMENT

Iran describes itself as "a constitutional hereditary monarchy."[1] The Shahanshah is the ruling Sovereign and Head of State. The government consists of three branches — the executive, the legislative, and the judicial. This is often misunderstood in the West as representing a system of separation of powers somewhat similar to that existing in the United States. What it is in fact, is the subject of this chapter and in part, that of the next.

The executive branch of government in Iran consists of the Prime Minister who is appointed by the Shah (technically on the recommendation of the Majlis). The occupant of that office at the time of this writing is Jamshid Amouzegar, who as Iran's oil minister, played a major role in increasing world oil prices in 1973-74. He succeeded Amir Abbas Hoveyda in August 1977. Hoveyda had successfully held that post for well over a decade — longer than any other Prime Minister.

The legislative branch of government in Iran consists of the National Consultative Assembly better known as the Majlis, consisting of some two hundred and eighty deputies. They are elected for a four year term and need not reside in the district they represent. There is provision for Christian, Zoroastrian and Jewish seats. The Majlis meets annually in Teheran on October 6, the anniversary of the opening of the first Majlis.

A Senate was provided for by the Constitution of 1906, but was not established until 1950. This Chamber has sixty members. Thirty of them are appointed from Teheran. Half of the members are elected and half appointed by the Shah. There are sitting women members in both houses.

The third branch of government, described as "independent" of the other two is the judiciary. It is headed by Minister of Justice with cabinet rank. The particulars of this branch will be considered in the last chapter.

Local government, technically a part of the Executive, is

provided for in Articles 90-93 of the Supplementary Law of 1907. They direct that provincial and district councils shall be set up throughout the country whose members are to be elected by the local populace.

There are fourteen provinces in Iran, including the Central Province of Teheran and six governorates (i.e., smaller, less developed areas). The executive head is known as the governor and he reports directly to the Minister of Interior. Each province is sub-divided into smaller administrative segments — country, district, village. Large urban municipalities have country or district status. The authority in all cases are appointed officers.

This is the way Iran appears on paper. In actuality, it is much different. Beginning with the Constitution itself, the present Shah at once professes loyalty to it but at the same time grumbles that "the Constitution was brought to us by the British and it was a defense against Czarist Russia. It was never really Iranian. It had been copied from the Belgian Constitution, with the power of the king stripped."[2]

In the Shah's view, it was his job to "Iranize" the Constitution. One of the effects of the Constitutional revolution was, in his view and others', to paralyze the central government and remove it as an active force in the Iranian political system. The great office of the Shah had been moved toward the exalted nothingness of the later Caliphate. The job, therefore, facing the Shah and his supporters was to re-establish the central authority. The intention and the effort made to do this was to be within the letter of the Constitution, however, rather than to press for an abrogation of it. As a consequence, the Shah came to take the public position that the Constitution was a positive thing ("It's good to have a Constitution"). Constitution Day in Iran has become one of the major observances of the year. In his message to the Nation on the 71st anniversary of the Constitutional Revolution,[3] the Shahanshah stated that "Iran would remain committed to its own concept of democracy and continue to avoid disruptive practices known as democracy abroad." His Imperial Majesty said Iran could not accept in the name of democracy "anarchy and disintegration of social criteria and institutions." "Destructive forces" that hurt the interests of the nation could not be tolerated.

"Constructive" forces, by contrast, were symbolized by the Rastakhiz Party (see below) which "for the first time since the victory of the Constitutional Convention embraced all Iranian men and women and facilitated their participation in national affairs". The "Rastakhiz dialogue", the Shahanshah concluded, "would constantly enrich and strengthen the nation's political consciousness, and its commitment to the achievement of increasingly greater goals".

The Shah was not alone in his encomiums on that day and most of the government leaders added to their praises of the Constitutional cause, the "Shahanshah's role in the development of Iranian democracy, power and prosperity". The Prime Minister paid tribute to the memory of Iranians who "sacrificed their lives" to gain the right to constitutional government. The Senate President, Jaafar Sharif Emami, and Majlis Speaker, Abdollah Riazi, both honoured the memory of the "freedom fighters" of 1905-06. The former drew parallels between the Iranian Constitutional Revolution and the French and American revolutions. He noted the "destruction of the shackles of absolutism and arbitrariness of government" as a result of the Revolution.

The Majlis Speaker noted that "anarchy and instability" followed the victory of the Constitutional Revolution and that "only through the establishment of the Pahlavi Dynasty" was it possible for Iran to recover the promise of those early years. First Reza Shah the Great and now the present Shahanshah, he recalled, have both given the dynamic leadership necessary to bring Iran into its own. In a closing note the Speaker proudly speaks of "an independent national policy, absolute sovereignty over its natural resources, prestigious world status and respectable military potential".

The Shahanshah now scrupulously seeks to preserve all the outward appearances of constitutional — or even Parliamentary government. He always opens the Majlis in a style reminiscent of the Queen of England opening Parliament and gives his own speech from the throne. Recently two new buildings to house the Majlis and the Senate were constructed of real architectural splendour that may not be up to the royal palaces but are very creditable structures indeed.

Government — Functional Aspects

When William Morgan Shuster, the American financial expert, was discharged as Treasurer-General of Iran in 1911, his legacy seems to have amounted to a steady succession of studies by western scholars — most of them American — as to what was wrong with Iran. Their frustrations over the years have been accompanied by such wry jokes as "You wouldn't believe what happened to me today." Response : "I'd believe anything you'd tell me."

In a sense, this is understandable. Iran does not function within the organizational pattern that is commonly accepted as the norm in the West. Even the simplest problems— getting a visa renewal or a carnet for one's car — seem in Iran to be fraught with enormity. So much of western political mythology hinges on the assumption that the function of government is to serve the public. This gives the average citizen the warm feeling of being important and of receiving services that he cannot otherwise afford.

Iran has fewer illusions than most about the nature and function of service. And this has been born out over the centuries by the unarguable fact that the Persians have had the reputation of being great administrators. When Aristotle was fussing with the problems of the Greek city-state, the Persians were successfully administering the greatest Empire the world had ever known. How is this to be explained ?

The explanation is to be found in the theory of concretisation that was explained in the Preface. All things point up into the prevailing political force, which in the case of Iran is to be found in the Monarchy. Thus the foreigner is really irrelevant to the exercise of political power in Iran — a hard fact to face. Indeed, he is a nuisance in a sense. There are any number of North Americans who have been asked in Iran why they do not stay home and worry about their own problems instead of coming to Iran to worry about those of that country. It is a good question but one that most people do not really appreciate. Voltaire's advice to cultivate one's own garden is one of the really difficult things for most people to learn. It is so much easier to make suggestions about somebody else's garden.

The functioning government of Iran, as is true elsewhere, builds upon the well-known relationship between political authority and its social setting. This requires the Westerner to shed many of his preconceptions and see Iranians as different from himself.

In 1954, a team from the University of Southern California went to Iran to establish an Institute for Administrative Affairs in the University of Teheran. When this writer was at the University 15 years later, that Institute no longer existed. It is not surprising. As remarked above, Americans — known for their administrative expertise are—both fascinated and horrified by what they encounter in Iran. After years of experience and personal knowledge, the impact is somewhat abated, but long tours of administrative duty are still the exception rather than the rule in the case of American advisers in Iran. And what is created today by *farman* and *fiat* with or without the advice of the foregone may simply cease to exist tomorrow.

A conspicuous characteristic of Iran is that it is a mosaic of peoples. The true Iranian is surrounded and infiltrated, so to speak, by Turks, Kurds, Arabs, even Americans and Jews. Consequently a very complicated social system has developed which fits into a concept of modern nationalism only with great difficulty. A part of the meaning of this mosaic is that divisions of labour are traditional in Iran. On Yom Kippur a large part of the bazaar will be closed in Teheran. Certain peoples do certain things. The mosaic, consequently, also represents status levels. Intellectuals are not merchants. They do different things. People in the upper classes do not wash their own cars or sweep their own floors. Neither does one, as the host, invite a guest to take his coat off and "be at home." No public officer of any rank in Iran would run around in his shirt sleeves let alone have his picture taken thus unattired.

On the face of it, all of this would suggest a high degree of inegalitarian behavior. In a sense, yes, one's friends are at the level of one's station. On the other hand, there is equality before Allah and this is no proferred opiate to the masses. In Iran, people are acutely aware of the differences that separate them. But the wealthy may not buy their space in the mosque as pews were once purchased in the Church of England. A beggar may be a beggar, but a monetary gift to him is an act of dignity. The donor understands that he is not giving a bone to a dog.

The mosaic system in Iran is generally organized on hierarchical lines.[4] Society is socially graded and a pattern of dominance and submission is pervasive. This is not at all inconsistent with that peculiar brand of Iranian individualism which will be remarked on below.

Even though the present regime seeks to promote a strong national image before the eyes of all Iranians it is nevertheless true, with only a few exceptions, that allegiance to family, tribe, religion, station is more important to the Iranian than his allegiance to the government.

Watergate shakes Americans to the point where they actually come to question themselves. The Iranian would not even bother to concern himself with it.

Public policy and its administration, then, begins to take shape in Iran as almost a familiar concept and way of doing things. National institutions therefore tend to reinforce rather than alter the traditional Iranian family pattern. Because this is true, public administration in Iran ceases to be, as in the West, a textbook version of what is conceded to be, efficient behavior. To list some of the variables :

(1) What the father is to the head of the family, so is the public official to those for whom he is responsible. The father's role in Iran creates a prolonged, dependent relationship that can extend into middle age and beyond. I can recall receiving a sad letter a few years ago from an old friend in Iran who had for years lived with his sister and a family of faithful servants. She had died and he was in great agony. His letter was a request that I — living then in North America — should find him a Persian wife because he was so lonely. I was his intellectual senior and confidante. It was natural that he should come to me in my role as a father image, his entire family now being gone.

(2) Dominance and submissive roles are learned early in life, starting with the family and continuing on thru one's working pattern and identity patterns. Committees therefore, work only with rarity in Iran. There can be only leaders and followers. The father may be a dominating one, even

tyrannical but it is his responsibility. He can't fob off that responsibility on his wife, his children, or the extended family. His total life — indeed the total life of the whole family — is inextricably bound into one.

(3) Safety lies in the family and with the father who alone will face the hostile world. Elsewhere, life is unstable and even dangerous. Interpersonal relationships are never completely trusted outside the family and indeed not always within the family, particularly if preferment is in the offing. Cooperation, therefore, which is so important to North Americans (to be "uncooperative" is a terrible stigma), is actually discouraged outside the family. Service clubs in Iran, as an example are really somewhat laughable duplications of what they are in North America or Japan. There is no such thing as external security. This is one reason why foreigners in Iran are beset with examples of evasion, delay etc. They have probably never asked themselves why anyone should cooperate with them. It's hard enough to get Iranians to cooperate with each other.

(4) Because authority in Iran is concentrated at the top, organizations tend to become top heavy. This is, of course, not an exclusive characteristic of Iran. Public and private bureaucracies the world over tend to suffer from this. The only thing is that in Iran, so many decisions must be made at the top, far removed from the immediate problem. And then, when the decision is made, it may not be administrative so much as a personal or an expedient one. A by-product of this concentration of power is that if political problems (and so many problems in Iran become political) can be moved through irregular channels, they may have a much better chance of getting solved. Work that follows a formal pattern in Iran takes a long time simply because so many things other than the immediate problem are at stake. To really move a problem into the maw of the machinery would in most cases be the height of folly. "Going thru channels" is so ingrained in North America that to do otherwise almost seems dishonest. In Iran, to do so, wins no plaudits and can make a lot of enemies.

(5) Appointments to government jobs in Iran depend on almost everything but Civil Service ratings (and there is a Civil

Service headed by a Director General). Dissident university graduates, for example, can be silenced by giving them a suitable appointment in the same way that a North American professor can be removed from the firing line by the offer of a lucrative consulting job. By and large, more administrative appointments in Iran depend on family and personal connections than not. This does not mean necessarily that nepotism — as that naughty word is known in the West — is the prevailing characteristic of governmental opportunity in Iran. It rather means dealing with a known quality rather than an unknown one. One can trust one's own people — at least hopefully — and Iranians are great believers in this. Further, in Iran, one has a great responsibility to one's family. An incompetent family member, of course, can only be pushed so far. Merit in Iran, as elsewhere, ultimately surfaces. But in the early stages of a man's career, this quality is not always easily discernible. Initial appointments, therefore, and the secondary stages of advancement, do not, in important instances, follow the rigid civil service pattern that obtained in early China, or later England, civil services that were a model to the world of how excellence can be made to serve the state.

The particular setting of Iranian political administration described above — a socially oriented one — also needs to be filled out with some brief recounting of the personal characteristics and traits of the Iranian people that are pertinent to the functioning of government.

Much has been written of the love of art and poetry, of discussion, of the strong emotions openly extended by the Iranian people. Some of these characteristics appear in the day to day functioning of government, and business goes better if due recognition is made. But this is not the place for an elaboration of what many foreigners learn to recognize as quite unique and wonderful when they have come to know Iran well.

What is less basic perhaps but more important for our purposes can be generally described as "cultural" traits which characterize the workshop of government.

The individualism so highly prized in the West — which is less fact than myth — is an obvious attribute of the Iranian. By western standards it is quite wrong headed — hence generalities about Iranian corruptibility, deviousness, slyness, etc.

In Iran, because of history, accident, and culture there is almost no sense of freedom. Hence a concept of individual responsibility and independence of action is almost entirely lacking. For an Iranian to initiate an action is unusual in the extreme. He waits and sees. He measures and assesses. He seldom acts. When the frontier barn burns down in Western movies, everyone pitches in and rebuilds it. There might be a joint effort of sorts in Iran in case of a family disaster — but there would be limits. Keeping oneself afloat is an arduous, full-time occupation in Iran affording little time for cooperative effort. Not that Iranians are callous to pain and disaster, they understand this better than most. But just as the Westerner is beginning to realize possible legal dangers in giving aid to an injured motorist, so the Iranian long ago learned that there is a chain of action that once set in motion may not come to the intended conclusion.

Hence the Iranian seldom offers. He refrains. Clearly his position dictates the course of action or inaction. In cooperative exercises, therefore, the Iranian is not at home. More likely than not he has more than his share of problems to worry about, his own and those of his family.

Westerners might say this is no individualism at all. But it is. It is different, however. It lacks, as a rule, the element of cooperation which is so important in the West. The Iranian is not particularly cooperative and certainly would not describe himself as being individualistic as would a Westerner. He is more interested in his place — where he belongs. Particularly, he is bound into a family in such a way that no creature of the great atomization of North America could immediately comprehend the attendant motivations of the Iranian.

Iranians are proud of their history and their history is very much a part of them. On the other hand, they have no such pride in government. The institutionalized virtues of government are quite foreign to them. Hospitality and friendliness are present. But it is a personal, not a public thing. The Iranian can be frank and honest. This is, to him, however, something quite different than what one might expect. In Iran, it is usually better not to anticipate the effects of one's own predilections.

People rather than things motivate the Iranian. This is a part of his individualism. Unless he is an intellectual, he doesn't really care about abstractions, theories, rationality, et. al. Persian speech, even political, is full of historical allegories and poetic illustrations. A well turned phrase is worth more than any logic. Hence, in government, objective values and standards tend to be vague, diffuse. Only when practices and procedures fall into personal focus do they come to have meaning. Decisions are highly subjective. One's manner, dress, attitude and connections are more apt to determine whether the foreigner gets an extension to his carnet than the merits of his case.

What appears to be unsystematic in Iran is merely so by western standards. If understood, things become quite systematic. The foreign business firms who have men on the ground who know Iran and the Iranians do much better than firms who send out an occasional representative to take orders.

Gossip is a great part of the Iranian ethos. It has a purpose. Iranians are highly competitive although they may not always appear to be so. To spread rumours — and after all this is a characteristic activity of most communities — is to seek particular ends by a method that the prevailing folklore rejects. Sometimes people are injured. This can also be the intent.

The great traditions of Iran have been remarked often in this writing. They figure as large in the thinking of Iranians. Iran has a history and a sense of history that perhaps only the Chinese can emulate. Iran has been in truth, the center of the Universe (as a headline in a Teheran newspaper read during the Trade Fair of 1970 when the writer was in attendance). Its poets, artists, philosophers are as great as any ever produced in any culture. The Westerner unfamiliar with Iran seldom understands this importance. In Iran past achievement is very important. The present is here, the future in the mind of Allah. Consequently the Iranian is very conservative and traditional. Conservatism is regarded as a virtue in Iran. Any deviation from established patterns is suspect. To do things as have been done before is understandably the norm. The present Shah has a major job on his hands as he pulls Iran kicking and screaming into the 20th century. The fact that he does it in ways that are not within the usual experience of the Western observer has made it difficult of explanation. Iran is here today, was here yesterday, and will be here tomorrow. It is a continuum of fact, but also of history.

The Council of Ministers

Iran's present Council of Ministers is of very ancient origin. It is not a cabinet as that term is used in parliamentary government even though it is often described as such. Neither are the members of Council sole advisors to the Shahanshah. Portfolios they may have in fact and they may have specific administrative tasks to perform. Yet the role of the Council is a singular one that does not identify easily.

As noted above,[5] there was a Council of State under the Sassanian kings which consisted of the various governors of the provinces, the high ranking generals who commanded the marches, the princes of the Royal Family and the great lords of the privileged families. This Council appears, however, to have served in a consultative role only. For example, on the question of the succession to the throne, "know that we have desired that in this decision the King of Kings should be unique among rulers, not consulting any man or being persuaded to an appointment."[6]

On the other hand, early sources, including the one cited, speak of "omitting no piece of council" and "consulting" with sufficient frequency to suggest that the earliest Councils did represent an important apparatus of State. The Sassanian kings tended for the most part to be prudent men and consequently one would have expected the role of Council to be an important one.

The pattern thus early established by the Persians of having the reigning Monarch surround himself by important men of his choosing continued on through the various changes and vicissitudes of Persian national life. Inevitably, the roles of Counsellor and administrator became overlapping ones. Tribal leaders, military leaders, sagacious men experienced in the ways of politics, all brought to Council great problems and responsibility of their own. So it was that the king's counsellors became on many occasions, as well, his administrators.

Under the Safavids, a more or less formalized Council of Ministers came into being. The *Tadhkirat al-Mulk* speaks of "Pillars of the Mighty State".[7] There were 7 of these persons which "since early times had constituted the body of council amirs." The most important of the Pillars of the State was the Grand Vazir or the Supreme Divan. A comparison might be to the Prime Minister of a parliamentary country. His orders and interdictions were pretty complete within themselves but he did, on occasion, refer important matters to the Throne and in turn was responsible for carrying out "whatever the King's sacred order may be."

The *Qurchi-Bashi* was the senior officer of all the tribes. The *Qullar-Aqasi* was in charge of the Royal Household. The *Eskik-aqasi-bashi* was 3rd in rank. "To his competence belong the affairs of the members of assemblies and the maintenance of order." In the most ancient of traditions in Iran, he was charged with ordering the places of those who were in assembly "from the highest to the lowest." The *Tufanqchi-aqasi* was the senior administrative officer including the army.

Other members of the Council included the Superintendent of the Royal Workshops and the chief judicial officer — an office that will be discussed below.

The Council of Ministers, during the Safavid dynasty, exercised varying degrees of influence. In periods of interregnum, for example, the Council became of particular importance. At the death of Shah Abbas, the Council, along with representatives of the Sufi organization, prepared and sealed a document confirming the succession. These deliberations leading up to and including the voting itself were recounted in detail by Chardin.[8]

There likewise existed, during the Safavid period, an established ceremony regarding the order of precedence. Added to the fixed rules of the administrative hierarchy, however, were such casual factors as time and political combinations as well as the personal prestige of the holders of office. Throughout it appears as though authority within Council was firmly placed in the hands of the Grand Vizirs, who were described by Chardin as the "real kings".[9]

Coincidental with the 237 years of Safavid rule (terminated in 1736 A.D.) there came to Iran a series of travellers who left written impressions of what it was they saw. They were modern men in a very real sense. When Marco Polo had travelled in the 13th century through Iran, he demonstrated all of the enthusiasm of a small boy.[10] Travelling within all the "eight kingdoms of Persia" he was intrigued with the land and the cities; the marvellous tales of the three Magi who set out from Saba to worship Jesus Christ and the Old Man of the Mountain; the road from Yezd to Kerman; humped oxen and fat-tailed sheep. But he was not a political observer.

By the time of the Safavids, the British Empire was moving toward India. Great commercial ventures like the Moscovy Company and the East India Company needed more precise knowledge of the countries through which they would move and with whom they would do business. Anthony Jenkinson, Sir Thomas Roe, the Sherley brothers, Captain John Stevens, Jonas Hanway were but a few of the new breed of businessmen who came to Iran. As is true today it was important for the success of their missions that they recognize the intricacies of political power and maneuver. To that end, they observed and wrote their reports.

Jonas Hanway, for example, writing in 1753, observed that "the favour of the Prince (Shah) and of those whom he devolved his authority, is essential to the security of foreign merchants; and this may be best preserved by proper and timely presents, by a good appearance, and a resolute support of their own dignity."[11]

John Pinkerton compiled in 1811 a general collection of "Voyages and Travel" which digested much of the work of what he called "the best authorities". The described period is that immediately following the murder of Nadir Shah (1750 A.D.)

Pinkerton states that "the Shah of Persia has no Council of State".[12] On the other hand, the author does go on to say that "he acts as he is advised by his prime minister and great officers". That is excepting the women. "That which most perplexes the ministry", he writes, "is the Cabals that are carried on by the women in the haram; the resolutions that are taken here frequently thwart their best laid schemes, and the ministers do not only run the risk of having their counsels rejected, but they very often turn to their own destruction, if they are not suitable to the inclinations of the ladies most in favour.[13]

The ministers of state, as listed by Pinkerton are, first, the "*atamadoulet*" (support of the Empire), or the grand Vizer or Vizier Azem. He is the first minister of State. "No business of consequence is transacted in the state but by the direction of this minister, nor any grant or act of state of the Shah's held to be valid, till counter sealed by him. Unlike the Grand Viziers of Turkey who seldom die a natural death, those of Persia are as a rule honourably retired", Pinkerton observes, "at the end of service to end their days in peace with their families."

The second ranking minister reported is that of *divan beghis* or bey. "This great magistrate is the last resort in all causes, civil and criminal, unless the Shah in person sits in judgement." The divan bey can command any case to be removed to his tribunal from any court in the land.

The third rank is that of generalissimo, the senior general of whom there is one only. Below him is the general of the *courtchis* (palace guard), the general of musketeers (dragoons, i.e. they serve on horseback but fight on foot), the general of ordnance, and the general of the royal slaves (the term slave is an honourable one in Persia. (The King's slave "is equal to that of Marquis of France," reports Pinkerton.) It is known that many of these "slave" soldiers were brought in from Georgia and the Caucasus and for that reason were considered more reliable than local soldiers exposed to the intrigues of local Chieftains and officials.

Sitting in fourth rank is the *vacanavish* or Secretary of State. He registers the public acts, has the care of records, appoints the deputies (not the governors) in every province of the Empire. These deputies whose function would be equivalent to what we would call a deputy minister, transmit all important affairs to the Secretary of State.

"The last great officer is the *mirab* or lord of the water. He coordinates with the provincial mirabs, the distribution of the water of the rivers and of the aqueducts.

"These are the principal officers of state". But there were other officers whose place in an extended council are noted by

Pinkerton. Those of the household are small in number and are concerned largely with finances he remarks. The most important is the *nazir* who is Lord Treasurer and steward. Ambassadors and foreigners transact their business with this man.

Pinkerton writes at some length of the ecclesiastical offices of the realm and believes them to be of great importance, not merely as religious leaders or administrators, but as well in keeping with that most ancient of Persian traditions "for Church and State were born of one womb, joined together."[14] So they likewise functioned as councillor.

The "Grand Pontiff is usually styled the *sedre* in Persia. They also give him the title of prince, head of the true church, substitute of Mahomet, and lieutenant of the twelve Imams."

Apparently there was continuing tension between the secular authorities and the Pontiff which suggests that the western "Doctrine of the two Swords" might also have existed in Iran. Apparently dominion of the laity "is in usurpation," he notes, and "government belongs of right to the high priest." On the other hand, the regal power exercised by Princes "is derived of God and the high priest and his brethren ought not to meddle with politics."[15]

Apparently, because of the extent and power of the ecclesiastical courts, "lawyer and divine are terms of the same significations in Persia." The *sedre* and his substitutes are the ordinary judges in all civil as well as ecclesiastical cases. Pinkerton is confusing on the respective roles of the *sedre* and the *divan beghis*. He does state that the *sedre* and the temporal judges under him "have no written laws to go by but their decrees are found on ancient custom". On the other hand he states that the *sedre* "is the Supreme judge in the ecclesiastical courts".

The second ecclesiastical judge "is the ancient of the land, whom the Persians style *cheik islam*." However, his jurisdiction is little inferior to the *sedre's*. The *cadi* is the third ecclesiastical judge in Persia. His authority is confined to a particular town or district.

The *mufti*, that well known figure in story, is the fourth. His position is inferior to that of the *mufti* in Turkey. His role appears to be advisory in the main.

The provinces, as in very ancient times, are officered as well, in the national pattern. According to Pinkerton, the two chief officers are the vizier who has the government "of all those towns and villages which are the King's demesne lands" and the *chan* who has the government of the province in general. The word *chan*, or *Khan*, denotes princely caste and as in the time of the Sassanians, he is deemed sovereign within his realm. They have "exactly the same kind of officers as are in the Shah's court, with the same titles, there being scarce any difference but in numbers and pensions." Pinkerton points out that functioning as they do as Kings, the "Shah of Persia is styled now, as his predecessors of old, King of Kings."

These *chans*, or governors of the provinces, hold their position for life and often their children after them.

These, then, are the great men of the realm described by Pinkerton as representing the Chief advisors and support of the Shahanshah. They form concentric circles of power. The small, intimate group of officers is the Grand Council or the inner Council. Beyond that is the extended council, still of no great size, but larger by perhaps three times. So writes Pinkerton.

In the autumn of 1889, almost 100 years after Pinkerton's observations, Lord Curzon made his memorable trip to Iran. He had gone out as a correspondent to the "Times" and his objective was to furnish to that paper a resume of the political situation in the Shah's dominions. No better observer could have been sent. His own great career, which stopped finally at the very threshold of No. 10 Downing Street, was itself a tribute to the political sagacity of this distinguished man and it would be expected that any political observations that he would make in other walks of power would be of the highest order.

By now, the Qajar dynasty had held power for almost a century. A distinguished family of Turkish origin — they had held the equivalent of the rank of an English dukedom under the Safavids — they had imposed a harsh and even brutal rule on the country of Iran. The dynastic founder had set the pattern. Castrated in the fierce struggle for power in the dying years of Safavid rule, Agha Mohammed became an iron man — harsh, shrewd, unforgiving — but with a great sense of balance in his political maneuvers. Though the seat and cradle of the Qajar family was at Astrabad, Agha Mohammed believed it to be too remote and too far situated to the East to suit his expanding ambitions. Consequently in 1788, he selected Teheran for elevation to metropolitan rank and named it his capital. Teheran had no particular history other than being a fabled home of Teherani troglodytes who lived underground in a semi-savage state, at war with their neighbors and in revolt against the sovereign. However it was well situated. Agha Mohammed was within easy reach of his own patrimony and tribesmen. He was in a better position to watch Russia. He could easily move, as he did for the next seven years after his accession to the throne, against rebellion in South. But Teheran contained a population of only 15,000 ten years after it became the Capital city.

The Council of State, which assisted the Shah in governing his Empire was a fluctuating size according to Curzon. All members of Council served as deputies to One who held plenary power. The ministers were appointed by the Shah and were elevated or degraded at his pleasure (also true of the royal family who could be reduced or elevated in position and power). Some of the ministers held portfolios, some did not. The Council seldom, if ever, exceeded 30 in number but those exercising real influence were considerably less. As a rule — and this is a long tradition in Iran — the Shah presided over his Council and it did not meet without him. More often he met with the ministers out of Council. As chief administrative officer, the Shah's duties could be extensive and demanding, requiring considerable time. Nasr-ed-Din Shah, the Sovereign, betrayed what Curzon (who himself possessed many of the qualities he attributed to the reigning monarch) described as "a voracious appetite for any and every affair of State." His mornings were devoted to audiences with his ministers and to matters of State. The smallest detail was submitted to him and not decided until he had made the final decision. Every department was subject to his scrutiny.

Lord Curzon states: "There are at present seven ministers who may be described as possessing portfolios, the division or concentration of which will strike European readers as both arbitrary and eccentric."[16]

The King's first minister, the traditional Grand Vizier (Sadr-Azem), was not at the time of Curzon's visit, filled. Apparently there had been, on the accession to the throne of the Qajar, strong contention between this office and that of Commander-in-Chief (Amir-i Nizam) with the result that for the next several years, the office was vacant for long periods of time.

The Prime Minister (not, therefore, the first Minister), as Curzon calls him, was a 34 year old man of great energy and acumen. His official title was Amin-es-Sultan or Trusted of the Sovereign. He was "the most important personage after his royal master." He united "in his own person, the Ministers of the Interior, Court, Customs, and Treasury, besides being Administrator of the Mint and Governor of the Persian Gulf Ports. He is also practically Foreign Minister as well." He had travelled with the Shah in Europe and "at any rate to English ears, was of Anglophile sympathies." Quite naturally given his age, he was seen as an upstart and schemer by other ministers.

The Amin-ed Dowleh was one Mirza Ali Khan, a man of middle age "and great cultivation." He stood second in rank among the ministers and was considered hostile to the Amin-es-Sultan.

He united in his own person the Presidency of the Council, with the Ministers of Posts, Pensions, and Church Properties. Curzon saw him "as the most attractive personality whom I encountered in Persia" who lived in a fine home decorated in the European manner. He did, however, give the impression of one "whose enthusiasms were dead" and there was, at the time, a notable lack of initiative and energy about him.

The portfolio of Foreign Affairs, the Kawam-ed-Dowleh (support of the State) was in the hands of Mirza Abbas Khan. Curzon describes him as belonging to the old school. He did not, unlike the Prime Minister, accompany the Shah on his trips to Europe and the real control of foreign relations does not lie with him but with the Shah and the Prime Minister. "In spite of his portfolio, he is little more than a political cipher. He is a man of great wealth and industriously administers his department in Teheran."

The Minister of Justice and Commerce, Yahia Khan, "probably is the cleverest of the public men in modern Persia".

He was married to the Shah's sister in a somewhat complex context reminiscent of Darius's day. The lady was the Shah's sister by the same mother. She was first married to a distinguished minister of Council who was murdered by the Shah in 1852. She was then given to the son of his successor in that post. Upon his disgrace and exile a few years later, she left him and married her uncle who died. Hence Yahia Khan was her fourth husband.

Other Ministers of Council listed by Lord Curzon are the Minister of War; Minister of the Press, Ali Kuli Khan, who combines Ministries of Public Instruction, Telegraph, and Mines. There are other ministers of Council but they are not listed, as being unimportant. Actually, Curzon notes two things about the Council. (1) There exists an *imperium in imperio* in the Council of State in shape of a small Council of Five who advise the Shah on the matters of highest importance. These five as listed by Lord Curzon are the Amin-es-Sultan, the Naib-es-Sultaneh, the Amin-ed-Dowleh, the Kawam-ed-Dowleh, and the Mukhber-ed-Dowleh. (2) As in the case of Safavid reign powerful men outside the Council do function, on occasion, in an advisory role. Lord Curzon singles out the Amir-i-Nizam, a former Minister, who had been Ambassador to Paris and Governor of Kermanshah and Kurdistan, who is considered the best provincial administrator in Persia and Fathullah Khan, a wealthy nobleman of Shiraz. The latter was also formerly a Minister who is now Governor-General of Khorasan.

So in Iran, as elsewhere, there exists the formal and the informal rule. Tables of organization have meant little in Iran. A trained observer, therefore, in a position to see and understand the operation of government, could, as in the case of Lord Curzon, describe for the western world the function and personnel of the prestigious Council of State as it stood on the eve of the constitutional crisis.

One thing to be noted in Curzon's observations on Qajar rule is the fact that no high ranking religious man sits in Council. This represents a distinct break in the long history of mighty men next to the throne. The reason for this omission is not accidental. Qajar rule ushered in a long period of conflict between the State and the religious leaders, particularly the *ulama*. Clerical influence was lacking under the first Qajar monarch, and it continued although some of the Qajar rulers were known to be religious — and even pious — men. The secularization of the Council of State was continued after Agha Mohammed's death. This is not to say that religious forces were not present and were not strong within the realm. To the contrary, much of the Constitutional Crisis after the turn of the century, could be attributed directly to the power of the *ulama*.[17] But much of this was of a retaliatory nature against the ruling house.

The Constitution of Iran adopted in 1906 mentions the Council and the Prime Minister twice. It speaks of ministers who are appointed and dismissed by the Shah (Art. 46). Article 67 provides for the dismissal of Ministers should the Majlis or Senate wish it. The attempt in Convention to fix the size of the Council — Majlis approval would be necessary were it to be enlarged — had not met with success.

The early years of constitutional jockeying between the Majlis and Shah will be recounted below. While the power and position of kingly rule was diminished in the early years, the accession of Reza Khan to the throne very early tipped the scales toward the princely power. Decisions were increasingly made at the Court level and were carried out by the Majlis.

The abdication of Reza Shah once again moved the see-sawing struggle between the Shah and the Majlis back into the political arena. 1941, like 1911 and 1921, before it, were difficult to say the least; unstable to say the most. Between 1941 and 1952, alone, 16 Councils were officially installed and eleven persons served as Prime Ministers. Hundreds of Council appointments came and went during those early years. Considering the fact that the Constitution does not give the Prime Minister the power to dismiss ministers, it was inevitable that the entire political procedure for appointment and replacement should become a political football.

Moving to the present, as noted, the naming and dismissing of ministers in Iran is a power that belongs exclusively to the Shah under the Constitution. He may also act independently of the Majlis in dismissing and naming Prime Ministers. It is not surprising, therefore, that the change over from Amir Abbas Hoveyda as Prime Minister to Jamshid Amouzegar on

6 August 1977 caused no public comment, let alone any disturbance within the Majlis.

The function of the cabinet is twofold (1) to draft and present to the Majlis for approval, the laws and decrees of the realm. The Shah will, on important matters, issue an "Imperial Farman", instructing the Government. The drafting of legislation will follow. The Shah is quite careful not to act unilaterally under the Constitution (2) to perform the necessary staff work for the actual operation of government. Unlike the President of the United States, the Shah does not have a large immediate staff that would be equivalent to the White House staff. This function is performed by Cabinet Ministers. Each ministry, of course, has its own under-secretary, under-staff, budget, etc. as do their counterparts throughout the world generally. But the minister in Iran is much more than a mere administrator. He is a power in his own right and while he is constitutionally responsible to the Majlis, in fact he is not beholden to the Majlis for his position. In this sense he more closely approximates his counterpart in the United States than in a parliamentary country such as Canada or Great Britain. He does not sit in the Majlis nor does he represent a constituency, either a voting one or an interest one. He is the Shah's man. He also sees himself in the role of a deputy. The only requirements for appointment are that as a Minister he must be an Iranian citizen, of the Muslim faith, and not a member of the Royal family. As a staff, the Council of Ministers functions in a particular way. The Shah sees the Minister of Court, the Prime Minister, the Foreign Minister, the Governor of the Bank Melli and the Director of the Plan and Budget Council on the same basis. The Prime Minister among other things is the liaison between the Shah and the Cabinet.

Actually in Iran, the really important policy making today is the High Economic Council. It is an extra constitutional body, having no real authority and consisting of an ad-hoc membership that the Shah selects from various ministries and other important institutions in the country. The Shah presides over this body and it is said that discussion is clear and frank among the members. The Shah listens more than he talks and then makes up his mind. If the discussion does not focus clearly, he advises the group to redefine the discussion for a later session. Most master policies are discussed by this group but not necessarily all and the formulation in its final form is the Shah's.

The Prime Minister is not necessarily a part of all this. As pointed out above, he has an important liaison role and even historic. His office really quite closely approximates that of the historic Vizier. As first Minister, the extent of his power is determined by the discreet amount of control he exercises. He may not, as in the case of Dr Musaddiq, challenge the Shah. On the other hand he must serve usefully and well. Officially he is recommended for his office by the Majlis. In fact, the real selection decision is known only to the Shah.

His office is saddled with day-to-day jobs. An astonishing number of sub-offices are attached to the Prime Minister's office — State Security and Intelligence Agency, State Organization for Administrations and Employment Affairs, Endowments Organization, Imperial Inspectorate, National Tourist Organization, and the various authorities attached to the former Plan Organization — which has now been turned over to the Ministries. The Plan Organization has its own planning council headed by the Prime Minister.

The Council of Ministers then can be said to be essentially a body for the delegation of authority rather than for determining policy for Iran. But it does not follow that membership in the Council is, thereby, unimportant. To the contrary, this membership is a highly desirable one in Iran. It places the member close to the Throne which is the prime consideration. It also provides prestige, patronage and a ministry of one's own.

The relationship between the Prime Minister and the members of Council is pretty straight forward. Procedures are quite informal unless the Shah is present. The old Muslim concept of consensus is important in observance. There is occasional voting but as a rule, sharp divisions are avoided. At any rate a vote would not be binding on anyone, anyway. Decrees must be supported by a majority of the Council. While it is possible for an individual minister to have particular legislation introduced into the Majlis, this would be an unusual procedure. Proposed legislation is funnelled through the Prime Minister. There are no committees within Council although naturally some Ministers are more important than others and an inner group, as inevitably exists, would be seen in Iran to be the key ministers. The fact that there are important groups outside the politically designated Council, is also important as noted. Many decisions are made in Iran that are not a matter of Council's consideration. Powerful groups such as the National Iranian Oil Company pretty well stand alone vis-a-vis their relationship to the Shah. (The NIOC profits in 1976 stood at 17.1 billion dollars US the highest in the world).

There is, in Iran as elsewhere, a considerable shuffling of personnel within the Council (cabinet). This does not mean any particular dislocation of administrative function. There is an Under-Secretary in each ministry, as mentioned above, who function as do under-secretaries elsewhere. The ministry carries on. Movement within the Ministries tends to be lateral, however. Throughout the years, various posts within the Council tend to be held by a limited number of individuals. There are some 24 portfolios within the Council. A few deserve mention here.

The most important minister does not attend meetings of the Council and is in no way responsible to the Majlis. This is the Minister of Court (the present Minister is Amir Abbas Hoveyda) who has charge of the royal finances, the permanent property of the Crown, including the many royal palaces throughout the realm, and is concerned with matters of protocol and ceremony. He is what is termed in Washington D.C. a VIPI (a Very Important Person Indeed).

The Ministry of Foreign Affairs is of course, an important post. At this writing the Minister is Abbas Ali Khalatbari. In recent years, however, Ardeshir Zahedi, has tended to move back and forth between that post and that of Ambassador to the United States. There are five political departments within the Ministry. There are consulates, legations, and embassies in about 30 countries. Iran does not, as remarked below, have "honorary" consuls abroad. All posts are staffed by Iranians.

The Minister of Defense is another, most important post. During the days of Reza Shah, this Minister and the Minister of Foreign Affairs were really the only ministers who seemed to play any kind of a prominent role in government. Official publications, of course, emphasize the Shah's role : "the Imperial Iranian Armed Forces, headed by His Imperial Majesty the Shahanshah Aryamehr, who is the Commander-in-Chief ..."[18]

The Minister of Finance presides over a very large ministry housed in an immense modern building in Teheran. There is a myriad of divisions within the Ministry — customs, taxation, budget, concessions, accounts and inspection, etc.

The Minister of the Interior is responsible for the internal administration of Iran. Provincial officials report to this Minister. Governors of the provinces were in earlier times, extremely powerful and quite independent men. Today they have been pretty well brought to heel but whether they report always to this Minister or on occasion to the Shah himself, is not clear. The Minister of Interior is also the responsible Minister for Internal Security.

The Minister of Justice holds a strategic position as Iran moves more and more into the area of legal reform. He and the Attorney General work closely together. Iran's judicial system is modelled after that of France. It is a hierarchy of courts leading up into a Supreme Court, as will be discussed in the next chapter.

There are two ministers dealing with education. The Minister of Education is charged with Public Instruction, Religious endowments and Fine Arts. In the field of education proper, the Minister is assisted by a Council of Education consisting of some 20 members. The Ministry of Science and Higher Education, on the other hand, is concerned with the higher educational system. This consists of both public and private institutions that grant degrees and institutions affiliated with government agencies. The University of Teheran, founded in 1934, is the most prestigious. Today, there are 10 full universities functioning and 5 more are in the planning stage. There are some 150 other institutions of higher education, 87 of them affiliated with the Ministries and the National Iranian Oil Company.

Other ministers, frequently the subject of press releases, are those of Agriculture, Energy, Industry, Transport and Housing (all replaced in a major shuffle announced in August, 1977);

the Minister of Planning and Budget; the Minister of Health; the Minister of Labour and Industrial Affairs. There are other ministries, less well known, including a new portfolio (since 1976) "to handle party affairs".

There are two Ministries that deserve special mention here simply because they present so well the two faces of Iran. One looks backward, a proud hold upon a great heritage. The other is ultra-modern, a model of what is seen so often in highly aspirational nations. These are the Ministries of Culture and Information that face each other in Council across the century and yet which are strangely alike in function and direction.

The Minister of Culture heads up an influential ministry with a large budget and staff. The activities of the Ministry include in recent years the publication of a large number of important books that are not to be found in bookshops or purchased from the Ministry itself. The Ministry also has a massive collection of original treatises on archeology, urban history of Iran, Persian mythology, Islamic thought, linguistics and architecture and it is rumoured that there are even volumes on the historic institution of the Monarchy in Iran. (I searched diligently and could not find them.)

The Ministry has also commissioned on its own, a large number of studies. A few years ago, as an example, a detailed and massive study of every aspect of life in Baluchistan as well as that region's history, topography, geography, natural resources and manpower potential was carried out by an Italian firm. No one — at least outside the Ministry — has ever seen it.

Again, the Ministry has, over the years, collected thousands of folk tales and recordings of folk songs. Contrary to popular belief, a comprehensive series on Iranian villages and tribes (western scholars are always getting grants to study Iranian villages on the grounds there is no information about them), that is probably unique in the world lies in the vaults of the Ministry. The Turcoman village of Incha-Buron in the Gorgan Plain, to take one of them, is one of the best documented rural spots in all of Asia.

Films ? There are tens of thousands of short documentaries that were commissioned by the Ministry that have not been shown.

All of the above, and much more, are contained in the archives of the Ministry and a non-library known as the Pahlavi Library. High officials in the Ministry of Culture will say they know nothing about all this. It is as good an example of Defensive Bureaucracy in operation as this writer has seen.

Why should a Ministry go to the trouble to assemble these massive materials and then not make them available ? The first part is simple. As any administrator knows, it is as important to keep your budget up as the RPM's on your car. This Ministry is a big operation and it needs money to function.

The second part is a little more difficult. Iranian traditions tend to be secretive. Pupils and disciples were traditionally never taught all by the "morshed" or the teacher. The latter always kept something back. He thought it impertinent to appear as if he knew everything about a subject because only God knows all. He did this in exactly the same way as the weavers of Persian carpets deliberately include "a mistake" in their work in order not to appear to be challenging God's. supreme perfection. Further, scholarship has always been seen in perspective as an individual matter in Iran. Scholars were suspicious of teams that uncovered the mysteries of nature. They themselves held themselves in reticence regarding these disclosures. Then, too, knowledge was sought in Iran for its own sake and more often than not, in abstract fashion. It was perhaps exciting to make discoveries in nature but the knowledge thus gained was seldom intended for practical purposes. It was simply beneath the dignity of an accomplished "hakim" to make use of his knowledge of mechanics, for example, for the purpose of designing and putting to work a simple and seemingly ridiculous machine which at best would appear as an act of offense against the Divine order.

All of this points to the existence of real ambivalence regarding the work of the Ministry of Culture.

Many of its employees are young, even western educated, "Hakims". They know the western ways of doing things like making documentaries and team studies and they approve of them. But, the line between doing something and making it known to the public in Iran is still to be drawn. The only text on Constitutional Law the writer has ever seen in Iran written by a living scholar, reads like a primer — sections, sub-sections, articles — in short a detailing of the various articles of the Fundamental Laws — no commentary, no elaboration of any kind.

So it is generally in Iran. How much should Iranians know about their country and its working? Clearly there is danger here. If political theory in the universities is cut off at a point prior to the American and French revolutions, which it is, clearly there are strong forces in Iran that would oppose the release of too much research into Iranian life. The Shah, of course, is pushing a literacy program. But there is solid evidence that he distrusts social and political studies as possibly opening Pandora's box. Obviously nobody is going to ask him how far to go in these matters as he is truly a busy man. But normally in Iran it is more prudent to sit on something than release it. To this extent, the Ministry of Culture is very much a sensitive arrangement of political expediency.

The Minister of Information is quite another type of Portfolio. Although the Constitution of 1906 provided for freedom of the Press, the Press Law of 1955, amended in 1963, redefines that freedom. In addition to establishing educational and financial criteria for persons desiring a license to publish a newspaper or magazine, the minimum circulation requirements, etc., the law stipulates that "no newspaper or publication may be suppressed without a court order except when they publish articles against religion, the Iranian monarchy, or when they report on troop movements, publish other military secrets, entice the people to resist government troops, or publish ... material of a pornographic nature."

The Ministry of Information is the principal government agency supervising the information media and enforcing legal provisions applicable to the Press. The present Minister (September 1977) is Darioush Homayoun, a former newspaper editor and political activist. This Minister is the government's spokesman to the Press and he orients the editors on current government policy. Criticism of the Shah and of the government's policies and programs is not permitted.

The writer can recall an example from his own experience that points this up. Engaged in discussion with a government official, the writer made some comment about certain aspects of education reform about which he had reservations. The official's eyebrows shot up and putting a severe look on his face, he said, "Ah, you are opposed to the Shah's White Revolution." There was simply no way to get through to this man that individual points of the reforms might profit by some discussion. For all these reasons, it is very difficult to assess the current White Revolution and the more specific aspects of the Plan Organizations that implement the White Revolution. Statistics must be handled with care. Formerly, organizations like the International Bank for Reconstruction and Development could and would provide accurate information. More recent policy, however, restricts such information and in fact refers inquiries "to official channels of communication of member countries." This, of course, puts the ball back in the old ballpark.

The Ministry of Information controls this ballpark as far as Iran is concerned not only in the manner described above but in more extensive ways as well. Because the Shah is skilled in western public relations and publicity techniques, he closely guards the operation of this Ministry. He — through the Minister — pretty well determines what the government information activities shall be and the Minister is charged with carrying this out not only for domestic consumption but foreign audiences as well.

The Shah is also — and this is an important mission of the Ministry — the central figure in the country's information program. A major phase of government publicity programs is directed toward a wide dissemination of information about the Shah's activities. Every newspaper carries a front page article on the Shah everyday. The fact that the White Revolution has become the Shah's personal achievement over the years is characteristic of the careful planning of information activities. Only Mao has perhaps done it better, but the Shah certainly runs him a close second. Even the Chairman and Managing Director of the National Iranian Oil Company, Dr Manuchehr Egbal, a very powerful person, carefully credits the Shah's wise leadership with being responsible for the oil windfall of recent years. To a large extent, of course, this is true, which gives a certain fascination to the person and position of the Monarch vis-a-vis his image.

So it is with the Minister of Information. It's an essential assignment as the Shah sees it.

Generally speaking, then, the present day Iranian Council of State consists of important men in the realm, as in the days of Ardashir, whose reliability and loyalty to the Shah is equally as important as their administrative ability. They are political men even though they are non-political, as noted, do not owe their position to a constituency, or even to the Majlis. They are a very special group, supplemented and complemented by other councils and other authoritative figures within Iran.

The Majlis

The Majlis is invariably seen by observers either as a rubber stamp for the policies of the Shahanshah or as a nuisance — sometimes by the Shah himself. It has, in fact, played a difficult role in modern Iran simply because there has been no tradition upon which it could draw. The Prime Minister, the Council of Ministers, the Ministry of Justice are in a very ancient tradition. Not so the Majlis. Nevertheless, this body functions today with dignity, an important arena for debate, discussion and publicity. If there is no great leadership here, there is no particular place for it at present.

The word itself "Majlis" means King's Assembly and in Safavid times it referred to the audiences granted by the Shahanshah, the proceedings of which were recorded. These in turn were put in due form as orders issued from the Throne. This labour was done by the Majlis-nivis ("Recorder of the King's Assemblies") who has variously been described by historians as a private secretary or an official historiographer.[19]

The Majlis, as noted above, consists of 280 deputies who are normally elected every four years by nation wide male and female suffrage upon attaining the age of 20. Separate deputies are elected to represent the principal religious minorities — the Armenians, the Assyrians, the Jews, and the Zoroastrians.

The Senate, also as noted, has 60 members, half of them popularly elected and half appointed by the Shah, with thirty members chosen from Teheran. The Senate, like Senates elsewhere, speaks to the historic greatness of the Roman Senate — even though in fact modern Senates are apt to be a faded carbon copy of Rome's great glory. Iranian Senators must be Moslem, 40 years of age with at least 15 years' experience in the public services. Employed, salaried government employees are excluded. Senators are to be selected from "among the well-informed, discerning, devout and respected persons in the country". (Art. 45, Constitutional Law of 1906). While considered co-equal to the Majlis, the Senate may not deal with financial matters.

Officially, the duties of the Majlis are quite simple and even restricted. Unfortunately, we have no authoritative studies of the Majlis. There are committees within the Majlis but we know little of their operation. Neither do there appear to be powerful geographical constituencies to push programs through their elected delegates. In short there is little solid information either in Iran or out on the function — as opposed to the duties — of the Majlis. Officially, one paragraph in an official publication on the 50th anniversary of the founding of the Pahlavi dynasty provides the nutshell :[20]

> Bills may be presented to Parliament by the Government, in the person of the responsible Minister or the Prime Minister, or by a member of the Majlis, provided in the latter case that the bill is supported by 15 deputies. Normally bills first pass through a committee stage before being voted on in the Lower House. If approved, bills are then debated in the Senate and after approval receive the Imperial assent and become law. Legislation may also be initiated in the Senate, but the annual Budget and bills concerned purely with financial matters are voted on exclusively in the Lower House, although the Senate may make comments and suggestions. Parliament must also approve any concessions, Government loans or disposal of State property.

The Majlis today could not be described as a strong institution. It is perhaps even weak by comparison with other Iranian institutions. Its membership has been variously recruited from the landowning class, from professional and business groups, from some of the new rich, but the Deputies could not be described as belonging to the aristocracy. Within the Majlis, certain politically advantaged Deputies could be said to dominate the leadership and control what few committees exist. They have not in the past, however, been necessarily the leaders of the political parties nor have they been particularly active in debate. Except for a small inner group gathered around the Prime Minister, the turnover of leadership has been high.

Wherein, then, lies the significance of the Majlis ? If it is not just window-dressing, what is it ? What it is lies within the interstices of what is described below.

The Majlis and the Shahanshah, since the Constitutional Crisis of 1906, have intermittently — depending upon the power of the Shahanshah at any given period — been engaged in a continuing struggle, each side claiming as a constitutional right and heritage the primary role in Iran of reformer and revolutionary.

It is easy to lose sight of this. The program of the present Shahanshah is an extensive one — oil nationalization, land distribution, plan organization, and above all the White Revolution. But these things could have belonged to the Majlis and there were periods where it appeared as if they might. The nationalization of oil, as remarked above, is a clear example.

Perhaps if one theme could be used to comprehend the continuing tension between the Majlis and the Shahanshah over the past 70 years, it might well be that of modernization. Both wanted it. Both claimed it. For the present the matter seems resolved. This would not necessarily continue if the present Shahanshah were succeeded by another.

But to return to 1906, and the great debate on the matter of rule. While one of the aims of the framers of these laws was to deprive the monarch of his arbitrary powers and to ensure the functioning of the government along more modern lines, it must not be assumed that the Persian Constitutionalists were in any sense seeking to remove their autocratic ruler. The establishment of the Persian Constitution must be regarded as a nationalist (i.e., patriotic) rather than a democratic movement. It was rather the threat of political force from without than the tyranny of an autocrat within that drove the Constitutionalists to devise, in such a comparatively short time, the Persian Constitution of 1906. One of the first acts passed by the Majlis when the Assembly met for the first time on October 7, 1906, was to veto a proposed loan of $400,000 which Great Britain and Russia were to make to Persia in equal proportions, in order to provide the Shah with funds for fresh extravagances. The action served to underscore the known fact that for years, the western nations had poured enormous amounts of money into the ancient kingdom for the purpose of corrupting its rulers and driving a wedge between the people and the national interest. In a very real sense, therefore, the purpose of promulgating a new constitutional regime in Persia was a patriotic one; one intended to restore the ancient integrity as between ruler and subject; one intended to preserve the heritage of a once-great Empire.

In this sense, the move for constitutional government in Persia is to be distinguished from similar moves in the Middle East, where very often, foreign advisers were instrumental in devising constitutional instruments. The Persian action should also be distinguished from many of the constitutional developments in Western Europe where so often monarchs were deposed as not representing the best interests of the people. To the Persian Constitutionalists, the Shah was still the key to government; more than the key, he was the cornerstone. It was inconceivable to the Persians that there could be government without the Shah. For unlike the more democratic Arabs, the Persians had been firm believers in the divine right of kings. The man who sat on the Peacock Throne was the descendant of Cyrus, who thought he was more than human by birth, but was not surprised or annoyed when Croesur suggested that he was only human.[21]

Reza Shah, the father of the present Shah, ruled from 1925 to 1941. He began by promoting his "new order" with great force but without disturbing the underlying power structure.[22] He eventually moved in his rule to a personal military dictatorship. In the early days of his reign, modernization and reform were the keynotes to action and much was accomplished — even if he did have to wear his boots into a mosque to make a point. Construction of the trans-Iranian railway, the creation of state-owned or financed industries, was a long step forward. Law reforms and the fostering of education were begun.

Because of his great position as founder of the present ruling dynasty and because he shares with Cyrus, the title "Great", it is important to give at least some brief accounting of Reza Shah's achievements. What follows is generally how Iranians themselves view this powerful personality.

Reza Shah is generally described as a soldier and statesman — as a rule being depicted in uniform. On 21 February 1921, he marched at the head of a column of the Cossack Brigade from Qazvin to Teheran and seized the city. It was a bloodless coup that lasted less than 24 hours. Reza Shah wasted little time in asserting his primacy over the new government. He took cabinet position as Minister of War and in 1923 became Prime Minister. In 1925 he was crowned Shahanshah. This ended his active career as a soldier. Despite the fact that he had served with the Cossack Brigade for a number of years, little or nothing is known publicly of his military service.

Once the Constitutional Assembly (Majlis) voted to transfer the Crown from the Qajar ruler (Ahmad Shah was a mere boy) to Reza Shah, the new ruler was faced with formidable tasks calling for qualities of statesmanship. The Treasury was empty, the government bankrupt and few expected Iran to retain its independence or territorial integrity. British and Russian troops were on Iranian soil and large parts of the country lay outside the central government's control. The tribal leaders were virtually autonomous in their provinces. The Qashqa'i and the Baktiari tribes (later dealt with severely by the present Shah) in particular are mentioned in official accounts. The most powerful single dissident in the realm was Shaikh Khazal, governor of Khuzestan. He exercised his office pretty much as a personal fief — having his own army, refusing to pay taxes, dealing with the English, etc. Along the Caspian, another dissident, Kuchik Khan, sought to establish an independent republic, and he like Shaikh Khazal had to be subdued.

Because of the Bolshevik revolution, Russian influence at the time of Reza Khan's ascension to the throne was considerably lessened from earlier times and the special nemesis was now Great Britain. Lord Curzon, who in 1889 had travelled throughout Iran was now British Foreign Secretary. His efforts to secure a treaty with Iran appeared — to the mass of Iranians — as an attempt to turn Iran into a British protectorate.

In short, during this most difficult period, Reza Shah was faced with the formidable tasks of restoring domestic order, collecting taxes, resisting foreign pressures, and stabilizing a government that admittedly had only a tenuous hold on its governing position.

Specifically, Reza Shah did a number of things. He started building the army from his days as Minister of War and eventually men like Shaikh Khazal were forced to capitulate in the face of military confrontation. The Gendarmerie was reorganized and strengthened and the Swedish officers of the original force were replaced.

The Iranians see Reza Shah essentially as a builder in the pattern of Ataturk, the Turkish "strong-man". He undertook a vast building program:— a network of roads to bind the country together; the rebuilding of cities; the opening up of resort areas along the Caspian — Ramsar, Chalus, Babolsar—; above all the construction of the trans-Iranian railroad, in its time one of the great engineering feats in history. One of the Shah's favourite poses was leaning out of the window of one of the cabs.

Trade and domestic commerce were, understandably, an essential concern of Reza Shah and for a man who was quite distrustful of foreign powers, it was a considerable achievement that he was able to accomplish as much as he did in that field. He abolished the concessionary tariff system designed chiefly to benefit English and Russian trade and he established in its place a system of protective tariffs. He imposed Government monopolies over key items, such as sugar, tea, grain, and tobacco. He sought to impose a uniform tax system.

While Reza Shah was himself not an educated man — the old madrasseh was dominant and there were few schools in the country — he recognized the importance of education. The University of Teheran was created and the first steps taken toward public support of education. At least in his public life, Reza Shah was committed to the emancipation of women. The university was created co-educational. He abolished the veil (and is said to have publicly kicked a *mullah* who refused to admit unveiled women to a mosque). Girls were entitled to attend public schools.

The glorification of the pre-Islamic past reached its zenith under Reza Shah who, of course, took the name Pahlavi for the dynastic title. Important families were encouraged to take historic names. National poets and ancient traditions underwent a considerable revival of interest. Statues, streets, mausoleums were created in their honour. No nation ever displayed in such a brief time so overwhelming a recognition of the glorious past.

The person of the Shah is an important part of his image. "Tall, straight, soldier-like ... powerful, piercing eyes ... a big man ... to the end of his life he remained an imposing figure." His tastes were simple. He cared little for dress, preferring the uniform. His taste in food was plain. He shunned luxury. When he arrived at Mauritius in exile, the governor of the Island had set aside his finest room (complete with a four-poster bed) in his finest house for the deposed Shah. Reza Shah asked that he be given a simple soldier's mat on which to sleep.

World War II marked the end of manhood's run for Reza Shah. There is little mention made in Iran of the domestic and foreign policies of the Shah during this difficult period. Officially Iran refused to expel a large German trading community in Iran at the request of the allies. The demand for expulsion was in any case partly an excuse. The allies needed a land route. On the night of August 24, 1941, British and Russian troops moved to secure their interests and Axis embassies were closed. September 16, Reza Shah signed the declaration of abdication. He travelled by ship first to Mauritius and then Johannesburg. One of his last acts was to stoop down and pick up a handful of Iranian soil.

When Reza Shah was taken into exile, the 14th Majlis which was elected in 1943 seized the purse strings — as was its constitutional right — and demanded that the cabinet and ministerial appointments, including the Prime Minister, receive a vote of confidence before taking office from the Majlis. The emergence of the Tudeh party gave a strong measure of strength to the parliamentary claims vis-a-vis the young Shah. This party which as pointed out above, is now outlawed in Iran on the grounds that it is a Communist inspired party originally consisted of some members of the Communist International but also had a large membership within the Majlis of loyal

Iranian deputies some of whom had been imprisoned by Reza Shah.

The Tudeh party gave strength to the Majlis. It created the concept of a Majlis as being something other than a rubber stamp and this was the position reached when Dr Musaddiq emerged in strength at the 15th Majlis in 1947. There followed — full sovereignty was restored to Iran the year previous — then a struggle in Iranian politics with the young Shah fulfilling the public role of a constitutional monarch while quietly trying to recover the absolute authority of his father.

The struggle for power in Iran — and it should not be forgotten that both the Shahanshah and the Majlis saw the Fundamental Law as a mandate — reached its climax in 1952 – 1953. In October 1947, the United States and Iran had signed their military aid pact. Up to that time, the Shah had no party. The Majlis saw this action as moving to restore the old military regime of Reza Shah. Consequently they sought a close check on the budget as well as a check on ministerial appointments (except for the Minister of War) as mentioned above.

This see-saw for power then continued up to 1951 when Dr Musaddiq became Prime Minister — the last Prime Minister not to be hand-picked by the Shah. The next year, he was able to force the War Ministry portfolio for himself as well as retaining the post of Prime Minister. The events of the next year are too well known to require recapitulation. On 16 August 1953, the Shah, his wife and the lone pilot flying his plane (late Chief of the Air-Force) left Iran.

The Shah's return to power inevitably swung the pendulum to the Shah. One of his first acts on his return to Iran was to dissolve the Majlis by Royal decree — the first time this had been done. The country was placed under martial law and remained that way for three years. SAVAK became a permanent government agency and Dr Musaddiq was placed under house arrest to eventually die. The modernization of the Army moved swiftly ahead and the Shah, his immediate family, and his close associates at Court moved to unparalleled positions of powers. Elections in 1954 and 1956 for the 18th and 19th Majlis were closely managed by the government even to the point of nominating candidates and supervising the balloting.

The 20th Majlis was elected in August 1960 and the election was nullified by the Shah as fraudulent. An election rerun in 1961 did not please the Shah more, so he dissolved the Majlis for the second time and again placed the country under martial law.

Many of Dr Musaddiq's former supporters — including some high ranking religious and military leaders — together with his student demonstrators and dissident leaders of the Majlis, now appeared to challenge some of these recent actions of the Shah. The Shah finally moved against them in a harsh counter attack. The army was purged at the highest level — many names disappearing from the public scene whose fates several years later were still unknown to former acquaintances. Religious leaders like Khomeini were arrested. Protestors before the bazaars in Teheran were gunned down. Tanks invaded the University of Teheran campus. As the rioting spread to other cities, it was put down by the army in bloody fighting. How many thousands were killed will never be known. But the Shah's power has never been challenged from that day. Elections were called in 1964 for the Majlis and no opposition candidates were allowed to run, previewing the single party system of eleven years later.

Such displays of power are, of course, not unusual in the history of Iran. What is perhaps interesting in this case — and it must be realized that the Shah felt himself justified in taking this action — was that the Shah felt his projected reforms were being thwarted.

When Dr Musaddiq emerged as the strong man of the Majlis in 1947, his supporters knew him as a man who not only had resisted the tyranny of Reza Shah, but who had publicly indicated that foreign influence — which was still very strong in Iran — must go and more important, that the old Iranian pattern of entrenched, inherited wealth, of landlordism, of nepotism, of all the forms of economic control of the life of the nation by the few, must be altered. This was, of course, seized upon by some, as being communistic and resistance developed accordingly. Nevertheless the Shah was not yet in a position to do much about it. Because his father had never built a political party, the concept of party was not clearly understood in Iran and has really never been understood in Iran to this day. The Shah's position was simply that the Constitution gave him great powers and it was his right to exercise them. Dr Musaddiq, on the other hand, saw the whole Constitutional Convention and the subsequent promulgation of the Fundamental Law as creating, above everything else, a Parliament that was to serve the nation. Logically it followed in his thinking that the Shah, as a constitutional monarch, was really above and outside the political conflict.

This is not to say that Dr Musaddiq was on the side of the angels. As a large landowner, he stopped the Shah's distribution of Crown lands because he feared this would create an example which he and other landowners would have to follow. This, despite his impassioned pleas against entrenched, traditional wealth. Further, Dr Musaddiq's assumption of dictatorial powers in 1952 – 1953 was a naked thrust for power. He abrogated the fragile structure of constitutional government with no promise of future alleviation. If the Majlis was to serve the nation, he gave no hint as to how that would be accomplished. Finally, Dr Musaddiq's alliance with the Tudeh party was not clearly defined and riding that particular tiger — communist organization — has never been the most fruitful of exercises as regards constitutional government.

As pointed out above, the two were on a collision course and in Iran the traditional power of the Monarch is not apt to be the one that gives way. For a brief moment, however, it looked as if it would. The immediate events surrounding the Shah's brief exile have already been remarked.

Dr Musaddiq's nationalization of the oil industry in 1951 had aroused the foreign community that attended closely upon developments in Iran's economy. His actions had also aroused many of the tribes who traditionally looked upon the Shah as being truly Shahanshah and who really did not understand much about parliamentary government anyway. Finally Dr Musaddiq, while certainly having a strong following both in and out of the Majlis, could not expect much support from traditional landlords who might have their problems with the Shah, as they had had under Reza Shah, but who were not really prepared to go along with the general reform movement that now appeared in the offing.

So it was that the forces to restore the Shah to his throne

from exile were set in motion. The most colourful support came from the Houses of Strength (Zurkhaneh). These unique types of gymnasia date from the days of Cyrus the Great and represent the traditional love of Iranians for chivalry, heroism, and pageantry.

Essentially the Zurkhaneh is a round hall with an octagonal pit in the middle in which these athletes perform traditional exercises to the accompaniment of a colourful ceremony led by the leader (Morshed). He sits on a raised platform beats the drum and recites verses from the *Shahnameh.* The verses exhort the athletes to cultivate humility, modesty, love of country, loyalty to the Shah, along with the physical strength.

When the word came that the Shah was returned, it was quite a spectacular sight to see these powerful men march along the streets swinging their exercise clubs, clearing the streets as they went.

Not unexpectedly, the CIA involved itself with, among other things, the purchase of a broadcasting station in Teheran.

General Zahedi, father of two recent concurrently serving Ambassadors to the United States and Canada, a third powerful supporting element, rallied his forces and moved his manpower into Teheran for the restoration. He was appointed Prime Minister to succeed Dr Musaddiq on the Shah's return.

With the restoration complete and Dr Musaddiq destroyed, it was clear that the Shah would have to come up with something. He did so on November 11, 1961.

The Shah's proclamation on reform was made public at the meeting of the Council of Ministers in the Marble Palace on that date. Thus was the modern sector created in the womb of what came to be known as the White Revolution.

The Shah has continued to guard his Revolution almost as an exercise of the prerogative. For example, Dr Ali Amini, Premier of Iran in 1962 and a member of the Qajar family, was being praised by United States officials — diplomats, economists, and engineers — for his work. The press releases were beginning to refer to the "Amini reforms" which put him close to the Musaddiq reforms of an earlier period. The Shah was said to be put out by all this as he felt references should be made to "the Shah's Reforms." On April 11, 1962, the Shah and his Empress arrived in Washington D.C., for talks with United States officials who expressed their hope publicly that his visit would bring his Imperial Majesty and Dr Amini closer together. The United States regarded this as important because they had been trying for months to put together a group of loans for Iran's five year development plan to be promulgated summer 1963.[23] But when the plan was finally promulgated, it was the Shah's — no one else was even mentioned.

The actual recounting of the essential reforms[24] — and they, of course, have been added to since that day — was prefaced by a statement in which the Shah expressed his concern "for this country and its people" and his determination to take immediate steps "for achieving the social, material and intellectual advancement of the realm" "for the comfort and well being of the people and the establishment of social justice and progressive development of individual members of the community," "to the end that a life for the nation would be achieved" "in keeping with the standards of the modern world."

The preface clearly limned the Shah's role as the architect of modernization. His personal responsibility, as well as his concern, was clearly set out. This role was emphasized by the fact that the Proclamation on Reform was pronounced when neither the Majlis nor the Senate was in session. This, it should be pointed out, was clearly the way the Shah wanted it. The Majlis had begun to make noises in this direction in 1958–1959 when two anti-corruption bills had been passed and again on 16 May 1960 when a land reform law was passed limiting land holdings to four hundred hectares of irrigated or eight hundred hectares of unirrigated land. But the Shah was apparently struck by the late President Kennedy's approach to the problems of social reform and his reference to "social justice" echoed the American voice on that subject. The Shah, therefore, was clearly prepared to take the initiative — although not without dissent. The National Front, for example, issued a strong statement describing the Shah's constitutional claim to this initiative as "a return to despotism fifty-five years after the Constitution was inaugurated." The statement went on to say that "the throne and the Executive Power do not have the right of enacting laws and the enactment of law is among the special rights of Parliament."

In 1962, the Shah had not yet decided on the course to

follow with regard to this dissent. In an address to the National Press Club in Washington, D.C. on April 13, 1962, the Shah's speech reflected some indecision. "This King business has given me nothing but headaches," he declared. He was living under constant "strain and stress," had suffered vilification and attempts on his life, and had presided over the liquidation of almost the entire royal fortune. In this speech, the Shah pleaded for sympathy and understanding and urged the Americans to refrain from hasty criticism of his regime.[25]

1963 ended this dialogue. When the Shah told E. A. Bayne in an interview in 1955, "I am going to rule," he succeeded to this validation in the bloody riots of 1963. Thereafter no one challenged the Shah's right to his Revolution. To return now to the Proclamation of 1961.

The essential reforms as named were originally six in number, later increased to twelve. The first (only the original reforms will be considered here) concerns Civil Servants. Rules for service are to be uniform among the several ministries. Close attention is to be paid to both recruitment and administration. The terms of promotion and retirement are set out.

The second proposal was actually a continuation of the first but more carefully defines the matter of priorities. The army, police, gendarmerie, Ministry of Justice officials and professors and teachers, in that order, are given priority. Thus, the top officials of these categories of state employees are early designated for what is termed in Iran "the modern sector".

The third proposal deals with agriculture. Mechanization is to be the order of the day. Land reform and limitations of proprietorship are to be put into effect. If the land reform laws prove impracticable, then "the government must embark on its revision in whatever way it is deemed necessary." The throne was clearly reserving to itself the right to adjust the nature of land reform as it went and this is clearly what happened as will be seen later. The peasants are, as in former times, to be guaranteed their welfare and well being. Development projects intended to increase agricultural production are enumerated—road construction, irrigation channels, chemical fertilizers, etc.

The fourth proposal once again blueprints the nature of what came to be known as the modern sector. Like the peasants whose wages do not go up despite other guarantees, the condition of labor in Iran is held to be "satisfactory" in the Proclamation on Reform. Working housing is encouraged but employers who do this are permitted to reckon this expenditure as a portion of the insurance they are to pay for worker protection. The government is to guide and aid in the matter of industrial installations.

The fifth proposal deals with tax revenues. It is pointed out that many of the wealthy still do not pay their fair share of revenues and that an "ethical relationship" should exist as between the tax payers and collectors. Clearly there were to be no "soak the rich" slogans in Iran echoing some of the more vocal aspects of F.D.R.'s New Deal.

The sixth program calls for a revision of the education program. Free elementary education should be broadened and vocational training provided. The Ministry of Education "must watch pupils from the very first day they enter primary school, keeping records of all with outstanding ability." Bursaries are to be made available to outstanding students from poor families. Students may go abroad to study but the "utmost care" is to be taken that this is a worthwhile expenditure if the government is picking up the tab.

The conclusion of the Shah's proclamation as presented in November 1961, ended with an appeal for "social justice" for all Iranians, a phrase without any tradition or possibly even meaning in Iran. It was, however, one that was considerably in vogue at the time, particularly in the United States.

It is not inconsistent that the establishment of a privileged economic sector in Iran — which was really the end result of the new reforms — should be described as revolutionary. The term "White Revolution" has in fact become the key phrase in Iranian modernization. In the Shah's mind, revolution, his revolution, is to follow a peculiarly Iranian pattern and not merely ape what is popularly associated with that term elsewhere.

The White Revolution also becomes a master plan. Iran is, at this writing, preparing for its Sixth Plan. The details of the successive Plans are of no concern here. But over-all Plans are increasingly associated with strong, nationalistic sentiment. At the Ramsar Conference held at the delightful resort on the Caspian in July 1974, the Shahanshah began to speak of the "Great Civilization" that was to become.[26] "Every Iranian", he observed, "must sense a special responsibility at this momentous crossroads in Iranian history." There are moments in history, the Monarch intoned, when nations are confronted with a convergence of opportunities and possibilities." "Fortunately these unique possibilities are available to us today. ... A failure to seize them would be both a pity and also a great sin." He warned the nation against the misuse of its wealth by imitating the bad example of the western powers; that Iranians must "vaccinate and immunize" themselves against these abuses. Unlike other countries, the Shah said, in Iran, the promised land was not "each day postponed for a few years later." The Great Civilization is not merely a "promised paradise." It was here. The Shah concluded his speech by saying that the country now had the means to assure the well being of every citizen.

The decision to create a modern sector with all the appurtenances of Plan Organization, and give to it the fruits of this modernization, followed an age old pattern that was peculiarly Iranian.

It was pointed out in the first Chapter that "controlled penetration" in the early days was the method by which the Shah provided for the security of his realm and assured the viability of the economy. This is precisely what is happening today. Political reliability is required of those who are to receive the fruits of modernization. Loans are in abundant supply because there really is no shortage of money in Iran. Furthermore interest rates are comparatively low. But the point is one must qualify. Not everyone is admitted into the promised land. So the penetration of individual members of the populace into the modern sector is almost entirely controlled by the government. Those that can provide a service and are politically reliable can come in. The rest stay out. This does not mean that the national income will not rise generally or that the per capita income will not rise. It does mean that the lion's share goes to a small group at the top with changes gradually being made that may eventually involve the whole population.

What does this lion's share look like — to the observer who has been in and out of Iran over two decades ?

The first thing that strikes one — and these observations are personal and impressionistic — are the changes in appearance. This writer can recall in 1959 watching the sheep graze on the slopes north of Teheran that today are covered with middle and upper class housing. He can recall staying in the best hotel in Isfahan — a modest bungalow-type unit owned and operated by a German couple. Today it sits quietly in the shadow of the Hotel Shah Abbas — one of the great hotels in the world that perhaps exceeds in luxury anything in North America. Twenty years ago, travel was not always safe. There was robbery and pillage and I can recall hearing of a small army garrison being wiped by tribal marauders. There was little to buy except marvellous handicrafts — and they were not expensive. The best night club in Teheran was more like an old-fashioned vaudeville than a Las Vegas production even though the attractive French entertainers were still around on the Middle East circuit (later they were banned in Iran).

So many things have changed and I should say most of them for the good. From a backward nation of forty years ago, Iran has been transformed into a cohesive country with a large, dynamic, and increasingly modern, economy. The basic strategy of development applied in these recent years aimed at creating a modern sector that is modern in its production methods, its consumption patterns, and increasingly in its intellectual outlook.

This pattern is not being followed elsewhere in the Middle East. Other revolutionary regimes aim at lifting the whole by the bootstraps. But Iran deliberately chose a different way and while it has been criticized for doing so, there is no doubt that given the objectives of the present government, the creation of a modern sector has borne much fruit. It must be understood that most of the fruits, and the means, of development have been given to this sector. The result, of course, is that while the rest of the country has not been wholly neglected it is this select group which has grown fast in per capita income and in relative population size. The frenetic activity of this group reminds one humorously of the Caucus race in Alice in Wonderland "Everybody has won and all must have prizes." The key explanation for this phenomenon is to be found in the extremely high investment and the impact of the large and fast increasing foreign exchange inflow from the oil sector. This has made the necessary money available to the upper and middle classes and to the educated bazaar group to permit them to make very high profits in order to keep the economy expanding at nine per cent a year. This means middle and upper class housing, cars for the rich, fashionable restaurants and hotels, holidays, etc. It also means, of course, that all supporting elements of the monarchy are intimately associated with and involved in the activity of the modern sector. High ranking officers are now as busy with their investment portfolios as are many of those in the Pentagon. The great families are generally and profitably consolidating their financial positions. Education in Iran is fashionable and eagerly adopted by the children of those who have rising economic and financial prospects.

Teheran was originally chosen as the model for the modern sector and the changes in that great city are obvious at every turning. While there are a few handicraft outlets, including an official government one directly across from the American Embassy, Teheran is no longer the simple town of a generation ago. While the great bazaar is still there, Teheran has industrialized to the point where it is now one of the dirtiest cities in the world. In the wonderful clear plateau country surrounding the capital city, Teheran from a distance is seen as a black, indistinguishable cloud. Actually Teheran has now reached the saturation point and while present industries may expand, no new ones can be brought in. It is for this reason that the great expansion has taken place out toward Ghazvin which, while supposedly being a new town, is actually one vast industrial park.

Other cities, most notably Isfahan, are beginning to follow the same pattern that is to be found in Teheran. The location of that city has been noted above. It stands in a wide and fertile valley far from any frontier. It has a good water supply. Its altitude of fifty-two hundred feet gives the city a temperate climate. Iranians, while expressing their admiration for the beauties of the city, speak of it as becoming the "Manchester of Persia." It is the center of Iran's textile industry — there are over sixteen mills — but perhaps more important for the future, it is the seat of the first steel mill ever in Iran. A massive operation, built largely by Soviet experts, is now turning out, among other things, steel for an automobile of medium class but high price which is marketed in Iran under the slogan "From Aryan chariots to Aria automatic of Iran." It is an outward and visible sign of the prosperity of the modern sector. But perhaps this is enough here. The economics of the White Revolution, the Plan Organizations, of modernization generally, is not the concern of this book. This book is essentially political. What is important to emphasize is the fact that these developments had their genesis in the early struggles between the Monarchy and the Majlis. Each participant in this struggle sought to legitimatize his position. The Shah finally took the initiative and to this day he holds it. The role of the Majlis today may be essentially a passive one. But it is a role, and it would be useful to know more of this role — of the relationship between the Majlis and the Shahanshah as well as the detailing of Majlis power. But whatever it is, as in times past, so in the future, it is a role that fate will deal to it as God sees fit.

The Party

Political parties in Iran have played an uncertain role in the life of the nation. There had been, through the centuries, no history of party and even in more modern times, no tradition as it was emerging in the Western World. Not until the bitter and even bloody years of the constitutional struggle did the concept of political party begin to take shape. Various protest groups were the first to appear.[27] At the extreme left were the *mujahiddin*, the guerilla fighters. They were aided by the democrats from the Baku oilfields who were eventually taken over by the nobility. Then there was a moderate group, the *Ittadali* which was jointed by the constitutionalists from Gilan. Other, less important groupings emerged, most of them highly personal as well as political. Generally speaking, one could say that there was opposition to the Qajar rule but not necessarily to the concept of a monarchy. Then there was the constitutional element, some of whom favored a parliamentary democracy and others who envisioned the Shah as a constitutional ruler. It was really an ill-defined menage at best. The Shah's regent (the Shah, of course, was a boy) had been a Balliol man and he demanded that the Majlis — when it was first convened during this tumultuous period — be divided into two parties — a government and an opposition. This English model was generally followed with the moderates in a very large majority. The so-called "democrats", the opposition, only had 20 members. But given the varied objectives of those within the larger party, it was inevitable that party government should fail to take hold. Quite naturally, when the Constitution was promulgated in 1906 — no mention was made of or provision for, political parties in the government.

Reza Shah came to the throne in 1925 and thereafter political parties in Iran ceased to exist. At one time during his reign a majority party was contemplated as a means of providing a supporting majority in the Majlis. But Reza Shah was distrustful of parties and didn't really understand their uses. Consequently nothing came of the idea.

When Reza Shah went into exile in 1941, a power vacuum existed. The successor to the throne, the present Shah, was a mere boy without political experience. World War II was proving to be bitterly divisive of the realm. Foreign occupation was merely one of the myriad problems calling for political solutions. Hence the time for political expression was at hand.

The first parties were formed in 1942. They were not well-organized or well-financed although some land-owner and merchant money was available. The elite stood clear. Roughly speaking, the parties divided into left and right with names reminiscent of the constitutional period. On the left there was the Comrades Party, the Freedom Party and the Justice Party. The last named became the later Tudeh party.

On the right there was the Patriot's Party which later became the National Will Party (Eradeyi Melli). It described itself as a reform party but its members sat in the Majlis in a private capacity, not as an organized party unit. It was said to have had British backing and did control at least one newspaper in Teheran. Its founder and leader, Sayyid Zia al-din Tabatabai, a former Prime Minister (1921) was arrested in 1946 and the party disappeared.

The Democrat Iran Party resembled in many ways the National Will Party. The leader of the party, Ahmad Qavam, was an aristocratic politician, also oriented toward the British.

The Tudeh party was of sterner stuff. It was organized by a group of educated men, many of whom had been imprisoned by Reza Shah. It had good organization. It supported the formation of trade unions and elected 8 members to the 1944–1946 Session of the Majlis. A militant branch of the party led the separatist movement in Azerbaijan which isolated that region during 1945 – 1946. The party was believed to have Soviet support and officially to this day, the Azerbaijan move has been seen as a Soviet move.

In February 1949, the Tudeh party was banned after an attempt on the Shah's life. Its leaders were for the most part jailed or fled into exile — many to the USSR. Reza Radmanesh, for example, who was executive secretary of the party attended the XIXth. Congress of the Communist Party of the Soviet Union in October 1952. However, the Tudeh party did not die. A large number of front groups appeared in Iran and party papers were readily available in Teheran. Though the party was illegal, it continued to function — and well. Cells were organized throughout Iran headed by trusted leaders. Soviet influence became increasingly evident. The propaganda directed against the Shah, the government and by now, the United States, represented really quite a torrent.

Other parties appeared and disappeared during these turbulent years. In 1947, the Democrat Iran Party won a majority in the national elections. The Iran party was active but never came to power. In 1950, the "Toilers" party was formed. It targeted two specific groups. One was the anti-Stalinist intellectuals who were for the most part, Marxist. The other had access to Court, the Army and once again, the British Embassy. Dr Mozaffar Baqai, the party leader, was the most charismatic of all the party leaders up to the time of Dr Musaddiq. But all of these parties, including the Tudeh, were overshadowed by the rise of Dr Musaddiq himself.

In 1950, Dr Musaddiq formed the so-called "National Front". It included the Iran Party, the Toilers party, religious leaders, and independent deputies in the Majlis. While in its official declarations, the Tudeh party opposed the new amalgam of political parties, it supported certain of his actions.

After his removal, its membership declined but it remained, and still remains, the *bete noire* of the present regime.

Because of his great importance as a political leader during this period, something should be said of Dr Musaddiq who emerged in strength at the 15th session of the Majlis in 1947.

Dr Musaddiq was a most interesting man and the writer was surprised to find as recently as four years ago, in private conversation in Iran, a high amount of regard and respect held for him by prominent people, some even in the government. His appeal, of course, was never really understood in the West largely because (1) he nationalized the oil companies even though the action was later rescinded and then re-nationalized by the Shah; (2) he constantly had his pictures taken in his pyjamas; (3) he cried a lot.

Actually this is the type of thing that points up the type of differences that make for misunderstanding between the East and West. Dr Musaddiq was born in 1879. He entered government service at eighteen and ten years later studied economics in Paris for two years, transferring later to Neuchatel in Switzerland where he took his doctorate in law in 1914. From 1915–1928 he served as a deputy in the Majlis. He ran afoul of Reza Shah and lived in retirement from 1928–1940 when he was arrested and imprisoned. He was finally released when Reza Shah abdicated. In March 1944, he reentered the Majlis and gradually assumed the leadership of the National Front. His refusal to compromise with Reza Shah's dictatorship and his vigorous efforts to rid Iran of corrupting foreign influence were the actions of a strong man. His public weeping was seen by Iranians of evidence of great earnestness and moral courage. His gaunt, almost saintly appearance identified him in much of the public eye as a Husayn-like martyr-figure. As pointed out above, the events connected with the Husayn are still commemorated during the month of Muhurram by mourning processions, performances of passion plays, weeping, even flagellation. It is a very old role, this, and is associated with sentiments associated with the basic problem confronting man as Being and man as Iranian :[28]

> "What rains down ? Blood ! Who ? The Eye ! How ?
> Day and Night ! Why ?

From grief ! What grief ? The grief of the Monarch of Karbala !
What was his name ? Husayn ! Of whose race ? Ali's !
Who was his mother ? Fatima ! Who was his grandsire ? Mustafa !
How was it with him ? He fell a martyr ! Where ? In the Plain of Mariya !
When ? On the tenth of Muhurram ! Secretly ? No, in public !
Was he slain by night ? No, by day ! At what time ? At noontide !
Was his head severed from the throat ? No, from the nape of the neck !
Was he slain in thirsting ? No ! Did none give him to drink ? They did !
Who ? Shimr ! From what source ? From the source of death !
Was he an innocent martyr ? Yes ! Had he committed any fault ? No !
What was his work ? Guidance ! Who was his friend ? God !

The struggle for power in Iran — and it should not be forgotten that both the Shah and the Majlis saw the Fundamental Law as a mandate — reached its climax in 1952–1953. In October 1947, the United States and Iran had signed their military aid pact. Up to that time, the Shah had no party. The Majlis saw the pact with the Americans as moving to restore the old military regime of Reza Shah. Consequently they sought a close check on the budget as well as a check on ministerial appointments.

This see-saw for power had continued up to 1951 when Dr Musaddiq became Prime Minister — the last Prime Minister not to be hand-picked by the Shah. The next year, he was able to force the War Ministry portfolio for himself as well as retaining the post of Prime Minister. He was likewise granted power to rule by decree for six months. The events of the next year are too well known to require recapitulation here. On 16 August 1953, the Shah, his wife and the lone pilot flying his plane (later Chief of the Air Force) left Iran and it appeared as if the Monarchy might be ended.

The Shah's surprising return to power was well supported and as noted above, one of his first acts on his return to Iran was to dissolve the Majlis by Royal decree — and place the country under martial law.

In April 1957, the political situation seemed sufficiently under control that martial law was lifted. Dr Eqbal was named Prime Minister and the announcement came from the throne that political parties could once more be freely formed. However, a multi-party system was in reality proscribed. From public announcements dropped informally, it appeared that the Shah really intended a two-party system, a system which he later defended. The Iran-Novim party consisting of men known to and owing allegiance to the Shah, a sort of "inner group", so to speak, became the ruling party and remained so until 1975, (except for the period 1961 - 1964 when Iran was again under martial law). Its leaders identified with the Shah's personal aims. Assadollah Alam, the Shah's long-time friend, was the first party leader. Hoveyda succeeded as party leader and Prime Minister. He successfully held this post until the creation of the Rastakhiz Party at which time he was named to the same position in the new party and Prime Minister.

The opposition party, *Mardum* (People's Party), once the name of a Tudeh party paper, was also formed and encouraged to present its program to the people in 1957. The party leader, Alihaqi Kani, was the 44 year old son of the distinguished *mujtahid* Ayatollah. His credentials were impressive. He had been the wrestling champion of Iran in his weight and held the Ph.D. degree in Political Science at the University of London. Of the 261 members over all in the Majlis, the *Mardum* Party held 32 seats. Its support was scattered. Even the guilds supported the Iran-Novim party. Nevertheless, there was now in Iran a two-party system, a majority and opposition minority, blessed by the Shah himself and described by him as representing an important move toward parliamentary government.

The 20th Majlis was elected in August 1960 and the election was nullified by the Shah as fraudulent. An election rerun in 1961 did not please the Shah more, so he dissolved the Majlis for the second time and again placed the country under martial law. Clearly the two-party system in Iran was in trouble.

Nevertheless, the *Mardum* Party, as the loyal opposition, did carry on until the bitter end. Its best leader, the late Nasser Ameri who was the official opposition leader in the Majlis, was an outspoken opponent to the ruling Iran-Novim party. He was a notable exception to the "me-tooism" that had originally marked the opposition. Whatever else may be said of him, it is nevertheless true that much of what he foresaw, did, in fact, come to pass, resulting in a major reshuffle of the government in summer, 1977.

Shortly after the Fifth Development Plan was ratified in 1972, Ameri warned that Iran would face a "rarely precedented inflation rate" if the government failed to take basic measures against the inflationary effects of heavy investment in the Fifth Plan. Extensive measures were needed to enable Iran to absorb the huge investments in the Fifth Plan. Two months later he became more specific. Lashing government "failures," he committed his party to a program of more equal distribution of wealth, far-reaching administrative reform, "quality" education, financial honesty and expanded welfare and housing programs.

Speaking before the Fourth Party Congress,[29] Ameri clearly called for an extension of the fruits of the modern sector. He also called for a limitation on urban land holdings and, interestingly enough, for "an independent judiciary."

Ameri made these specific points in his address:

(1) high land prices barred low income classes from securing adequate housing;

(2) limits must be established on land ownership in the cities and heavy taxes imposed on unused land both in and out of cities;

(3) there was great need for a 'vast housing construction program' along with regulations to prevent profiteering on such government subsidized housing;

(4) trade guilds, workers' syndicates and cooperative members were being forced to join the ruling Iran-Novim party;

(5) the government " 'had not tried' to reform tax policy in ten years in power." A considerable part of large incomes either remain free to taxation or are not collected. He described tax policy as one of the most

important tools for ensuring more equal income distribution;

(6) despite the Shah's decrees providing free education for all Iranians, the government had failed to provide adequate educational and recreational facilities for the youth. He also emphasized the need for "quality" education. In this respect, the writer can recall that in 1970, the Shah made a visit to Shiraz to check on the literary campaign. The local officials found to their horror that illiteracy had actually risen that year (largely due to the settlement of tribes in the area). So they changed the figures to show that illiteracy had declined. (The writer knew personally an official who resigned his position rather than be a part of this).

Finally Ameri hit hard at Prime Minister Hoveyda's party. He accused it of using public funds to win votes, of failing to carry out administrative reforms, of corruption ("which important officials have been brought before the courts ?" he asked), and of using its position to restrict the freedom of individuals to join the party of their choice.

The November speech to the Party Congress, which, incidentally, gave a new mandate to Ameri, was a block buster but a costly one. The first week in January, he was summarily removed as Secretary-General of the Party. A statement issued by the central committee said that his removal was due "to objections by members of the committee on his policy;" that Ameri had pursued "individualistic" policies; that his accusations against the Iran-Novim party added to his unpopularity.[30] The *Kayhan* did not report any interview with Ameri following the action of the committee.

Two weeks later, Mohammed Fazaeli was named Secretary-General of the Mardum Party. In his first interview he denied that Ameri's ouster had weakened the party. Rather he noted that Ameri, who had once served as vice-governor of the Central Bank of Iran and President of the Agricultural Development Fund before entering politics, "was not experienced in politics." Fazaeli pledged that the Mardum Party was "only concerned with patriotism, service to the Shahanshah and the nation."[31]

The first week in February — the exact date was not given — Ameri was killed in a traffic accident on the Bandar-Pahlavi-Rasht road. The next month, March 1975, the Shah brought to an end a 15 year experiment in permitting the existence of opposition parties and created a new one-party system. This was an abrupt about face, even for the Shah. He had long maintained in interviews and in print that a two party system was required for the evolution of democracy in Iran. He now took the position that Iran could no longer afford such a "luxury".

It was the Shah's intention, through the creation of a new party, to be called the Rastakhiz Party, to end divisiveness within the realm and — anticipating a future all-inclusive adult membership — to create what then Prime Minister Hoveyda called "unity without uniformity."

Dariush Homayoun, then Deputy Secretary General of the Rastakhiz Party was a little more specific. At a party meeting in Sari in May 1977, he stated that the Party was not a temporary one, "nor is it to be replaced by a multiparty political order." He pointed out that Iran had tried "other systems" but there was general agreement in Iran that there should be a simple political entity "which embraces all the nation." He saw the party as having three functions, or tasks to perform: (1) for the people, the mobilizing of popular strength, (2) for the government, a supervisory role to provide guidance and if need be to criticize and scrutinize Government work, (3) the destiny of the nation.

Homayoun briefly reviewed for the party activists the developments leading up to the creation of the Party. He pointed out that at one time there were no parties, at another time, a multi-party system, at still another, a two party system. None of these, he said, could work "because of the specific institutional aspects of our society."[32]

Details of the Constitution of the Rastakhiz Party which has been printed as a complete text[33] are of no particular concern here. There is, simply stated, a provision for the following organs:

(1) The Congress (the highest organ which meets once every four years, the members of which are elected by the party chapters on the basis of 1 delegate for each 1,000 members).

(2) The Central Council (formed by the assembly of the representatives of the district, city, township, and provincial councils. It meets twice a year).
(3) The Executive Board (implements the resolutions of the Congress and the decisions of the central council. It has various subcommittees).
(4) The Political Bureau. (formed by the Prime Minister and his designates. The Prime Minister is the chairman. There are deputies and one representative of the Majlis and of the Senate respectively the total number is not to exceed 14).
(5) The Secretary General (responsible for the administration of the Party, his duties are largely organizational i.e., appointing deputies and other units).

There are Party Councils — the Village Council, the District Council, the Town Council, the Township Council, and the Provincial Council. Membership to each is not necessarily elected. The wording is that the Councils "shall be constituted." Membership in the party is open to Iranian citizens, 18 years of age and over. Headquarters are in Teheran.

The future of the party appears to be identified now exclusively with the Shah himself. The "treacherous and fake parties" of the past are no longer. The Rastakhiz party is "a new wave along the path of revolution,"[34] a confusing simile that may or may not presage much for the future. The Teheran newspapers give considerable play to what they describe as "debating the party." It is one which asks few difficult questions. Perhaps it were better described as a "platform" for a good discussion. Iran's "special system of democracy" is at the center of the debate. The party is seen as encompassing the interests of all the Iranian people and not just certain groups. It is the instrument of the whole nation "it is a party in which people can speak openly and express their views and problems." An editorial in the *Kayhan* described it as a Party designed to give institutional expression to the new political climate. "It is not exclusivist or elitist; it includes and represents all Iranians. It is not monolithic or inflexible; rather it permits the expression of all views and opinions. It allows for the development of different channels of ideas ... and it is open to a wide variety of views and ideas." Ironically there appears to be something of the aura of Mao about all this. The flowers are invited to blossom — except the Iranians say it better: "Pens should write and tongues should speak so that the clash of ideas should light our path toward the ideals of the Revolution."[35] It is noted that people are hesitant to speak out. The people have been "conditioned" by past experience. They hold a "negative attitude". The party gives them faith and confidence. The image of the great constitutional debate of 1905 is even involved. The debate concludes : "this party was established by the people of the nation themselves in response to an invitation by the Shahanshah, who stands above all these things. His relationship with the people is that of father, supporter, protector and symbol ... the Rastakhiz Party is founded on the spiritual relationship between the Shah and the People, and this in turn, is founded on love and devotion."[36]

The close association of the government, the Majlis, and the Party is a constant theme in today's political rhetoric in Iran. "We all move forward in the same direction" is the way Abdol Majid Majidi, leader of the progressive wing of the Rastakhiz Party puts it (when asked what distinguishes one party wing from the other, his remark was that "both wings aim at rendering greater service to the Country;" they "reinforce party solidarity"). Majlis Deputy Halaku Rambod reiterates this unity of theme. "Deputies", he said, at a press conference in August 1977, "should not think it necessary to be either 'pro' or 'anti' on every question". Their aims "should not be to trip the government." Their aim should rather be to "strengthen and improve legislation." "The Majlis", he said, "must act as intermediary between the people and the executive organs." Proposed legislation involved both party and government. Essential to this must be "the higher interests of the progress of Iranian society." This clearly takes priority over "individual views."

Hushang Ansary, a former Cabinet leader, now Chairman of the NIOC has placed this concept of unity within its peculiar Iranian format. Other nations, he has pointed out that "consider themselves democratic" do not march to the same music as do Iranians. "Neither capitalism or Communism or any other 'ism' has proved capable of dealing adequately with the problems of the times, he has noted. "Our social system", he says, "has come into being under a special set of circumstances and stems from the Monarchy, the Constitution and the Sixth of Bahman Revolution". Western democracies, he noted "operate through the manoeuvrings of pressure groups and this situation, essentially one of conflict and antagonism has given rise to dangerous economic and social problems". "In Iran", he said, "there is no danger of such fragmentation and chaos. The Iranian system does not allow the presence of either pressure groups or individuals with vested interests. ... The Monarchy and the special bond between the Shahanshah and the people constitute Iran's power base".[37] Princess Ashraf, in a formal address in Tabriz a few years ago, gave that special bond further elaboration. "Throughout the history of Iran", she said, "the Monarchy has been synonymous with unity, stability, and sovereignty".[38]

NOTES

1. Iran Today, *op. cit.*, p. 34.
2. Bayne, *op. cit.*, p. 76.
3. *Kayhan*, August 6, 1977. p. 1. All speeches reported below on pp. 1-2.
4. Bill and Leiden, *op. cit.*, Chapter III.
5. Chapter III, p. 116.
6. Book of Tansar, *op. cit.*, p. 61.
7. *Tadhkirat al-Mulk*, *op. cit.*, p. 44.
8. IX, 425-67. Quoted in *Ibid.*, p. 114.
9. *Ibid.*, p. 115.
10. *Book of Ser Marco Polo* (ed. Yule) (2 vols.) London, 1926, I, pp. 78ff.
11. Hanway, Jonas, *An Historical Account of the British Trade Over the Caspian Sea with a Journal of Travels* (4 vols.) London, 1753. I, p. 335.
12. Pinkerton, John, *A General Collection of the Best and Most Interesting Voyages in all Parts of the World*, London, 1811, p. 214. The spelling is as given in Pinkerton. See Savory, R. M., "The Principal Offices of the Safawid State during the Reign of Isma'il", *Bulletin of the School of Oriental and African Studies* (Parts 1-3) 1960, pp. 92-105.
13. *Ibid.*, pp. 214-15.
14. Book of Tansar, *op. cit.*, p. 33.
15. Pinkerton, *op. cit.*, p. 215.
16. Curzon, G. N. *Persia and the Persian Question*, London, 1892 I, pp. 426-32. (The spelling is as given in Curzon).
17. *Algar*, op. cit., p. 259.
18. *Iran Today*, *op. cit.*, p. 50.
19. *Tadhkirat al-Mulk*, *op. cit.*, p. 121.
20. *Iran Today*, *op. cit.*, p. 37.
21. Hopkins, E. W. "The Divinity of Kings", *Journal of the American Oriental Society*, vol. 51, no. 4 (December, 1931), p. 315.
22. Bayne, *op. cit.*, p. 58.
23. *N. Y. Times*, March 22, 1962, p. 4.
24. For details, see Bill and Leiden, *op. cit.*, pp. 137-38.
25. *N. Y. Times*, August 15, 1962, p. 1.
26. *Kayhan*, August 10, 1974, p. 1.
27. Cottan, R. W. "Political Party Development in Iran", *Society for Iranian Studies*, I (No. 3) 1968, pp. 82-94. See also Wilbur, D. H., *Iran, Past and Present*, Princeton University Press, 1958 pp. 4-10.
28. Browne, *op. cit.*, IV, pp. 177-80. See Savory, *op. cit.*, p. 85.
29. *Kayhan*, November 30, 1974, p. 3.
30. *Ibid.*, January 4, 1975, p. 1.
31. *Ibid.*, January 18, 1975, p. 2.
32. *Ibid.*, May 21, 1977, p. 3.
33. *Ibid.*, May 3, 1975, p. 5.
34. *Ibid.*, August 6, 1977, p. 4.
35. Ansary in *Ibid.*, July 30, 1977, p. 1.
36. *Ibid.*, May 28, 1975, p. 4.
37. All speeches reported in *Ibid.*, July 30, 1977, pp. 1-2.
38. *Ibid.*, June 19, 1971, p. 1.

Chapter 7

THE LAW OF THE MONARCH

Law

For Westerners who tend to think in terms of homogeneity, the law of Iran represents a riot of history and tradition, many and diverse cultures, Islamic law, kingly power, constitutional government and more recently the influence of French and Belgian legal models. Aspects of these materials have been built into the preceding chapters. For example, the relationship between law and religion has been seen as a constant theme in Iranian history. Traditional roles have been played out by king and aristocrat alike in still other of the narratives composing earlier chapters. The manifestations of kingly rule have been clearly limned. And Islam "which is our refuge" is shown to be a powerful and constant force. For that reason, it seems prudent not to labour the reader with a detailed accounting of law from the Achaemenid period to the present. It seems best to deal with it in most summary fashion. Any other course would reveal such an awesome repository of history and law that any writer and reader would share the dilemma of Daniel in the lions' den. The decree under which that historic action was taken — a decree which Daniel himself, as the Shah's adviser, had submitted to the Sovereign — could not be rescinded because of the "law of Medes and Persians that altereth not."[1] Prayer, in the face of such irreversible and overwhelming odds, therefore, was clearly the answer — now as it was then.

Up until comparatively recent times, Iran has been served by a parallel system of laws which have corresponded roughly to the English Common Law and the medieval Canon Law. The latter was based on the Koran and was known as the Shari'a. This was an elaborate system of religious and civil law which had been evolved from a study of the teachings of the Koran and the traditional sayings of Mohammed. While the Shi'ites of Iran shared with the Sunnites these chief sources of their legal system, there were differences, largely involving principles of legal interpretation. The Sunnites developed two principles, one allowing judgement on the ground of a consensus of opinion and the other on the basis of a legal analogy. The Shi'ites, while not completely rejecting these principles, did introduce a supplementary use of Reason which was completely at odds with their religious brethren. This was known as *aql'al-fitri* or "inspired reason" and involved the declarations of the successors of the Prophet, the Twelve *Imams*. It will be recalled from above that these Imams were the spiritual successors of the Prophet who would have also — if events had transpired as desired — been Caliph as well. This office, continued both by heredity and special designation, was continued until the series of Twelve Imams was terminated in 873 A.D.

The Shi'ites ascribed to the *Imams* — as well as Mohammed and to his daughter, Fatima — the authority of this "inspired reason". Human reason was seen as a subordinate principle for legal deduction. Clearly there was a degree of elasticity here that was congenial to the subtle mind of the Iranian.

Theoretically the Koran comprehended all things relating to the affairs of man and his relationship to God. Over the centuries, however, religious law was gradually restricted to matters of faith and morals, inheritance, domestic relations, and oaths. The regulation of inheritance put problems of land tenure under the jurisdiction of the clergy which accounts for the early opposition to the Shah's land distribution scheme. Oaths, corresponding to our notarial acts, likewise gave to the clergy authority over commercial affairs.

The common law of Iran (*urf*) represented local customs in various parts of the realm and in some cases dated back to the Achaemenid period. In point of fact, according to Firdawsi's *Shahnameh*, narrated in the first chapter, the first person to establish a court of law in Persia and exercise the functions of judgement was Kaumers. Generally speaking the customary law dealt with such matters as water rights and grazing rights; the relations between landlord and tenant; and in some instances, taxes. The *urf* itself was administered by the King, the governors of the provinces, and the mayors of the cities, the managers and collectors of districts, the squires and heads of the villages. The lowest officers invested with the administration of the *urf* heard complaints of all kinds and some in evidence. Even the heads of the villages were allowed to inflict punishment and impose fines. If the crime was severe, the delinquent was sent to the magistrate of his district whose power was more extensive. When a governor was given his high office by the King, he was also given the power to put the criminal to death. However, there was, under certain circumstances, provision made for an appeal to the Shah. A well known story tells of such an appeal where the person returned to the governor with a positive *firman* from the Shah. The governor at once ordered the man's chest open and removed his heart so that he could see it, seeking him to be a very brave person with an extraordinary heart for appealing to His Majesty the Shah.

The decisions of these courts of Persia were obtained without much cost as the administrative work was much less than in the case of the Shari'a. The *urf* dealt with all criminal cases, although the criminal laws were administered in a manner conformable to the Koran. The tribes in Persian territory technically were under the jurisdiction of the central government, but they were ruled by their own customs and habits almost until the present.

The Shahanshah provided a third dimension to the two parallel systems of law thus described. His authority, as pointed out elsewhere in this book, was theoretically absolute. Clearly, however, he would not fly in the face of immemorial custom. Nevertheless certain areas of legal competence were reserved to him. Public safety was his concern. So was conspiracy. Robbery under some circumstances was his concern. The administration of the death penalty lay with him alone although under some circumstances this needed the approval of the ecclesiastical courts.

If the Shah could punish, he was also required to observe the tradition of *bast* or refuge, remarked in an earlier chapter. Certain mosques and shrines and even the person of the Shah himself could afford *bast*. The so-called "cities of refuge" in the Old Testament are historic examples of provision being made for temporary escape of involuntary manslaughter until the blood had cooled.[2]

Centuries of working out these parallel systems of the law of Iran prior to modern times resulted in a clear division of labour.

There was no contending in the courts for jurisdiction. Rather there was agreement as to purpose and goal of law. "If anyone neglects or transgresses either the Law representing Right and Reason (i.e. the Islamic Law)", begins the Safavid word of authority," or the customs established by long practice (mustamarra) or the usages of the realm (mamlakat) or by the rules of righteousness, he must be prevented from doing so and if the armies and Pillars of State commit unlawful acts ... the Grand Vazir submits the matter to the Throne and carries out whatever the King's sacred order may be."[3]

In neither the law of Islam or the customary law of Islam was there any sense of public justice as we understand that term. The concept of the State as a party in interest had not yet developed in jurisprudence. A crime was a crime against the injured party except for the few exceptions noted above respecting the position of the Sovereign. The principle of *lex talionis* was a principle of retaliation and was as much observed in Iran as in Israel. The wronged party could exact satisfaction in kind.

In civil suits, arbitration was generally followed, with or without state intervention.[4]

Until the middle of the 19th century, this was the system of law that obtained. Throughout the rest of the Islamic world, however, the Shari' a reigned supreme, suffering no real parallel systems of law to challenge its authority as in Iran. But even so there were lacunae. In matters of commerce and trade — for much of these matters were foreign to the Prophet — the rules of the Shari'a were ill-defined. Customary law generally prevailed here just as administrative regulations edged toward the domination of control and punishment of serious crime. Nevertheless, it was true that the Shari'a was officially the only law in Islam — pronounced as law — and its influence was everywhere apparent.

The tremendous commercial and industrial expansion of the Victorian era in England had its effect on the world of Islam. The great Ottoman Empire, traditional arch-rivals of Iranian power and influence, was the first to respond. It was clear that the law of the Shari'a could no longer grapple with the complexities of the new era. Consequently the Ottoman Empire embarked on what has been known as the Tanzimat

Reforms. From 1850–1865, new codes were promulgated, based largely on French models. They included commercial and penal codes.

In Iran, these developments did not go unnoticed. In its case, of course, because of its long and singular history, Iran was in a sense much more independent of the all pervading influence of the Shari'a than other Moslem countries and consequently the actions of its great neighbouring Empire did not necessarily presage particular legal changes in Iran. But the climate was right.

The Qajar rule — in a sense, always an imposed rule in Iran (if one can compare it with the munificent reign of the Zands who immediately preceded the Qajars) — was stumbling to its bitter end. The tenets of Islam, custom, the Monarchy were challenged again and again by reigning Heads.

A bitter story is told in Teheran of a Qajar ruler who apparently had interpreted an English admonition as an affront and decided to show the English that he was still master in his own house and would administer justice as he saw fit. He invited the Ambassador to the palace and then in his presence proceeded to blind fifty subjects. The Englishmen who have their faults but whose lack of courage is not one of them, were, on this occasion, represented by an ambassador who sat through the savagery, then excused himself, stationed himself at the gate and as the blind men were led out gave to each of them a handful of gold coins. Apparently the Shah was furious but this was a period where England used its great force for good as well as its own advantage. One recalls Gladstone dispatching a fleet to the shores of Turkey about this same time to halt the Turkish mutilation of Armenian Christians.

It first began — the move to liberalize and modernize the law in Iran — with the growing demand for a "House of Justice", and the issue of underground literature, of which "*Yek Kalema*", was the best example. (See below) *Yek Kalema* means "one word" and the one word was Law. Two of the early moving forces in the move to modernize the law were Jamal al-din al-Afghani, an Islamic nationalist teacher and Malkom Khan, a former Iranian minister to Great Britain. Both of these men called for the adoption of a fixed code of laws and the assembly of a representative parliament.

Nasir al-din Shah was assassinated in 1896. His successor, Muzaffar Shah, under great pressure, finally promulgated an imperial rescript that has been called the "Magna Charta of Iran." In this document, the word "law" and "constitution" do not appear — a concession to historical Iranian tradition — but nevertheless it was clear that an "assembly of delegates" would be constituted to 'render' the necessary assistance ... in such reforms as are designed to promote the happiness and well being of Persia."

The constitutional period will be considered briefly later in this chapter. What is of importance here was the move to liberalize the laws of Iran — to liberalize them and to bring them more into line with the practicalities of the 20th century.

The old law books in Iran — the Islamic law — were all in Arabic. Only the shorter manuals — for the most part ceremonial laws — were available in Persian. Two things, therefore, were required. One was to put the law into the language of the people. The other was to put it on paper. A strong beginning was made during the early sessions of the Majlis when not only the proceedings of the constitutional conventions were published and distributed, but rules of procedure for each government department was issued, with carefully prepared indices. Direct legislation was normalized and the scope of that legislation increased with each session of the Majlis. By the time of Reza Shah (1925) there was in existence not only the Constitution with its amendments, and the fundamental provisions for the four great provinces and the eleven departments of administration, but bureaux had been organized for census, for the recording of deeds, for the government of registration of marriages.

The common law of Iran was similarly brought into line[5] There was now put in print, clearly stated provisions in regard to property, wills, partnerships, etc., the rules of order for court trials, legal ways of hastening decisions in particular cases, the means afforded for legal arbitration without formal trial, rules for giving security, rules governing citizenship, criminal laws with the procedure for the trial of government servants charged with criminal cases, all systematically arranged and briefly stated.

In all of this, foreign codes were freely utilized and in some cases actually adopted. The French codes, particularly, were much in evidence. In 1925, an extensive commercial code was enacted by the Majlis. The next year, a criminal code was adopted. In 1928, a civil code of some 900 articles was promulgated. These three basic codes formed the hard core of the new legal system. Since then, there have been revisions, additions, and even new legislation. For example, a new Maritime Law went into effect in October 1973. Maritime courts in Iran were established. Regulations relating to Maritime Insurance, appointments of ship-captains and crew-members, etc., were promulgated, and in general Iranian law was brought into line with those of other nations involved in vast oil shipments and other cargo.

A law of 1928 abolished the so called "capitulations" which up to that time had given foreigners resident in Iran immunity from arrest as well as the right of trial by their own consular representatives. Laws passed in 1931 and 1935 established the legal ages for marriages and enhanced the divorce and property rights of women.

Laws of 1928 and 1935 did away with the ancient Persian dress, and made Western clothing and headgear compulsory. This, of course, was a windfall to second hand clothing merchants in New York and elsewhere. The early traveller in Iran can recall endless racks of this clothing — ill-fitting, unmatched jackets and trousers — offered for sale in Teheran. The veil was abolished. Iran became the official name of the country. Honorary titles were abolished. So carefully has this provision been observed that even at present, Iran has no honorary consuls abroad — a practice — a minor diplomatic sinecure — followed by many western countries.

After 1933, the Minister of Justice was given full power to put laws into effect and then submit them to Parliament for approval after they had been tried out in practice.

What had been accomplished, then, in Iran in a period of roughly a century, had been to all effects and purposes a modernization of the law. Contrasted with the previous system already described, the primary characteristic of modern Iranian law was that it was now based on direct legislation and the first question was no longer the intent of the Koran and the Traditions but the purpose and preference of the Government.[6]

To turn now to the administration of the law. Prior to the modern period, reference to the courts meant reference to the courts of the Shari'a. As Moslems could have no written law but the Koran and Traditions, there could therefore be no official courts other than those administered by the theologians and the doctors of the law. In Iran, even with its long precedent of custom, this was still largely true. There were secular magistrates who decided the cases brought before them according to the precedent but this law was never written. It was, in essence, the King's law as he could be said to be the head of the *urf*, and yet the King's law was itself not written.

Since 1927 – 1931 the dual system of religious law and customary law in Iran has been brought together in a hierarchy of civil courts under the supervision of the Minister of Justice.

At the top of the hierarchy is the Supreme Court of Iran.[7] The Supreme Court of Iran presently functions under the authority set forth in the "Law relating to the organization of the Judicial Body" of the Code as enacted in the year, 1956. This law has not been translated into English. The Code itself, of course, (parts of which have been translated into French) runs to several volumes, but for the convenient use of lawyers, professors, and other interested persons, the most important sections have been compiled into a single volume presently edited by one man — a private lawyer — much in the same manner as the early United States Supreme Court Reports were compiled and edited by a single person — Wheaton, Cranch, etc.

Approximately 25 Articles of the Code to the Supreme Court. Some 7 Articles are concerned with the censure of errant judges, including those on the Supreme Court.

The Supreme Court of Iran, as presently constituted, consists of eight branches, each with four judges assigned but with only three sitting in any given case. The odd number presumably is a precaution against deadlock. Each of the judges, in turn, prepares the decision of the Court as the cases come before it.

The branches — this is the terminology, not committees of the Court — are divided according to the work load and to the skills of the judges as adapted to the needs of the Court. In other words, some branches sit primarily to interpret the criminal code, some, the civil code. There is a court of felony (a branch), etc. — all depending on the docket and business pending. A judge, however, once appointed to the Supreme Court is expected to serve where he is assigned and would not think of himself as having been appointed primarily for his competence in the fields of torts, contracts, etc. It should be noted that a personnel breakdown of the Court would show no sectional or regional representation or primary area of judicial responsibility.

The judges of the eight branches as well as the presiding judge of each branch are appointed by the Minister of Justice. The Chief Justice, known in Iran as the President of the Supreme Court, is nominated by the Minister of Justice to the Shah and is appointed by the latter on executive order. This appointment requires no approval of the parliamentary body.

In case of heavy dockets, or for other reasons deemed sufficient by the Minister of Justice, he is empowered to increase the number of branches up to four additional. The Court can also have alternate judges — also appointed by the Minister — up to half the total number of judges.

The President of the Supreme Court, who functions rather as the senior judge than as the Chief Justice (i.e. the administrative aspects of the Court's work are largely the responsibility of the Attorney-General — see below) must be at the time of his appointment or have previously been president of one of the branches of the Supreme Court, or an ex-Minister of Justice who has had a judicial career on the Supreme Court. He, along with other members of the Court are not permitted to hold any other public office nor to act publicly in a non-judicial role.

Supreme Court judges are appointed for life. The retirement age is 70 (Lower court judges retire at 75).

The Disciplinary Code is an important part of the judiciary apparatus and applies to Supreme Court judges as well as lower court judges and lawyers. By comparison with the American agony over a Code of Ethics applicable to the Supreme Court, the Iranian code seems simple, direct, to the point — and completely unacceptable to the western tradition. The code provides for two disciplinary courts, one for judges and one for lawyers. They are separate. There are 8 degrees of punishment under the code for judges.

Offenses which invite disciplinary action are — at the reprimand level — excessive absenteeism or unwillingness to carry one's judicial load. The middle-level suspensions and demotions are for drinking alcoholic beverages (prohibited to Moslems) or smoking opium in public or other unseemly behaviour. At the dismissal level, one is talking about serious public scandal, although this would seem to be a somewhat relative matter by comparison with what has been known to happen on occasion to high court judges in North America.

A further aspect of the Supreme Court is its association with the Minister of Justice and with the Attorney-General.

The office of Minister of Justice predated both the creation of the Supreme Court and the adoption of the Code. According to the *Tadhkirat al-Mulk*, that authoritative manual on Safavid administration, the Divan-Begi directed the interrogation of those guilty of capital crimes (murder, rape, blinding, and breaking of teeth), controlled the tribunals of legal authority, and tried cases of oppression and transgression and civil actions in cases involving more than five toumens. (67) $. He was Justice Officer.

A Ministry of Justice is therefore today in Iran, a ministry with considerable historical prestige. In fact, when the present Ministry of Justice was established under the present Code, a Minister of Justice was appointed to set up the Ministry — not a Committee of the Majlis. The Code provided that all judges should be Iranian nationals and qualified lawyers. At the time, there were not sufficient law school graduates to qualify with the result that the Minister of Justice — who held the appointive power for Supreme Court judges — was obliged to appoint some judges with a background of ecclesiastical studies and some from the Civil Service who had shown ability in legal matters. Most of these first appointees have retired, but a few still sit on the Bench. Today, of course all appointed judges hold law degrees, most from the University of Teheran, a few from universities in France and Switzerland, a few from the United States and fewer still from Great Britain, although one degree holder from the University of London did rise from the Supreme Court to the post of Under-secretary of Justice. It should be noted that Supreme Court judges are normally selected for appointment by the Minister of Justice from within.

Although there are a very few exceptions, the normal procedure of appointment is from the court of first instance, to the Court of Appeals, to the Supreme Court.

Below the Minister of Justice, in the hierarchy of the Judiciary, sits the Attorney-General and the President of the Supreme Court. They are considered co-equal. They have offices next to one another and seldom grant interviews except when together. The President of the Supreme Court is considered to hold the judicial portfolio and the Attorney-General, the administrative. For that reason, the line of communication is from the Attorney-General up to the Minister and not from the President up. The latter, in fact, because his position is considered to be exclusively judicial, has very little personal contact with the Minister of Justice.

The functions of the Attorney-General can be comprehended under two headings :

1. He supervises, directs, and gives advice to the public prosecutors of the Courts of Appeal and to the public prosecutors of the courts of the first instance. His function here is administrative. There are three echelons of prosecutors — the court of first instance, for example, has several of them working under the direction of the public prosecutor of appeals.
2. He has several associates who work under his direction and control with the branches of the Supreme Court. As a general rule, when the General Assembly of the Supreme Court is convened, the Attorney-General himself appears before the General Assembly to carry the prosecution.

Below the Supreme Court sits a criminal high court which operates in the provincial capitals as a court of first instance. Members of this body consist of 3 judges in minor cases and 5 judges in the case of felony. In civil actions, this court functions as a court of appeals.

Originally, the lowest courts of first instance, the district courts (Dadgah-e-Bakhsh) had civil jurisdiction in matters involving controversies in amounts under 50,000 rials (about $ 650). Judges sat alone. Their criminal jurisdiction was restricted to imposing sentences of less than a month. These courts were abolished in 1977.

The primary court of first instance (Dadgah-e-Shahrestan) has civil jurisdiction over controversies involving more than 50,000 rials and criminal jurisdiction over offenses punishable by more than a month and less than 5 years imprisonment. A session of this court likewise requires only a single judge. In August 1977, these courts were expanded to take over the district courts. New responsibilities have been given to these so-called "township" courts. They can now deal with classes of cases such as inheritance, landlord and tenant disputes, disputes relating to family courts, etc. There are now 101 of these courts in the Teheran area.[8] About 20% of the elected members are women.

In 1965, rural courts or Houses of Equity were created to investigate and settle disputes arising among the inhabitants of a village. Ten years later over 3000 of them existed. In a sense, they replace at the lowest level, the formal judiciary—the judges do not have to be lawyers. They are ordinary citizens elected by the community (3 serve as regulars, 2 as alternatives). While their judgements have been reviewed in the past by a judge of the nearest court of first instance, their record is very good and very few cases have been reserved. In fact these Houses of Equity in the reorganization of the courts by the Ministry of Justice in summer, 1977, were given considerable expanded power.[9] According to the directives of the Ministry of Justice, they may now try civil suits in 13 different categories — trespass, wife support, inheritance certifictes, bail, estates of the deceased, property management, protecting the holdings of minors, mental cases, and "those lost forever", etc. They may not try criminal cases.

At the city level, the counterpart of the Houses of Equity are known as the Adjudication Councils. Their base was considerably expanded in the reorganization of 1977. Roughly their jurisdiction parallels that of the Houses of Equity except the trial value of disputed cases is double that of the village (i.e. 100,000 rials in the city against 50,000 in the village).

Penal cases may be tried by these courts where no more than 50,000 rials are involved. However, traffic fines are reserved to the police. (Traffic violations in Iran are criminal. While theoretically criminal procedure in Iran places the burden of proof on the State, great weight attaches to police reports. Hence a prudent foreigner carries sufficient cash in Iran to make on-the-spot settlement of his traffic disputes before he gets tossed into the maw of the police machinery.) The Minister of Justice has made clear that the Adjudication Councils could resort both to the law and also to traditional practice in settling cases. This statement makes clear that despite the promulgation of the Constitution in 1906 and the subsequent secularization of the law, the old customs of Iran — the *urf* — and the Islamic Tradition are still present. There is no such thing in Iran as "instant law" in the sense that some developing countries are said to impose it. Law in Iran is not a fragile thing. It is old and tough. It is familiar. The substantive law of property in Iran, for example, the law of the family, succession after death, have all been secularized but generally speaking they still follow the teachings of Islam. Hence lawyers are not really essential in the lower courts, as the people know the law through long tradition.

The Shahanshah, as pointed out above, has traditionally provided the iron dimension to the ancient parallel systems of law. Certainly areas of competence belong to him. These areas come together in the system of courts martial as they obtain today in Iran.[10]

Article 87 of the Supplementary Law of the Constitution states ; "Courts martial shall be established throughout the country in accordance with special law." The so-called special law was passed further to this provision shortly thereafter. It established three categories of courts martial of which only one is of concern here, that is the "ordinary courts martial" Articles 10–15 of the court martial law provide that in each district where a military unit is established (unit is not defined. It seems to apply to corps headquarters), a courts martial composed of three army officers shall be established. There is provision for an appeal to a higher court which consists of four officers. It will be noted that the civilian courts have no jurisdiction even on appeal.

The ordinary courts martial have jurisdiction over (1) spies; (2) those carrying arms against the government; (3) collusion with or giving information to a foreign government on matters regarding military affairs; (4) any action incompatible with the "security and order" of the country; and (5) action intended to further the organization and objectives of communism.

It should be noted that Iran's courts martial system stands in general contrast with western tradition. Jurisdiction is not confined to soldiers in uniform. (There have been cases, however, in the United States, involving the trial of civilians by courts martial). It tends to be more security oriented and it is curious how detached Iranians are about what would be considered to be an anomalous position vi-a-vis the civilian courts in the West.

For example, this writer has heard leading attorneys in Iran speak of this as "dirty work" with which they did not want to be associated. They speak of "known criminals" even before they are brought to trial. Some go so far as to compare the courts martial with summary justice, an idea to which they do not seem averse in these circumstances. Certainly courts martial trials in Iran are brief and almost invariably administer the death penalty. Execution is carried out almost immediately.

The peculiar status of the courts martial system is to be found in — or rather not to be found — the omission of any description or even mention of this system in texts on law in Iran. In a sense, the system reflects a direct extension of kingly power and this is reflected in the procedures followed. In 1970, the writer was told by a leading attorney (courts martial were not then open to the public) that no defence attorney was provided to the accused. In fact the case was prepared and prosecuted by a prosecutor known as "the Inquirer". This man has all the details so, as the attorney described it to me with indisputable logic, why does the accused need a defence ? The Inquirer would not present the case unless the culprit was guilty.

Criticism of military courts acting in the case of civilians, has been mounting for several years, not only regarding Iran but in the United States and throughout the world. As a consequence, in the summer of 1977, certain amendments to military court rules were adopted in Iran — without, it should be remarked, any particular public discussion or debate.

The Ministry of War and the Ministry of Justice are now jointly charged with seeing that in every case, the accused is represented by counsel. In the case of service personnel "one or two" active or retired military officers will act as defense lawyers. In the case of a civilian, the lawyer shall be recognized by the judiciary. No provision yet provides for a court-appointed counsel at public expense.

The accused and his attorney are given 15 days to examine the charges against the accused. If the accused or his lawyer have objections regarding the authority of the court, or the statute of limitations, or if they regard the investigations carried out in any way amiss, they must submit their objections to the court office during this period.

The prosecutor still retains his important powers. He is charged with undertaking the "preliminary interrogation of the accused" and issuing charges. However, this must be now done within 24 hours after the appearance of the accused. The prosecutor and not the court, still issues the relevant order (i.e. release on personal cognizance, release in custody, release on surety, commitment to jail). However, the order must be in keeping with the importance of the crime and the severity of the punishment projected. Further, the past record of the accused must now be considered, "his physical condition, age and social standing."

Defense attorneys in military courts are to be free to speak to the charges against their client and they may not be prosecuted in this regard. If charges are brought against a defense lawyer arising from his appearance in a military court, the case shall be heard in a military court if the lawyer is a military man, but if the lawyer is a civilian, the case shall be heard in a civilian court.

Sessions of the military court are now to be open unless the prosecutor shall feel that a public trial is prejudicial to public order and public interest or to public morals. In this case the prosecutor may request the court for a secret trial. If the court accepts the prosecutor's request, it shall issue the order for a secret trial. At the end of the trial the judgement of the court shall be read only to the prosecutor, the accused and the defense lawyer.

Article 203 of the new amendments reads : "Judges shall

act with due regard to God, Shahanshah, and Justice, within the framework of the law and with regard to the character of the accused. They shall be entirely free and independent in reaching their judgement."

Security is at once monolithic and component. In Iran, the Courts Martial, as noted, is at once a system of law and a matter of security. As a marriage, it is coordinate and effective. If it is a creature of the Shah's will — as well as representing his sense of government — it is difficult to argue that in the historic context of Iranian law it does not represent what it says it represents — God, Shahanshah, Justice. There is dissent to this, of course. An easier argument sees the individual in continuing conflict with the collective life of the nation. The contentious issues between what we, as individuals want and even demand, and the security of the State has always been a subject for great political mileage. In Canada, for example, under the Diefenbaker administration, human rights became legislative rather than at common law. To this date most matters involving human rights before the courts are interpreted, still, under the criminal code. Canada has no Bill of Rights as does the United States. But even in the United States, interpretations of the Bill of Rights as passed down by the Courts have been a continuing matter of contention.

Iran has had the same problems as other nations — only they've had them longer. When Xerxes told Themistocles that laws in different countries differ, he was making the observation that any older, more experienced man would make to one whose background and experience were limited. (For all their intellectual curiosity, the Greeks suffered from a certain provincialism.) Today is not that much different from yesterday. The most vociferous proponents of free expression can, in fact, be pretty intolerant at all times and in all seasons.

In Iran, matters of human rights are, as elsewhere, the subject of continuing dialogue. When Hushang Ansary, a prominent public figure in Iran, says that freedom of the press and access to information are "among the most indisputable rights of the Iranian people"[11] he means what he says. When Empress Farah criticizes the "faceless bureaucratic culture in Iran that disregards human relations in their encounters with the public,"[12] she is not talking law but she is speaking to a matter of law and she also means it. Iran has not always received a good press in the West, in matters affecting human rights. Yet it is not consonant with law elsewhere — and its problems — to single out Iran as an example of high disregard of human rights. The system of courts martial in Iran just dealt with does speak to the matter of life and death in the security of a nation. On the other hand, since the days of Cyrus the Great, the Iranians have shown a very real sense of balance in matters involving the citizen and the state. The first declaration of the rights of man to be found anywhere is inscribed on a terra cotta cylinder that lies in the British Museum, two blocks from where I write this. This cylinder of Cyrus was discovered in 1879 by British archaeologists and speaks to the conquest of Babylon. In the text, terrorism is prohibited in the lands of Akkad and Sumer. Homes are to be restored to the people and made secure to them. Slavery is abolished. Religious tolerance is instituted. An ancient story from Achaemenid times speaks of the enforcement of it. A dishonourable and corrupt judge of this dynastic rule was flayed alive and his skin used to recover the judgement seat upon which was placed his son, his successor, with the grim reminder not to forget the seat whereon he sat.

In Iran, as with all nations, human aspirations must be equated with the realities of enforceable law and enforcement. The interests of the individual are surely involved. But so are those of society and ultimately those of the state itself. The law speaks to these matters as best can. In North America, there is great emphasis on free speech. Yet even the great Holmes reminds us that free speech does not give one the right to should "Fire" in a crowded theatre. Human rights can only be understood in relation to such political rights as independence, national sovereignty, and internal security. Even in England, that fountainhead of Western freedom, when the Crown is being challenged, the rules change. "If the Chancery and Courts of Westminster be shut up, it is war."[13] If the sheriff cannot execute the king's writ, then it is *tempus belli*.

In Iran, the process of the transformation of freedom to rights has at times been a painful one — certainly it has been an arduous one. Defining rights in terms of legal and constitutional sanctions is not at all self-evident. I can remember years ago travelling in a foreign country with a wise old Jewish friend. Something happened and I began exclaiming about my rights. "Your rights", he said scornfully, "you had better find out what they are before you demand them."

Probably the greatest difficulty in forming a consensus on the substance of human rights stems from differences and disparities within systems of government. What may be considered a legitimate right in one society may easily be construed as an abuse of such a right in another. Furthermore, situations may drastically alter within a given system at any given time. In the fall of 1977, Germany abrogated certain human rights as they related to imprisoned terrorists — access to a lawyer, refusal of *habeas corpus*, etc. The Left made much of this. But it is in the nature of the political dialogue that this is bound to happen. Countries of recent constitutional origin — and Iran is one of them — struggle incessantly with disruptive and separatist movements. Understandably the right of dissent will lie in a narrower focus than those countries with a long tradition of constitutionalisation. The fine line between dissent and disruption is not an easy one to walk.

In Iran there has been a concerted effort to identify rights with the Monarchy rather than the Fundamental Laws. "Every step taken during the Revolution under the Shahanshah's leadership has been aimed at building the infrastructure for the expansion of the people's liberties."[14] Such liberties are now considered a cardinal principle of Iran's overall development. Where is the line ? "As the Shahanshah has pointed out, within the framework of Iran's social system, there is freedom for everything — except treason."[15]

The demands of justice and kingly rule, as will be shown below, address themselves further to these matters. Perhaps it were best now to turn to them.

Justice

In a memorable sentence, Aristotle writes : "Fire burns both in Greece and Persia; but conceptions of justice shift and change."[16]

In the house of every Greek and Roman was an altar. On this altar there was kept a small quantity of ashes and a few lighted coals. This fire was kept by the master of the house and was extinguished only once a year. Every evening the fire was banked and in the morning revived with a few twigs. Not just any sort of wood would do. The keeping of the sacred fire was a concert of special rites and rules, including the trees from which the twigs would come.

On the first of March the sacred fire was extinguished and lit again immediately, not with flint and steel but by rubbing pieces of wood together as was the custom of early peoples everywhere. Only when the entire family had perished did the fire become extinguished forever.

The fire was pure. No unworthy object could be cast into it; no blameworthy deed committed in its presence. The fire was divine. Offerings were made to it; prayers offered up to it. An Orphic hymn runs thus : "Render us always prosperous, always happy, O fire; thou who art eternal, beautiful, ever young; thou who nourishest, thou who art rich, receive favourably these our offerings, and in return give us happiness and sweet health."[17]

Fortune and misfortune came in sequence to the fire, When the palace of Priam is destroyed, Hecuba draws the old man to the fire. Arms could no longer protect them, but, she said, "this altar will protect us all." Alcestis, who is about to die, giving her life for her husband prays for her noble husband and for her children. When Agamemnon returns from Troy covered with glory, his first act is to make a sacrifice of thank-offerings to the fire in his own house.

Meals were eaten before the fire. Horace, Ovid, and Petronius all attest to this. The first fruits of the food was the fire's portion. No one doubted that God was present and that he ate and drank.

The sacred fire was a just God. No ignoble thought or conversation disturbed the serenity of the hearth. Man measured himself — for good or evil — before the shadowed embers. Here was his moment of truth. Not in the presence of the enemy; not in vain glory or wild excess. But here, in the heart before his God. So we moderns, too, lie and look into our fireplaces or into the campfire not plotting evil but basking in the immemorial good that lies in all humans and is here distilled through the flickering flames.

The worship of the sacred fire, as Aristotle tells us, did not belong exclusively to Greece and Italy. It was Eastern as well.

The ancient Aryans knew the fire God. The Laws of Manu scrupulously describe the essential religious acts and as in Greece warns the guilty man against approaching his hearth before he had purified himself. The Orphic hymns but echoed the earlier Rig-Veda of the Aryans. "O, Agni, thou art the life, thou art the protector of man; thou are a prudent defender and a father; if we have committed a fault, if we have gone far from thee, pardon us."[18]

The Laws of Manu assign the fire a special role in Kingship. The King was holy because of his descent from the Gods. His person was of a divine character. He was the brother of the Sun and Moon and his home was among the Stars. But his real nature was fire and in ancient Persia, this fire nature was always symbolized by the nimbus of fire surrounding his head.[19]

The central position of the Shahanshah distinguishes fire worship between the West and the East. In the former, it remained familial and personal. In Iran, while this was also true — even the Shah had his personal fire which was extinguished at his death — the nature of kingship lifted it into the public weal. As a consequence fire worship in early Iran became an integral concern of the State. The evidence of this can readily be seen by the traveller in Iran who has any interest at all in the archaeological ruins which are so prevalent throughout the realm.

There is a very fine Achaemenian ruins at Naqsh-i-Rustam, Ka'bâ-i-Zardusht, which has inscribed on its walls a long trilingual inscription in Pahlavi-Sassanian, Pahlavi-Parthian and Greek of the struggle between Rome and Persia. This is perhaps the most photographed of the fire temples in Iran as it is in a fine-state of preservation and is conveniently located close at hand to Persepolis and modern Shiraz. There are others, of course, to be seen throughout the kingdom and they all bear witness to the great importance of the sacred fire. In point of fact, under the Seleucids, the princes of Persis bore the title *Fratadara*, or fire guardians. Not until the Parthians was this illustrious nomenclature superseded by that of Shah.

The Sassanians re-established a state religion. It was not Zoroastrian, however. It was rather, the ancient Mazdaean faith that seems to have been affected by Zoroaster's reforms.[20]

Into that faith, Artaxerxes II introduced the cult of Anahita which was especially associated with fire worship. The chief sanctuary was at Istakhr. It was served by fire priests (herbads). In the northwest, Iranian religion similarly centred on fire worship, most notably at the great temple of Shiz. The familiar magi were priests at this temple.

Fire worship, then, in ancient Iran, was a matter of state.[21] Worship was public. In the centre of the leading cities there was always a fire-temple. They were not small structures. At Bishapur, the temple adjoining the Palace was 46 feet square and 46 feet high. The stone fire altar, consisting of base, column, and table, is in disarray, but its components can still be seen.

The three fires most especially venerated within the Sassanian Empire were Adhar-Farnbagh at Kariyan in Fars belonging especially to the priests; Burzin Mihr, the Peasants Fire, on Mount Ravand in Khurasan; and Adhar-Gushnasp, the Warriors or Royal Fire at Garjak in Azerbaijan. The Kings were very generous to these early sanctuaries as they were to the mosques later, after the Arab Conquest.

Ruins of fire temples constructed as late as the 7th Century can still be seen in Iran.

Public worship, of course, required the services of a vast priesthood, arranged hierarchically from the lowest class to the highest rank.[22] The Grand Mobad, or Chief of the Magi, had the supreme direction of religious matters. He was chosen by the Shah and in turn nominated the members of the priesthood. He sat at court in very much the same role as the Chancellor of ancient England. He was the King's conscience. He was also the Chief Justice.

The Chief Herbad, who apparently was also at Court, was the "Chief of Fire." He represented the thousands of minor herbads (fire-priests) throughout the realm. Unlike the Chief Mobad, he had no judicial functions.

As a further example of the power of the clergy, under the Sassanians (only 5 Sassanian Shahs chose their successors) when the monarchy moved to an elective procedure (within the Sassanid family, of course) the designation of the king in case of dispute became the choice of the Grand Mobad.

Aristotle's simile of the burning fire reflects the poet in the man. We see it in ourselves as we lie in front of the fireplace or gaze into the campfire. We make our plans, we have our recollections. But it is true, too, that as the fire warms us, its laziness comes to us and our thoughts tend to idleness. Strong resolve is lacking. Xerxes brings us back to the reality of it. When he granted Themistocles an audience, he said this:[23]

"Laws, O Stranger, are naturally different among different men; there may be legitimate differences of opinion, but all men are agreed that it is a noble endeavour to respect and keep the laws. ... Among us, who have many noble laws, this is pre-eminently binding : to honour the king and worship him as the image of God who saves all."

The divine and priestly role of the king has been considered in an earlier chapter. If Persian subjects of Xeres day fell to their knees and addressed him as a divinity,[24] this did not thereby relieve the Shahanshah of the responsibility to see that justice was done. Justice, in fact, is seen in Persian literature as being the Supreme virtue. It depends upon the divine commandment and therefore, in the words of Tusi, "the first concern of the king."[25] Throughout the literature of the early and later period of Persian kings, there is a strong emphasis on the fact that the ruler should use his intelligence, knowledge, instincts and ideals in the service of justice. "The ruler should understand that leadership is a bride, whose dowry is the lives of men."[26]

There is every reason to believe that law under early Persians was enforceable and enforced. Judges were held in high respect. For the most part (except for the very high families) the functions of the judge were reserved for the priests. "Among the Persians," Agathias writes, "nothing is considered lawful and just unless it has been approved by a Magus."[27]

The laws were much feared among the Persians. Three kinds of crime were recognized — against the Shahanshah which consisted of treason, rebellion and flight in battle; against God, when a man turned against the State religion (applied chiefly to Manichees) and against one's neighbour.

The King, in theory and early in fact was the supreme judge. On certain occasions — a tradition dating back to Achaemenid times — the king appeared on horseback to overlook the crowd and render justice to those who complained of oppression.

Usually, however, as will be described below, Sassanian kings held formal court twice a year. Shortly before the Arab Conquest (under Yazdigird I) this custom was abolished.

Plato and Aristotle both make brief note of the Persian concern for justice and the right way. "The Persians steered a middle course between subjection and liberty," Plato writes of the Achaemenid period, "if the subject was a man of wisdom and a capable adviser, the king showed no jealousy of him, but permitted free speech and bestowed instructions on such competent counsellors, so that the gift of wisdom was freely placed at the disposal of the public service."[28] He remarked that the Achaemenid "won the hearts of the common people by his liberality and munificence." He caught the essence of justice in noting that in judgement the text is "within his judge's own breast" and thus becomes "the State's preserver as well as his own."[29]

Aristotle was less generous than Plato. In examining Persian kingship he noted the paternalism present in the relationship of the king toward his subjects but remarked that it "resembles tyranny" (i.e. injustice).[30]

Men, for better or worse, sit this seat, he reminds us. There is no escape. It was the custom of the Persian Kings, he tells us, to give special audiences for the common people at the festival of the autumn equinox and at the vernal equinox (No-Ruz, the Persian New Year). Several days before these audiences were to be held, proclamations were read telling the people to be ready. Cases were prepared, documents collected and petitions received. When the day came, the king's herald stood outside the gate of the bazaar and shouted : "If any man impedes another from submitting his needs, the king will be innocent of his blood." The king then took his position with the *mubad-mubudan* (Chief Justice) sitting at his right hand.

Then the king would turn to his Chief Justice and say, "In the eyes of God, there is no sin greater than a king's sin. The right way for a king to acknowledge God's grace is by looking after his subjects, giving them justice, and preserving them from oppressor." When the king is a tyrant (and the Persians warned themselves against tyranny as much as Aristotle did) all his courtiers practise tyranny. When a king forgets God, then God abandons him in His wrath. With this abandonment "the world goes to ruin ... then the kingship is transferred to another house". Then the king addressed the *mubad* more specifically. "O, God-fearing *mubad*", he said, "take care that you do not favour me against your conscience, because everything that God demands of me, I ask of you; so I hereby make you responsible."

Then the Chief Justice considers the case and awards judgements. When all is done, the king returns to his throne, puts on his crown, and turns to his nobles and retainers and admonishes them to see that these matters are carried out. "On that day whoever was nearest to the king was furthest and who was strongest was weakest."[31]

This book is concerned, however, primarily with the concept of justice (adalaj 'adl) as developed in historic Iran. Plato and Aristotle have both been read in translation for centuries by Iranians and they hold a place in the pantheon of thought that is second to none. But their works have been added to and multiplied by generations of Iranians who themselves have demonstrated great qualities of mind addressed to the problems of justice within their own environment which surely was much different from that of the Greek city state.

Four names stand out — Nizam al-Mulk, Mirkhond, Ali, al-Farabi. They are representative thinkers in that they are Moslem, essentially Shi'ite; Iranian or identified with Iran. Each was a man of importance in his day and each was a thinker, and a doer. They saw concepts of justice and their meaning in terms of human interpretation and eventually, application.

Between 1086 and 1091 Nizam al-Mulk served with distinction as Grand Vizier. His book, *Siyasat-nama* or *Book of Government*, was written by him for the edification of Sultan Malikshah of the Seljuq dynasty who was then ruling Persia. The Seljuqs were a wild tribe of Turkish nomads who, through fierce fighting, had ascended to the throne. They knew nothing of administration and Nizam al-Mulk, as the King's first minister, took it upon himself to instruct his master in the art of running a civilized country as contrasted with a mobile tent city. His justification for writing the book, was, however, presented with great delicacy. "In order that the Master of the World", he starts out, "may know how zealous different kings have been in the pursuit of justice and equity; what care they have taken that the oppressed should receive their rights; and what measures they have adopted to remove evil doers from the face of the earth", he Nizam al-Mulk, deigns to write this book.[32]

The *Book of Government* contains fifty chapters and devotes much of this space to the matter of kingly justice. All aspects of government are considered of course — as they easily relate to justice — and the sage advice of the great Vizier comes through clearly and interestingly. Throughout, consultation is advised. "Holding consultations on affairs is a sign of sound judgement, high intelligence and foresight" (Chap. 18).

The first two chapters deal with the ruler and God. "In every age and time," he writes, "God chooses one member of the human race, and having adorned and endowed him with kingly virtues, entrusts him with interest of the world and the well being of His servants." It is the ruler's job to impart such dignity and majesty in the eyes and hearts of men, that under his "just rule" they may live their lives in constant security and ever wish for his reign to continue.

The keynote, therefore, is struck at the beginning. The purpose of government is to bring justice to the people and to safe-guard it. "Just rule" is a phrase found again and again in Persian history. It is not possible for a ruler to avoid this awesome responsibility no matter what his personal predilections.

Chapter 3 provides the implementation of this ideal. "It is absolutely necessary that on two days a week the king should sit for the redress of wrongs, to extract recompense from the oppressor, to give justice and to listen to the words of his subjects with his own ears, without any intermediary." The Vizier states flatly that "when the king sits in a palace protected by gates, locks, vestibules and screens, self interested and oppressive persons can keep the people back and not let them go before the king."

Nizam al-Mulk then relates several stories of the kings of the Sassanid line which are studies in the problems of justice. Some of them recounted are "The Story of the Just Amir and the Saffarids" (Chap. 3); the story of Bahram Gur and Rast-ravishn (Chap. 4); the story of the bakers of Ghazhain (Chap. 6); and others. By far the most famous, however is "The Story of the Just King" (Chap. 5) which is a well known and oft repeated story in Iran. It is about Nushirwan, the Just, and is one of the famous stories about this great King, whose reign during the Sassanian dynasty was looked upon as the epitome of just rule.

Shortly after ascending the throne as a young man, one of Nushirwan's army commanders of great wealth, seized the land of a widow woman without recompense. After two years of trying to get some kind of settlement, the old woman, hearing that the Shah was hunting in a nearby area, went to him and asked for justice in her case. The Shah promised he would look into it and sent a page to check out her story. His report bore out the truth of her contention. The Shah then called his court together and had both the page and the old woman testify. The nobles comprising the court agreed that the army commander had acted wrongly whereupon the Shah issued the penalty :

> "I require you to strip the skin from that man's body, throw his flesh to the dogs, stuff the skin with straw and hang it upon the palace gate. Then let it be proclaimed for seven days that if any man commit oppression, taking even a bag of straw, a chicken or a handful of grass wrongfully from somebody else, and if a complainant comes to court, the same will happen to him as happened to this man."

Nushirwan then went on to warn the court personally, "I shall protect the ewes and the lambs from the wolves, I shall restrain grasping hands, I shall remove evil-doers from the face of the earth and fill the world with justice and equity". The Shah then commanded that a chain should be set up with bells attached to it "within the reach of even a child of seven years old" so that any complainants who came to court would not have to see a Chamberlain, but rather would only have to pull the chain and the bells would ring and Nushirwan would hear it and redress their grievances.

Mirkhond (Rauzat-us-Sala) was born in 1432 A.D. and was attached to the Court of Herat. His history is a general work, running originally to seven volumes, brief enough considering that the author treats of Persian history from the creation to the conquest of Iran by Alexander. It is a mixture of fact and fiction, quite typical of the parallel Iranian history that was described in the first two chapters of this book.

The most familiar portion of the text is the famous oration of (Minucheher), beside which the oration of Pericles, much studied by Western students, appears pale by comparison.[33]

After beginning with praises of the Almighty, the King speaks to responsibility of monarchy. "That Monarch is the most fortunate," he tells us, "who renders his flock most happy, devotes every time and season to the care of his subjects." He never demands more of his subjects than is established by tradition, avoiding the introduction of "new rules and capricious innovations".

The King, he tells us, has certain rights over the military and husbandmen, but they in turn have certain rights over him. For example, the soldier is expected to obey orders and to give battle to the enemy. The King, on the other hand, should supply their maintenance "without delay or evasion".

The relationship with the husbandmen is likewise reciprocal. They are to work, improve the soil, pay the King's Tributes "obediently and cheerfully". Their claim on him is as follows: "he is to dispense impartial justice on all their concerns; to levy the necessary imposts with leniency. He is not to place tyrannical governors over them, nor permit any intolerable vexation". In years of drought, the husbandmen are to be exempted from tribute.

Minucheher then speaks of the qualities of kingship. There are three essentials (1) the king should speak in truth; (2) he should be liberal and not penurious; (3) "he must be clement and not prone to anger." It is far better, he says to err on the side of clemency than of severity.

The King is never to suppress charges brought to him about administrators but rather he should "require the accused governor to appear before him and then investigate the matter with scrupulous attention."

Punishment is to be exemplary so that "no other person hereafter should practise the same conduct."

"The King is not himself to inflict punishment but to deliver up the perpetrator to the heirs of the murdered person who may either put him to death or make him pay the price of blood".

Accusations, in general, must be subjected to the strictest investigation and if proved guilty, punishment must follow. "Such are the institutions prescribed by righteousness to the King".

The King sees role in a sense as viceregent. "Human wisdom", he tells us, "cannot ward off the decrees of omnipotence." There is no fleeing the Divine Will. "The people of this world are like travellers", he reminds us, "laden with their respective burdens who set out on a journey". All that they carry "is borrowed" which at last they must leave behind. "Nor can any part of it accompany them except gratitude, recognition to the Divine Will and good works".

Minucheher closes his oration with words addressed particularly to his governors. "I charge you to do justice", he tells them, "and refrain from oppressing the cultivators for to them both you and I are indebted for whatever we eat or drink". In justice, the world flourishes; in injustice the world remains uncultivated. "Take heed", therefore, he concludes, "to act with justice".

In an urban society, it is not always easy to understand ancient admonitions regarding husbandmen, the cultivators of the soil, taxes, droughts, and their relations to principles of justice. To many of us, justice is a sophisticated compendium of relationships, of freedom, of maximum flexibility. As we move toward al-Farabi, we see this. But there is still one step to go between the hard-headed ministerial advice of Nizam al-Mulk and the abstractions of the philosophers. Ali, the beloved of the Iranians, a soldier and administrator, Caliph and saint, speaks to the matters that lie deep in the historical consciousness of the Iranian society.

The present Shah has stated that he does not want the peasantry (the husbandmen) of Iran to fall below the present figure of 60% of the population. Instead, he has announced, he will bring in 400,000 labourers if necessary to man the plants of industrialization. In expressing himself thus, he is stating an historical position as well as a present intention. He places himself firmly in a tradition that is Muslim — and in Iran this begins with Ali — but is yet even more ancient than Iran.

In the Avesta, that ancient Aryan treasure-house of Persian lore, the peasant held an honoured position. The Avesta is unequivocal in its praise for the life of the peasant and the practice of agriculture. The reclamation of wasteland is encouraged as well as planting.[34]

> "Creator of this material world, Thou Holy One; Where is the earth most gladdened ? Ahura Mazda answered : Wherever grain is most produced ... and grass and fruit-bearing trees; wherever arid land is changed into watered and marshy into dry land."

The early Aryan prototype of the Persian Shahanshah was Yima who is described as the Feeder, Protector, and Overseer of the world. The function of the Shah, therefore, was to fill this role. It was for him to provide whatever was necessary for the cultivation of the land — water, protection against marauders, seed. He was to see that there were sufficient cultivators of the soil. There were to be stores piled up as against bad years.

The land, of course, supported the prosperity of the early state. The activities and well being of the peasants was the base of society. Furthermore in the early days the main revenues of the kingdom were derived from the land. A depressed peasantry was a non-productive peasantry. Prosperity for all depended on the prosperity of the peasant. In a society of classes, as the early Aryan society was and as the Iranian became, the peasant might be at the bottom of the heap, but his importance was never denied. So it was that the peasant sought *bast* with the Shah. Their relationship was direct and woe betide the avaricious landlord who got in between.

When Iran became Moslem, this early tradition was carried on and merged with Islamic tradition. The classic Islamic conception of the ruler was that he was the shepherd of his people. As most people were peasants and nomads, it was the ruler's special charge that this class should not only be protected but they should be nurtured. Ali was a master administrator. There is a famous letter from the Commander of the Faithful, the fourth Caliph, the first Imam, to the tax collector in Egypt. Ali admonished the administrator to give greater attention to the development of the land than collecting the taxes because if the land is not developed, the country will fall into ruin, and the people will be destroyed.[35]

> "If the people complain of the heaviness of taxation, or of some natural calamity, the interruption of irrigation, misfortune, or that the land has been changed by becoming waterlogged or parched, lighten their burden in such a way as you would expect would lead to the putting right of their affairs. You should not regard it as a burden to do anything which will lighten their burden. Verily it is a store which they will return to you in developing your district and in adorning your province. In addition you will win their excellent praise and pride in having justice spread among them. Further you may count upon the surplus of food which you have caused them to store up on account of what you remitted to them, and on account of the confidence which you gave them, because of your justice towards them in your compassion for them.... The ruin of a country comes from the destitution of its people and the people are made destitute when the minds of their governors are concentrated on amassing wealth and when their tenure is insecure and when they do not take warning."

al-Farabi (c. 870 – 950) was born in Transoxiana (north of the Oxus River). As a mature scholar he transferred himself to the court of the Shi'ite ruler of Aleppo where he did most of his writing.

al-Farabi was, in fact, the great bridge between the East and the West and later Arabic philosophers depended on his achievement. His translations of both Aristotle and Plato and his commentaries were world renowned. In his own writings, *Views of the Citizens of the Perfect State, the Book of Government*, and *Aphorisms of the Statesman* have gained him a permanent place in the history of political philosophy.

In the last named book, the Aphorisms[36] al-Farabi writes at length of justice and of kingship. His opening comments are reminiscent of Sassanian rule. First the world was created. Then came the "ordering of the classes of the world". Included are their mutual relationship and man's station with reference to God. "This is the beginning", al-Farabi writes, "the end is happiness".

The philosopher develops his concepts of man's station in

this life and the classes that make up those belonging to a common station. Once each person has been secured within his class ("each man's portion has been fixed"), then it must be preserved to him. Justice consists of things "having once been divided, remain preserved to the people". Injustice is the upsetting of this balance. When it occurs, the pain and penalty to the perpetrator "must be measured, so that every injustice may be confronted with a commensurate punishment."

Justice is identified as well with work as with station. "Everyone must have assigned to him a single art with which he busies himself solely and a single work to which he attends ... nor must he go beyond it." The author does not believe that man can properly pursue many works or more than a single art and lists his reasons for so thinking.[37]

al-Farabi does not equate justice solely with money. He recognizes the sickness inherent in greed. Any man, he says, who "out of desire or gain" leaves undone the better portion of that for which he is responsible can no longer be said to exercise his stewardship. This is hurtful to justice.

The master or the governor has responsibility even in larger portion than that of the servant or the worker. If he is a man of intelligence, he will combine within himself the several virtues that properly make his own station in life. To do this, he must (1) have an excellence of discrimination with regard to which actions are to be taken and which avoided, and (2) having determined this distinction, he must employ his will to pursuing that action that is "the most excellent of all."

The man who lives by "intelligence in action" is described by al-Farabi as virtuous. The virtuous man loses by death "simply the ability to multiply his actions". Hence the first responsibility of the virtuous man "must not hasten death". He must seek means to survive as long as possible — not only for his sake but because he must not lose his usefulness to those who are dependent upon him. "He must go forward to death only when his death is more useful to the people than his survival". Only ignorant people, he says, are anxious about death. Even the soldier, he points out, must approach death in a particular way. Never rashness, never vainglory, or even that "perhaps he will escape". "Rather he risks his life when he knows that what he desires he will lose unless he endangers himself".

Desire, of course, can never be base. Virtue is the consort of desire and the word "virtue" appears often in the text.

As in the case of the master, or the governor, or the officer, so it is with the ruler. The King must identify himself with what he does, in his station, in such a way that the two become inseparable. Therefore to al-Farabi, "the ideal polity is that in which the ruler attains a kind of virtue which he could not possibly attain except in it."[38]

This is the highest virtue.

The concept of man and his work, man and his place, al-Farabi reminds us again and again in his writings has become, in our time, quite foreign as a way of life. Yet over the generations, al-Farabi pulls us back with great persistence to what is basic to any concept of virtue, of justice, of polity. He speaks to the total interpretation of life and work. He speaks of a concept of justice that must be rooted in the actualities of position and responsibility. To him, these things are not unattainable. They are real and ever present. Life so obtained "is the best possible". Of course there may be deficiencies; there may be corruption in low or in high places; there may be ignorance; there may be defects (a favourite word of the author). But if justice is to be accomplished it will be through a well-ordered scheme of things, "justice which consists in making a division and in preserving what has been divided" (differentiation of function) to the end that all attain happiness.

Once the State has been ordered, the people assigned, justice proclaimed and virtue commended, al-Farabi turns his attention to the ruler himself. "The true king", he writes, "is he whose aim and purpose in the art ... are that he should afford himself and ... the people true happiness, which is the end and aim of the kingly craft."[39] It is essential that the king himself be "the most perfect of them in happiness, since he is the cause of the happiness of the people".

The author then goes on to examine the nature of kingship. "Some think", he says, "the end and purpose in kingship" is greatness and honour and domination and commanding and forbidding and being obeyed and made much of and praised, and they choose honour for its own sake". Others think the aim of rule is riches. Still others think the end of rule is the enjoyment of pleasures. "None of these", says the author, "was called king by the ancients".

"The king is king by the kingly craft", writes the author in a phrase reminiscent of Plato. Rule by force, subjection, terrorising, fear, do not belong to the "essential conditions" of kingship, he notes, although certainly they may be in evidence given particular times and circumstances. As the author says "they may be useful to the kingly craft".

The author's description of the ruler is one in which are combined certain conditions : wisdom, practical wisdom ("what the common people call intelligence"), excellence of persuasion, excellence in producing an imaginative impression, power to fight the holy war (*jihad*) in person, that there should be nothing in his body to prevent him attending to the matters which belong to the holy war. "He in whom all these are united is the model".

al-Farabi recognizes the fact that one man may not possess all of these qualities of kingship, hence he distinguishes between "the ideal king", who possesses knowledge and the king "who rules according to the laws".[40] In the latter case, while many of the qualities of kingship belong to the king, he needs, in addition, "knowledge of the ancient laws and Traditions which the first generation of *imams* acknowledged and by which they ruled."[41]

In the concern expressed throughout Iranian literature and history for justice, excerpted as it has been here, it is important to realize that justice in Iran is based on the hard facts of life that give meaning to thought and to action. There has been little time for idle speculation. Applied justice is the only justice. In Iran, traditionally, this has meant three things — tranquillity in the bazaars, security of the harvests, the place of the highways.

A final question now needs to be answered. What of the king's personal goodness — what of the fount of justice itself ? The West may argue this and Christians may argue this. But the matter was brought to rest in Islam in the famous case of Hulaga. When the great Mongol conquered Baghdad in 656 A.D., he ordered that a ruling be obtained from the doctors of law as to whether a just infidel ruler were better or a believing unjust ruler. Radi 'ad Din 'Ali was present at this meeting.

He was senior and respected. When he saw the reluctance of the others, he took the paper and signed it as preferring the just infidel to the unjust believer. The others signed after him.

"A ruler lacking knowledge," runs an old saying, "is like an elephant in heat which passes by nothing without knocking it down. He has not intelligence to warn him or knowledge to restrain him."[42]

Kingly Rule

The true meaning of the much misunderstood phrase "law and order" now emerges within the Iranian context. It does not mean arbitrary rule or police oppression. It does not stand in violation of human rights. It is, rather an arrangement of things, orderly, carefully constructed, life forms within an essential being.

In the preface, the theoretical framework of this book was described as one of concretization, flowing downward from its apex, the *Grundnorm*, and seeking its stabilization at terraced levels, distinct within each level but a part of the whole. A simple analogy might be the vineyards on the steep slopes of the Rhine.

This political, legal, and social concept is very old. It did not originate with Hans Kelsen and the Vienna School. For untold generations it has been recognized, particularly on the Asiatic continent, as being necessary to political life.

"The King is like the First Cause, which is the cause for existence of all other beings. Then the ranks of order of the beings keep descending, each one of them being both ruler and ruled until they reach down to those that possess no ruling element whatever, but are subservient and always exist for the sake of others. If the King wishes to enjoin the people or a certain group among them to take a particular action, he intimates this to the ranks closest to him. These will then hand it on to their subordinates and so on down the scale. Thus all is linked and fitted together by giving precedence to some over others."[43]

Kingly rule as Plato said long ago is a craft. The present Shahanshah was 58 on 26 October 1977. He had, on that date, ruled 37 years. His continuing presence, as well as his continuing office, in a world torn by assassination, revolution, and angry scars everywhere, is a measure of how well this man has learned his craft. In his life span, starting with wobbly beginning, he came to understand what wise old Harry Truman meant at the Teheran Conference in 1945 when he told the boy "to rule".

This book has dealt with the many aspects of kingly rule in Iran, its components, its manner, its theory and its fact. It has set out in suitable focus for book of this size and intent, the complicated structure of the oldest continuing monarchy in the world. It has shown how this monarchy was established, how it adjusted, how it survived. It has moved from highly personal rule over the centuries to constitutional rule. It has witnessed periods of great gloriousness. It has known periods of poverty and humiliation. It has suffered countless invasions and has seen the scorched earth. It has been betrayed by its friends and faced the imperatives of its enemies. Its survival is one of the great political phenomena of the world.

There are two essential matters involved in kingly rule. One is the exercise of that rule and the others are the limitations upon that rule. The exercise of that rule has been very much the subject of this book. In closing this chapter on the Law of the Monarch, it seems important to set against that rule, its limitations.

Perhaps the proper place to start is with the Constitution of 1906, better known as the Fundamental Laws. By its very nature, a Constitution, of course, is a limitation on rule. This is the reason for it and the reason it is generally adopted throughout the civilized world. A Constitution is law. It embodies rule and it embodies justice. Normally, however, it demonstrates a great flexibility in these matters.

Simply because Iran describes itself as a "constitutional hereditary monarchy" as pointed out at the beginning of the sixth chapter does not mean that it is the same thing as constitutional government in the West. The reason for this is, of course, that as any constitutional lawyer knows, a Constitution is the living embodiment of the people's needs and their aspirations. Therefore, of necessity, all constitutions must differ. This accounts for the present Shah's statement, also in the sixth chapter, that he seeks to "Iranize" the Constitution. If, in fact, the Iranian Constitution was modelled on French and

Belgian lines, then patently it would not be a suitable vehicle in itself to express the Iranian experience. This, of course, is what constitutional law is all about. The American Constitution may have been modelled on the writings of Polybius, but the American nation is not therefore Roman. It has chosen its own way and consequently a vast corpus of constitutional law has grown up in the United States which speaks to the meaning of the Constitution. If, on occasion, the Emperor appears with no clothes as the time that Chief Justice Hughes remarked that "the Constitution is what the judges say it is", the Americans are not thereby upset. Of all the sacred cows in the United States — and there are many of them — the principle of judicial review is the most sacred and as an article of faith among Americans that principle is almost as good as the laws of the Medes and Persians that altereth not.

Prior to the promulgation of the Constitution of 1906, the powers of the Shahanshah, as described above in successive chapters, were of such an absolute nature that it would appear as if there were no limitations upon them whatever. Reputable scholarship could state : "they have been the most absolute monarchs in the world." The people were at the mercy of the king. "He can do what he chooses." He is absolutely exempt from responsibility and owes no duty to the State. Men were required to obey him "whether his commands be just or unjust." The King's powers of dismissal were absolute. He could seize property or take away the life of any of his subjects. "The only thing that can define his exact limitations is his personal disposition."[44]

Traditional society, despite the theory, seldom operates this way. This was true in Iran prior to the Constitutional period. It might be assumed, for example, that the lot of the Persian peasant was analogous to the French peasant under the majority of the Bourbons or the Russian muzhik under the Romanovs. This was simply not true. Of course there were rapacious landlords and there was mismanagement and misfortune. But as has been pointed out above, justice in Iran was closely identified with the peasantry and may well account, in part, for the fact that militancy among the peasants in Iran has never moved to the breaking point.

Similarly with regard to the use of counsel, as pointed out

above, the Sassanians firmly set for Iran a strong tradition of counsel to the King. The Shahanshah may not always have taken it, as related in the first chapter in the *Shahnameh*, but he ignored it at his peril.

Counsel was not always formalized in pre-constitutional Iran. In Achaemenid times, it was merely a meeting of priests and high persons. By the 17th century, a Council of State, as pointed out above, began to sit in somewhat regular session. But not until 1871 was a Council of State, as conceived in Europe, instituted by Naser ed-Din Shah. This was an important step toward Constitutional rule. In creating the Council of State, the Monarch apparently gave actual indication of intent to restrain his authority.[45] Wishing to assure himself of a proper limitation upon kingly rule he carefully chose, besides his Ministers, members of the law and fifteen councillors of career, tied in with sub-offices representing the provinces. This Council continued until the Constitutional period, meeting the conditions, as best it could, necessary for the financial, administrative and military reorganization of Iran. The creation of the Majlis brought this Council to an end, as recalling too explicitly the character of the old regime.

It should be pointed out that Naser ed-Din's projected reforms included administrative reforms as well, further limiting the capricious exercise of kingly rule. In point of fact, as administrators of a great Empire over the centuries, the Iranians offered successive prescriptions which wedded kingly rule to imperial administration. A letter from Ali was quoted above. As Fourth Caliph, Ali issued his *Instructions* in form that included excellent principles of administration. Nizam al-Mulk's *Book of Government* has already been remarked. The *Tuzuk-i-Timour* published by Tamerlane in the 14th century, the *Destour al-Amal* of Shah Ismail the Safavid, both formed important and comprehensive preliminaries to the administrative reforms of Naser-ed-Din.[46]

In all of this, there was no concept of the State. Hence limitations upon authority took the form of counsel, of administrative regulations, the presence of a formalized hierarchical structure, of tradition and traditional ways of doing things generally. This, in itself, created a particular type of kingly rule. Louis XIV identified himself with the State : "L'Etat, o'est moi." This would have sounded odd indeed to an Iranian monarch. In the Safavid period, there was not even a word expressing the concept of the state.[47] The term *dawlat*, meaning bliss or felicity referred to the aura of beneficence surrounding the just ruler and the canopy that sheltered his kingdom. It was a highly personal word and related only to the Shah.

Nevertheless this canopy existed and in a very real sense imposed upon the Monarch an abstract concept of just rule. This particularly related to the common people. The Shahs always treated their peasantry, their soldiers, their artisans, even the small merchants, with considerable tenderness. The present Shah's "My people" may grate on Western ears but it is a concept of long life. The fact is that the absolute nature of the Shah's authority was "not a threat to, but rather a guarantee of the individual freedom and security of the lower classes."[48] As pointed out early, woe betide the man who stood between the Shah and the people. Anyone who served the Shah directly was, in Iranian tradition, his personal slave. His property, his life, his wife, his children — these were all at the disposal of the Shah. Hence court functionaries, officials, even the nobility, did not find proximity to the seat of power an assured one. The Shah's anger could come without warning and he could act without restraint. But at the lower levels, there was the *urf*, the traditional law. The death sentence was pronounced in the courts and there was appeal to the Shah. Malcolm makes an interesting observation regarding this procedure as found in the *urf*. "This summary proceeding" he says, referring to the execution of those whose appeal to the Shah was rejected, "added to the mode of execution which was generally in his presence, and is always inflicted by executioners who attend his person, often give a character of barbarous tyranny to acts of the most exemplary justice."[49]

Chardin, an astute observer, quoted elsewhere in this book, makes the flat statement that there was no arbitrary exercise of the power by the Shah.[50] He is speaking of the Safavid period, of course, and certainly during that dynasty as well as before and after, there are cases where individual Shahs have been capricious, cruel, and unjust, as cases have been so cited in this book. But by comparison, if the competent historians are to be believed, there are relatively few examples of this over the centuries except, as stated above, where those who immediately surround the Shah and serve him incur his human displeasure. This was particularly a check on subordinate governors. The tradition in Iran was that any subject had the right of appeal to the Shah without let or hindrance. He could not be prevented from making his appeal and having his day in Court.

Enough has now been said to show that prior to the Constitution of 1906 there were traditions in Iran, traditions and arrangements were better, which represented very real limitations upon the exercise of kingly rule. Not being privy to the mind of the present Shah, I would hesitate to say that these traditions might be present in his thinking when he is speaking of "Iranizing" the Constitution. But it is no secret among public lawyers that formal legislation exemplified in a written Constitution needs a good many years of glossing and filling out before the bare bones of the law begin to take on a quality of life.

The years immediately, preceding the formulation of the Iranian Constitution were years of conscious movement toward the westernization of law. Of the many underground pieces of literature distributed in the last half of the 19th century, none was more influential than *Yek Kalama.*[51]

Yek Kalama, as noted above, means "One Word." It was really quite a tantalizing revolutionary slogan. Only in the reading of it would one finally discover that the one word was "Law". Written by a former member of the diplomatic corps who had travelled in England and on the Continent, he was much struck by the equity and the impersonality of Western law. Particularly he liked the British system, in true Iranian prose referring to it as "a fragrant flower."

There was other literature of this type coming off the presses in Constantinople, Ghirat, even as far away as India. There was much of it circulated in Iran and it did have its effect. On one occasion, over 2,000 people marched on the Palace to submit a petition for a "House of Justice", an unheard act of boldness. But Naser-ed-Din Shah, involved in his own reforms, was perhaps the most tolerant of Qajar rulers. When he was killed by an assassin's bullet in 1876, the bitterness of the constitutional struggle broke, subsided, and broke again. There are many people living today in Iran whose fathers were active during this period and a few of the very oldest members of the Senate can personally recall those years. Muzaffar-ed, Din Shah (1876 - 1907) in succeeding his father to the throne, didn't give a great deal away but unlike his successor, Muhammad Ali, he at least kept the cap on the struggle. As there is no real tradition in Iran of political science or public law, there is no comprehensive scholastic history in Iran that speaks to this period. Not until the National Assembly itself met based on a decree to his Grand Vazir by the Shah did some kind of systematic account of proceedings emerge. Quite complete records of the Constitutional Convention — if one can use that term — were kept and are available in many university libraries throughout the world although no copies are available in Iran. The opening session met in the presence of the Shah who carefully reminded the delegates that he was the architect and they were the workmen.

Muzaffar-ed Din Shah signed the constitution a few days before his death. On January 19, 1907, his successor, Muhammad Ali, was crowned. He promptly bombarded the Majlis and abrogated the Constitution. Blood flowed for 2 years until an uprising dethroned him in 1909 and crowned his minor son Ahmed with a regency.[52]

The Constitution began then, auspiciously or not, depending upon one's point of view, with two revolutions and one dethronement. These facts, in themselves, would suggest limitations of some magnitude.

The original Constitution of 1906 contained 51 articles. The Supplementary Law, adopted the following year, contained 101 articles. Both of these, together, are known as the "Fundamental Laws of the Constitution of the State of Iran."

The text of the Fundamental Laws is straightforward enough.[53] Except for "General Principles" discussed below, it reads pretty much as any other Constitution.

Under the law, the Shah is a constitutional monarch (i.e., his powers are in trust from the nation). In his oath of office, he swears on the Koran (1) to preserve the independence of Iran; (2) to protect the frontiers, (3) to guard the Constitution; (4) to reign according to the law; and (5) to promote the constitutionally established religion. The constitutional powers and prerogatives of the Monarch are set forth in articles 43-57 of the Supplementary Law. He appoints and dismisses ministers and department heads of the home and foreign services. While the Shah is free of ministerial responsibility, his ministers are not, and under the law they are responsible to both chambers. All bills of the Majlis must be signed by the Shah before they become law and the Shah may not delay or postpone enforcement of a signed bill. The Shah may dissolve both houses but elections must be held within thirty days. He may also call the houses into special session.

The declaration of war and the conclusion of peace are functions of the Shah. So is the conduct of foreign relations — receiving ambassadors, etc. While treaties require ratification by the Majlis, temporary secret treaties may be made by the Shah if in the national interest.

Article 57 of the Supplementary Law of 1907 limits the royal prerogatives and powers of the Shah to those expressly cited in the Constitution and the Supplementary Law.

On the matter of succession to the throne, Articles 36 and 37 of the Supplementary Law vest the monarchy in the eldest male descendant of the Shah. The mother must be of Iranian origin. Descendants from the Qajar line are denied eligibility to the throne. Thus the offspring of Reza Shah's three sisters and his daughters are ineligible and because two of his wives were of Qajar blood, the present Shah's half-brothers who are their sons are ineligible. The Shah had only one brother not related to the Qajar line — Ali Reza — and he was killed in an airplane crash in 1954.

It is important to reiterate that when the Constitution was adopted in 1906 it was not really designed to introduce democratic government by abolishing the monarchy or even by excessively limiting it. On the contrary, as pointed out earlier in this book, the Iranians had always been firm believers in the divine right of kings and they showed no intention during the crisis years of destroying an institution that was so integral a part of their nation's history. Further, when the imperial rescript (farman) was forced from the Shah on August 5, 1906, four months prior to the drawing up of the Constitution, the word *law* as remarked above, does not appear. The separation of the Shah and law was clearly not contemplated. When the Constitution was adopted in December, the Shah retained awesome powers. Twenty-three articles spoke to this power. The three here cited are typical.

> The sovereignty is a trust confided, by the Grace of God, to the person of the King by the Nation, (Art. 35). The person of the King is absolved of all responsibility (Art. 44). The Shah is the 'guardian' of the Constitutional Law of Iran (Art. 39).

In short, what is found in the Fundamental Laws is very much the same — vis-a-vis the monarchy — as had always been traditionally present. Beginning with the Achaemenids, the Shahs of Iran have been the very epitome of the Austinian concept of law. Law was a command from the superior to the inferior. It was absolute and imperative. At first we speak of the war-leader. Later, it is the marriage of priest and war-leader. Then it was the lawgiver. Thus, it was continued with further additions of power into the present as described in earlier chapters.

Concepts such as these are admittedly difficult for western observers to accept. There is, after all, the firm recollection of western history that Lord Coke once told King James I that he was under the law — even if afterwards he had to fall "on all fours". But, the western experience is not the Iranian one. The Constitution of Iran, if studied carefully, can be seen to be essentially administrative and executive, but not legal. The essence of legality is reserved. For that reason, it must be argued that the Shahanshah still — as historically he did — holds the law in this command. He is the *Grundnorm* of Kelsen mentioned in the Preface, and repeated in other form in this chapter, just as the British Constitution was argued by Kelsen to be the *Grundnorm* in Great Britain. But the difference is clear. There is agreement in England that the Queen is under the law. There is no one in Iran who will say this of the Shah. The writer discussed this matter with eminent lawyers and scholars in Iran four years ago even though it was not a particularly welcome question. Nevertheless the conclusion could only be drawn that law in Iran is seen in principle to lie with the Shah. In a sense he could be said to be above the law — as the command in the Austinian sense — or he can be seen as the law-giver in the historical tradition of Darius (none of this means, of course, that the Shah is necessarily lawless). But, whatever be the fact of the matter — and no one in Iran, including the Courts, can really speak to this with authority — the one thing that does emerge with clarity from the Iranian experience is that the Shah does not share his command position with anyone.

There are three components of power contained in the Iranian Constitution directly relating to kingly rule which suggest further limitations upon authority.

The first is Article 57 of the Supplementary Law of 1907 which limits the powers of the Shahanshah to those expressly stated in the Fundamental Law. From a political point of view, limitations are mischievous. Power is not so easily contained. Richard Nixon, who fancied himself in a position of supreme power, a belief not shared by his fellow countrymen, spoke much of "executive privilege" and pushed it to its limits. Elizabeth I, as hard a fighter but a more intelligent person, sought to give legal authority to political reality and the great struggle during her reign over the "prerogative" is a classic accounting of legal confrontation to this day.[54]

No such confrontation has appeared in Iran over the interpretation of Article 57. If Lord Coke could argue that the exercise of the prerogative was in violation of the freedom of Englishmen, as previously remarked, there is no one around who wants to argue this position with the Shah.

He sees his actions as representing the benefit and interest of the people. He is quite frank about his intentions "to reserve exceptional royal powers to the monarch"[55] in order that these interests may be best served. The fact that the Fundamental Law is quite clear on what the Shah's prerogatives are would seem to suggest that a unilateral interpretation of them by the one holding them leaves something to be desired in a legal sense. If the Shah wants to exercise his prerogatives to a certain end — for example, in the matter of granting exclusive monopolies to members of his family — there are no guidelines that apply as there are in England simply because there has never been a legal confrontation on the matter as there was in the days of Elizabeth I. There are no available studies and no court decisions that speak to this matter of the Shah's power. It is possible that studies of this type were made after the Fundamental Laws were adopted, but if so, they are now locked up. Lawyers and political scientists do not, today, concern themselves with such matters in Iran.

Mention was made earlier of the fact that the original journals of the Constitutional convention as well as the journals of the early Majlis debates are really non-existent in Iran even though at one time thousands of copies of them were available. This, coupled with the fact that no real studies of the monarchy are available, suggests not that there is some dark conspiracy of silence, but rather that it is the Shah who intends to provide the blueprint not only of the exercise of his powers but of the concepts of law and justice that obtain in Iran. Despite the Constitution, the Shah, like his predecessors before him, sees himself in what might be called an extra-constitutional tradition.

The second possible limitation contained in the Fundamental Laws is the general grant of power given to the Shah in the Constitution. This is not a *non sequitur*. Logically, a grant of power implies something not originally present in the nature of the office. But in Iran this is not sound doctrine and the present Shah knows this. As pointed out above, in the Fundamental Laws, over 23 articles speak to the power of the Shah in concrete terms. These include the conduct of war, of foreign affairs, of appointing and dismissing ministers, of signing all bills, etc. Yet these were all powers traditionally held in Iran by the Shahanshah. The constitutional articles added nothing to powers that Shahs had not for centuries possessed. Consequently as a limitation it is difficult to argue that the position of the Shah relative to the conduct of affairs in and for Iran was really any different after the adoption of the Constitution from what it was before. Indeed, was it even a limitation on authority at all ?

The third limitation upon the power of the Shah under the Constitution consists of three so-called "General Principles". They are (1) the state religion — Shi'a Islam — shall be formalized and observed according to the Ja'fari doctrine of the twelve *Imams*, (2) that no enactment of the Majlis (which must, of course, be signed by the Shah) may be at variance with the

Shi'a doctrine, and (3) the state religion, so defined, is to be "unchangeable for eternity".

The effectiveness of these limitations has never really been tested. At the beginning of the Shah's land reform and distribution scheme, the *ulama* objected to the draft law as possibly being contrary to the law of Islam. The law was withdrawn, redrafted, and re-submitted. It passed the Majlis with no debate and was signed by the Shah.

Simply because a constitutional limitation is not being constantly read into individual texts does not, thereby, mean that it is without meaning. In an increasingly secular age, one often hears the remark that religion doesn't count any more in terms of real power. In Iran, the same remark will be heard but it is not a measurable observation.

The fourth chapter of this book dealt at considerable length with the doctrine of the Imamate. Briefly it should be reviewed in its constitutional context. The twelfth *Imam* disappeared in 878 A.D. in the cave of the great mosque of Samarra without leaving offspring. He is considered by the Shi'ites to be immune from death and that he sleeps, to rise again at a future date. In the fullness of time, he will appear as the *Mahdi* or divinely guided one who will restore time, conquer the world, and usher in the millennium. Though hidden, this *Imam* is the "master of time". In 1502, the Safavids, who claimed descent from the seventh *Imam*, established this belief as doctrine and the Shah was seen as the *locum tenens* of this hidden *Imam*.[56]

During the Qajar dynasty, this doctrine was called into question by both the political and religious leaders, and it was certainly never advanced as a claim by the Qajars. But its importance did not die.

The Qajars, who ruled Iran for over 200 years, were of Turkish descent and had been mentioned in the chronicles of the times for 700 years before they came to power. They came from north of the Oxus river, at that time the north-eastern boundary of the Persian Empire. Possibly identified with the Turanians, described in the first chapter as traditional enemies of ancient Persia. They had tremendous resiliency and survival value. Under Tamerlane they were banished to Syria. Later, they attached themselves to the Safavids and assisted in raising them to the throne of Cyrus. In return for service rendered, they were included in the kizelbash or Seven Redheaded Tribes, Their power became so great that Shah Abbas found it expedient to divide them into three branches and put them to fighting against the Tartars, the Turkomans and other tribes. They were successful in this and Iran finally became the main settlement of the tribe. Their leader, Fateh Ali Khan, was made Commander-in-Chief by Shah Tahmasp I in the latter half of the 17th century. He was assassinated by Nadir Kuli Khan, later Nadir Shah, and consequently a blood feud developed which ended only in the death of Nadir and the death and torture of his relatives. The Qajars had seized the most coveted throne in the world.

The disagreement that so long plagued the relationship between the religious community and the Qajars surfaced immediately upon the ascent to the throne of the first ruler. Being of Turkish descent, the Qajars were looked upon by the Shi'ite community as interlopers and even disbelievers. This had some basis in fact. Mohammed Ali Mirza Shah disavowed the doctrine and principles of the Koran and refused to support the Shi'ite faith. (He was deposed, possibly on that account.) Furthermore, Qajar rule was sufficiently fearsome that the leading *mujtahids* repaired to Irqu, to Najal and Kerbala, and remained there. They, collectively, took the position that the Qajars could not, in truth, be seen in proper succession to the Safavid claims and consequently the religious doctrine developed that the *locum tenens* of the Imamate lay collectively with the *mujtahids*.

The present Shah, as pointed out above, walks this tightrope with great skill. He is not in the Qajar tradition. He may be in the Safavid. He speaks of the *Iman* and its influence in his personal life and he assiduously cultivates the religious community. In turn, he has become acceptable to the Shi'ite leadership. It is highly improbable that he would fly in the face of any constitutional limitation that was a reflection of religious influence. He would in fact work with it. There have been differences to be sure, on occasion, but to the constitutional question as to which is superior, the unalterable General Principles stated above or the constitution apart from these principles, clearly at law the former holds the primacy. In this sense they form a limitation. But the Shah has turned it around. He accepts his responsibility for promoting the Ja'fari doctrine of the Shi'a sect of the twelve *Imams* and for seeing that legislation is not opposed by the theologians. In turn, it is in the latter's interest to support — or at least not oppose — the Shi'ite doctrine that the Shahanshah is the *locum tenens* of the Imamate.

Kingly rule in Iran, then, is constitutional, but clearly it is more than that. It is Monarchical. This is the older tradition in Iran, and there is no constitutional law that speaks to the contrary.

This chapter has been concerned with the Law of the Monarch — law, justice, kingly rule. It is the triad that composes the essential fabric of Iranian society. It is the culmination of the national experience. It is truly Iranian. The motto on the Imperial Standard of the Pahlavi Dynasty speaks to the matter with feeling, in trembling. In its very austerity, it echoes the elegance of conceptuality that has been honed in experience.

Mara dad farmud va
Khod davar ast.
(Justice He bids me do
as He will judge me.)

NOTES

1. Daniel 6:12.
2. Numbers 35:6; Deuteronomy 19:7-9; Joshua 20:2-8.
3. Tadhkirat al-Mulk, *op. cit.*, p. 45.
4. Daeneoke, E., "Constitutional Law in Iran", *American Bar Association Journal*, (Vol. 49, 1963) pp. 568-70. This is not, as its title suggests, a study in constitutional law. It is by a private lawyer who is dealing primarily with actions before the courts.
5. *Ibid.*
6. Donaldson, D. M. "Modern Persian Law", *Modern World*, Vol, 24 (1934) pp. 341-49.
7. Inlow, E. Burke, "The Supreme Court of Iran", *Osgoode Hall Law Review*, Vol. VIII (No. 3) pp. 549 ff.
8. *Kayhan* 6 August 1977, p. 3.
9. For details, see *Ibid.*, passim.
10. Inlow, E. Burke, "Courts Martial: the Iranian Experience", LAWASIA, Vol. II (1971) pp. 112-20.
11. *Kayhan*, 30 July 1977, p. 1.
12. *Ibid.*, 16 July 1977, p. 4.
13. G. Halsbury, *Laws of England*, 499n (m) (2nd ed. 1952).
14. *Kayhan*, 30 July 1977, p. 1.
15. *Ibid.*, p. 2.
16. *Ethics*, 1154 b. 18.
17. Quotations in Carpenter, W. S., and Stafford, P. T., *Readings in Early Legal Institutions*, New York, 1952, p. 46.
18. See Hocart, A. M., *Kingship*, Oxford, 1924, pp. 10-11.
19. Widengren, F. "The Sacred Kingship of Iran" *Numen*, Supp. 4, 1959, pp. 442 ff.
20. Ghirshman, *Iran*, *op. cit.*, p. 121. The spelling is as given.
21. Today the fires in Iran burn low. Perhaps 15,000 worshippers will live in the area around Yazd. Several times a year they celebrate the ancient Zoroastrian feasts. The ritual is always the same. On the morning of the day they awake to the special sound of the Dastoor's musical instruments. They rise and go to the roofs of their houses. There they spread a special tablecloth on which a variety of fruits, a bowl of water, an open fire and a lighted lantern are arranged. Before it they sit in worship, cross legged, head covered and recite hymns from the holy Avesta Pahlvi. It is all very old, very sacred.
22. Huart, *op. cit.*, p. 153.
23. Themistocles, 27 in Plutarch's Lives (Loeb Classical Library) II, p. 73.
24. Panegyricus, 151-52 in Socrates (Loeb Classical Library) I, p. 217.
25. Nasir ad-Din Tusi, *The Nasirean Ethics* (trans. G. M. Wickens) London, 1964, p. 230.
26. Al-Fakhari, *On the systems of government and the Moslem dynasties* (trans. C. E. J. Whiting) London, 1947, p. 34.

27. Agathias, *De Bello Persico*, ii, 26, Quoted in Huart, *op. cit.*, p. 155.
28. Plato, *The Laws*, London, (Dent, Everyman's Library) 1966, p. 76.
29. *Ibid.*, p. 352.
30. Aristotle, *Ethics*, (ed. J. A. K. Thomson) Baltimore (Penguin Books) 1966, p. 247.
31. Nizam al-Mulk, *op. cit.*, p. 90.
32. *Ibid.*, passim. Chapters as cited.
33. *The History of the Early Kings of Persia*, translated from the original Persian of Mirkhond, put in its present form by Shea, David (London, 1832) pp. 177ff.
34. Lambton, A. K. S., *Landlord and Peasant in Persia*, Oxford University Press, 1953 pp. xviii-xx for quotations and observations offered.
35. Quoted in *Ibid.*
36. al-Farabi, *Fusul al-Madani* (Aphorisms of the Statesman) ed. by Dunlop, D. M., Cambridge, 1960.
37. *Ibid.*, pp. 55-56.
38. *Ibid.*, p. 69.
39. *Ibid.*, pp. 40-42 for account of kingship.
40. *Ibid.*, p. 18.
41. *Ibid.*, p. 51.
42. al-Fakhari, *op. cit.*, p. 15.
43. Lerner, R. and Mahdi, M., *Medieval Political Philosophy*, New York, 1963, p. 39.
44. Mirza, Y. B., *Iran and the Iranians*, Baltimore, 1913, p. 79. See Savory, R. "Notes on the Safavid State", *Iranian Studies*, Vol. I (No. 3) New Haven, Conn. 1968, p. 97.
45. Bouvat, L. "L'Administration de la Perse". *Revue du Monde Musulman*, Vol. XXIV (1913), p. 225.
46. For details, see *Ibid.*, pp. 219-45.
47. Savory, *op. cit.*, p. 96.
48. *Ibid.*, p. 99.
49. Quoted in *Ibid.*, p. 99.
50. Quoted in *Ibid.*, p. 100.
51. Inlow, E. Burke, "Yek Kalama" Pt. I, *Middle East Forum*, XLVIII (Summer, 1972) pp. 63 ff. and Pt. II, XLVIII (Winter, 1972), pp. 143 ff.
52. See Fraser, D., *Persia and Turkey in Revolt*, Edinburgh, 1919; Browne, E. G., *A Brief Narrative of Recent Events in Persia and a Study of the Constitution*, London, 1909.
53. Lockhart, L. "The Constitutional Laws of Persia," *Middle East Journal* (Autumn, 1959), pp. 372-88.
54. Inlow, E. Burke, *The Patent Grant*. The Johns Hopkins University Press, 1949, pp. 23 ff.
55. Bayne, *op. cit.*, p. 74.
56. Hitti, *op. cit.*, p. 441.

SELECTED BIBLIOGRAPHY

The life and history of Iran has been well documented. Good bibliographies, therefore, are available in substantial numbers. I have used the standard bibliographical references: J. D. Pearson (ed.) *Index Islamicus*, 1906 – 1972; Wickens, G. M., Savory, R. M., Watson, W. J. (eds.) *Persia in Islamic Times, A Practical Bibliography*. Other standard references used were *The Encyclopedia of Islam*, *The Cambridge History of Iran*, Lewis, Bernard (ed.) *Islam*; *The Holy Bible*, and *The Holy Koran*.

Materials in the British Museum and the London School of Oriental and African Studies were consulted and used as footnoted.

The files of the following were used as footnoted: Iran Tribune, Teheran Journal, Kayhan (International), The Guardian, The New York Times.

BOOKS

Adams, C. J., (ed.) *Iranian Civilization and Culture*, McGill University Press, 1972.

Al-Fakhari, *On the Systems of Government and the Moslem Dynasties*, (trans. C. E. J. Whiting) London, 1947.

Algar, Hamid, *Religion and State in Iran*, 1785 – 1906, University of California Press, 1969.

Anon., *The History of the Early Kings of Persia*, (trans. from the original Persian of Mirkhond) London, 1832.

Anon. *The Letter of Tansar*, (trans. by M. Boyce) Rome, 1968.

Anon., *Tadhkirat al-Mulk*, (trans. by V. Minorsky) London, 1943.

Arberry, A. J., *Classical Persian Literature*, London, 1958.

Arberry, A. J., (ed.), *The Legacy of Persia*, London, 1953.

Bayne, E. A., *Persian Kingship in Transition*, American Universities Field Staff, 1968.

Bill, J. A., Leiden, C., *The Middle East, Politics and Power*, Boston, 1974.

Binder, Leonard, *Iran, Political Development in a Changing Society*, Berkeley, 1962.

Browne, E. G., *A Brief Narrative of Recent Events in Persia and a Study of the Constitution*, London, 1909.

Browne, E. G., *A Literary History of Persia*, Cambridge University Press, 1969.

Browne, E. G., *A Year Amongst the Persians*, London, 1893.

Cambridge Ancient History IV, Cambridge University Press, 1930.

Carpenter, W. S., and Stafford, P. T., *Readings in Early Legal Institutions*, New York, 1952.

Chew, Samuel, *The Crescent and the Rose*, New York, 1965.

Christensen, A., *L'Iran sous les Sassanids*, Copenhagen, 1944.

Cottam, R. W., *Nationalism in Iran*, Pittsburgh, 1964.

Curzon, G. N., *Persia and the Persian Question*, London, 1892.

De Lorey, Eustache and Fladen, Douglas, *The Moon of the Fourteenth Night*, London, 1910.

Drekmeier, C., *Kingship and Community in Early India*, Stanford University Press, 1962.

Donaldson, D. M., *The Shi'ite Religion*, London, 1933.

Dunlop, D. M., (ed.), *Fusul al-Madani* (Aphorisms of the Statesman), Cambridge, 1960.

Eddy, S. K., *The King is Dead*, University of Nebraska Press, 1961.

Fraser, D., *Persia and Turkey in Revolt*, Edinburgh, 1919.

Frye, Richard N., *Iran*, New York, 1953.

Ghazali's Book of *Counsel for Kings*, (trans. by Bagley, F.R.C.) Oxford University Press, 1964.

Ghirshman, R., *Iran*, London, 1962.

Ghirshman, R., *Persia*, London, 1964.

Ghoshal, U. N., *A History of Indian Political Ideas*, Oxford University Press, 1959.

Greaves, R., *Persia and the Defense of India*, University of London Press, 1959.

G. Halsbury, *Laws of England*, London, (2nd ed.) 1952.

Hanway, Jonas, *An Historical Account of the British Trade Over the Caspian Sea with a Journal of Travels*, London, 1753.

Heeren, A. H. L., *Works I*, London, 1846.

Hocart, A. M., *Kingship*, Oxford, 1924.

Huart, C., *Ancient Persian and Iranian Civilizations*, New York, 1927.

Inlow, E. Burke, *The Patent Grant*, The Johns Hopkins University Press, 1949.

International Institute for Strategic Studies, *The Military Balance, 1974-75*, London, 1974.

International Institute for Strategic Studies, *Strategic Survey*, London, 1973.

Lambton, A. K. S., *Landlord and Peasant in Persia*, Oxford University Press, 1953.

Lerner, R. and Mahdi, M., *Medieval Political Philosophy*, New York, 1963.

Lenczowski, G. (ed.), *Political Elites in the Middle East*, Washington, D.C.,

Lenczowski, G. *Russia and the West in Iran* 1918-48, Ithaca, N. Y., 1953.

Millspaugh, Arthur C., *Americans in Persia*, Washington D.C., 1946.

Mirza, Y. B., *Iran and the Iranians*, Baltimore, 1913.

Motter, T. H. Vail, *The Persian Corridor and Aid to Russia*, Washington, D.C., 1952.

Najafi, Najmeh, *Reveille for a Persian Village*, New York, 1958.

Nasir ad-Din Tusi, *The Nasirean Ethics*, (trans. G. M. Wickens) London, 1964.

Nizam al-Mulk, *Siyasat-nama*, (trans. by H. Darke), London, 1960.

Noldeke's "The Iranian National Epics" or *Shahnameh*, Bombay, 1930.

Olmstead, A. T., *History of the Persian Empire*, University of Chicago Press, 1966.

Pinkerton, John, *A General Collection of the Best and Most Interesting Voyages in all Parts of the World*, London, 1811.

Plato, *The Laws*, London, 1966.

Renniger, E. D., *The Story of Rustam* and other Persian Hero Tales from Firdawsi, New York, 1917.

Rice, Cyrian, *The Persian Sufis*, London, 1964.

Ross, Denison, *The Persians*, Oxford, 1931.

Shah of Iran, *Mission For My Country*, New York, 1961.

Shuster, W. Morgan, *The Strangling of Persia*, London, 1912 and 1913.

Skrine, Clarmont, *World War II in Iran*, London, 1962.

Sykes, Sir Percy, *A History of Persia*, London, 1958.

Thomson, J. A. K. (ed.), Aristotle, *Ethics*, Baltimore, 1966.

Wilbur, D. N., *Iran, Past and Present*, Princeton University Press, 1958.

Wills, C. J., (ed.) *The Adventures of Hajji Baba of Ispahan*, London, 1897.

Yule, (ed.) *Book of Ser Marco Polo*, London, 1926.

Zonis, M., *The Political Elite of Iran*, Princeton University Press, 1971.

ARTICLES

Bouvat, L., "L'Administration de la Perse," *Revue du Monde Musulman*, XXIV (1913).

Cottam, R. W., "Political Party Development in Iran", *Society for Iranian Studies*, I (No. 3) 1968.

Daenecke, E., "Constitutional Law in Iran", *American Bar Association Journal*, (Vol. 49, 1963).

Donaldson, D. M., "Modern Persian Law", *Modern World*, Vol. 24 (1934).

Hopkins, E. W., "The Divinity of Kings", *Journal of the American Oriental Society*, Vol. 51 No. 4 (1931).

Inlow, E. Burke, "Courts Martial : the Iranian Experience", *Lawasia*, Vol. II (1971).

Inlow, E. Burke, "The Divine Right of Persian Kings", *Journal of Indian History*, Vol. XLV, Pt. II (August 1967).

Inlow, E. Burke, "Manu and Hammurabi, A Study in Legal Theory", *Journal of Indian History*, Golden Jubilee Volume, 1973.

Inlow, E. Burke, "The Politics of Reform", *Middle East Forum*, Vol. XLVII, (Nos. 3, 4) (1971).

Inlow, E. Burke, "The Supreme Court of Iran", *Osgoode Hall Law Review*, Vol. VIII (No. 3).

Inlow, E. Burke, "Yek Kalama" Pt. 1, *Middle East Forum*, XLVIII (Summer 1972) and Pt. II, XLVIII (Winter, 1972).

Lambton, A. K. S., "Quis Custodiet Custodes", *Studia Islamica V*, 1956.

Lockhart, L, "The Constitutional Laws of Persia," *Middle East Journal* (Autumn 1959).

Savory, R., "Notes on the Safavid State", *Iranian Studies*, Vol. I (No. 3) 1968.

Savory, R. M., "The Principal Offices of the Safavid State during the Reign of Isma'il", *Bulletin of the School of Oriental and African Studies*, (Parts 1-3) 1960.

Widengran, G. "The Sacred Kingship of Iran," *Numen*, Supp. 4, 1959.

Wright, Denis, "The Changed Balance of Power in the Persian Gulf," *Asian Affairs*, Vol. 60, Part III (October 1973).

CORRECTIONS

Page	*Line*	*For*	*Read*
29	7	womon.	woman.[12]
,,	2 from below	met."	met."[13]
30	12	ceremonies.	ceremonies.[14]
50	4 from below	throne.	throne.[18]
52	12	Babylon.	Babylon.[19]
65	8 from below	character."	character."[2]
183	2	Pinkerton,	Pinkerton,[15]